I0834639

SKETCHES AND CHRONICLES

OF THE

TOWN OF LITCHFIELD,

CONNECTICUT,

HISTORICAL, BIOGRAPHICAL, AND STATISTICAL;

TOGETHER WITH A

COMPLETE OFFICIAL REGISTER OF THE TOWN.

BY PAYNE KENYON KILBOURNE, M. A.,

SECRETARY OF THE LITCHFIELD COUNTY HISTORICAL AND ANTIQUARIAN SOCIETY.

HARTFORD:
PRESS OF CASE, LOCKWOOD AND COMPANY.

Notice

In many older books, foxing (or discoloration) occurs and, in some instances, print lightens with wear and age. Reprinted books, such as this, often duplicate these flaws, notwithstanding efforts to reduce or eliminate them. The pages of this reprint have been digitally enhanced and, where possible, the flaws eliminated in order to provide clarity of content and a pleasant reading experience.

Originally published:
Hartford, Connecticut
1859

Reprinted by:

Janaway Publishing, Inc.
732 Kelsey Ct.
Santa Maria, California 93454
(805) 925-1038
www.janawaygenealogy.com

2007, 2011

ISBN: 978-1-59641-102-9

Made in the United States of America

PREFACE.

The Town of Litchfield was first settled by emigrants from Hartford, Windsor, Wethersfield, Farmington and Lebanon, in 1720–'21. In 1751, the County of Litchfield was incorporated and organized, and at the same time Litchfield was established as the county-seat, and such it still remains. The township is located near the centre of the county, which occupies the north-west corner of the State of Connecticut. It is agreeably diversified by hills, vallies, mountains, lakes, forests and cultivated fields; and is inhabited, for the most part, by an industrious, thriving, intelligent and happy people.

Thus much for the information of the stranger whose eye may casually glance at this Preface.

It has been the design of the author of these pages, to trace the rise and progress of that little settlement in the wilderness, during the lapse of one hundred and forty years, to the present time. The history of many a town at the West, tells of a sudden and gigantic growth at which our fathers would have marveled. I have no such stories to relate. The early history of *Litchfield* is one of peril and privation—of patient industry, and slow development. Our fathers, the pioneers of this region, were earnest, hardy and fearless men, who, in addition to the labors of backwoods-men, found abundant opportunities for the display of their heroism in guarding their humble fire-sides from the prowling wolf and stealthy savage. The annals of such a people, and their successors, cannot be devoid of interest to any one ; and should especially be cherished with the liveliest satisfaction by those who are able to claim descent from them. I have long been engaged in collecting the records and traditions possessing a local interest, with a view of ultimately giving them to the public. My "labor of love" for the good old town that gave me birth, is at length concluded, for the present at least. I trust the reader will share, in some small degree, the pleasure which the author has felt in gathering up and sending forth these Memorials of the Past. Much more of perhaps equal interest, still remains unpublished ; but it will be seen that I have already exceeded my promised limits. The Family Genealogies in my possession, and for which I had hoped to find room, would alone fill a volume of the size of this. In the latter part of the work, especially, the power of *condensation* has been thoroughly tested.

I take this opportnnity to express my acknowledgments to those who have preceded me in my field of exploration, and whose footsteps I have sometimes found it convenient to follow. In 1818, a pamphlet by James Morris, Esq., was published, entitled—"A Statistical Account of Several Towns in Litchfield County," which contains much valuable information relative to this town. In 1845, our fellow-townsman, George C. Woodruff, Esq., published a History of Litchfield in a pamphlet of sixty pages—an excellent work.

Litchfield, Conn., June 15, 1859. P. K. K.

INDEX

CHAPTER I.

CHAPTER II.

CHAPTER III.

CHAPTER IV.

CHAPTER V.

CHAPTER VI.

CHAPTER VII.

CHAPTER VIII.

CHAPTER IX.

CHAPTER X.

APPENDIX.

HISTORY OF LITCHFIELD.

CHAPTER I.

EVENTS IN CONNECTICUT PRECEDING THE SETTLEMENT OF LITCHFIELD. BANTAM, ETC.

In 1630, about ten years after the landing of the pilgrims on Plymouth Rock, the whole of the territory of the present State of Connecticut was conveyed by the Plymouth Company to Robert, Earl of Warwick. On the 19th of March of the succeeding year, the Earl executed under his hand and seal the grant since known as the Old Patent of Connecticut, wherein he transferred the same tract to Viscount Say and Seal, Lord Brooke, John Hampden, John Pym, Sir Richard Saltonstall, and others. In the summer of 1635, the towns of Hartford, Wethersfield and Windsor, on the Connecticut river, first began to be settled by emigrants from the vicinity of Boston in Massachusetts. Still a year later, the Rev. Thomas Hooker and his congregation made their celebrated journey through the wilderness, from Cambridge, Massachusetts, to Hartford, where they took up their permanent residence. In 1637, the Pequot War was begun and terminated—resulting in the expulsion and almost total annihilation of the most formidable tribe of Indians in the colony.

The first Constitution adopted by the people of Connecticut bears date, January 15, 1638–'9. This continued to form the basis of our colonial government until the arrival of the Charter of Charles II., in 1662, when it was nominally superceded.

Alternate troubles with the Dutch and Indians kept the settlers, for many years, in a perpetual state of discipline and alarm. But while the political commotions in the old world sometimes agitated the other American colonies, the people of Connecticut had from the first felt that their civil rights were guaranteed to them beyond the reach of any contingency. The

Royal Charter was but a confirmation of privileges which they had long enjoyed. No king-appointed Governor or Council annoyed them by their presence or oppressed them by their acts; but the voters were left to choose their own rulers and enact their own laws. Indeed, the influence of the crown was for a long period scarcely felt in the colony. On the accession of James II., however, in 1685, the whole aspect of affairs was changed. It was soon rumored that His Majesty had determined to revoke all the charters granted by his predecessors. The arrival of Sir Edmund Andros at Boston, in December 1686, bearing a commission as "Governor of *New England*," was an event not calculated to allay the apprehensions of the people of Connecticut. His reputation was that of a selfish, grasping despot, bent upon enriching himself and immediate friends at the expense of the colonists. At this time, the entire region now known as the County of Litchfield, (except a solitary settlement at Woodbury, on its southern frontier,) was an unexplored wilderness, denominated the *Western Lands*. To save these lands from the control and disposal of Andros, the Legislature granted them to the towns of Hartford and Windsor—at least so much of them as lay east of the Housatonic river. When the usurpations of Andros were over, and the charter had found its way back from the hollow of the oak to the Secretary's office, the Colonial Assembly attempted to resume its title to these lands; but the towns referred to steadfastly resisted all such claims. The quarrel was long kept up, but no acts of hostility were committed until efforts were made to dispose of the tract. Collisions then became frequent. Explorers, agents and surveyors, of one party, were summarily arrested and expelled from the disputed territory by the contestants. On one occasion, several offenders belonging to the Hartford and Windsor party, were imprisoned by the colonial authorities. A mob assembled, broke open the jail, and set the prisoners at large. A compromise followed, confirming to the towns and the claimants under them, the lands of Litchfield and a part of those of New Milford. The other portions of the territory were intended to be equally divided between the colony and the claiming towns. Thus Torrington, Barkhamsted, Colebrook, and a part of Harwinton, were appropriated to Windsor; Hartland, Winchester, New Hartford, and the remaining portion of Harwinton, were given to Hartford; the other lands in dispute, now constituting the townships of Norfolk, Goshen, Canaan, Kent, Sharon and Salisbury, were retained by the colony. It should be added, that a small portion of the township of Litchfield was claimed by certain citizens of Farmington, by virtue of a deed of purchase from the Indians, dated August 11, 1714. On the 11th of June, 1718, the Farmington claimants relinquished their rights to Hartford and Windsor, and in lieu thereof received one-sixth of all the lands of the town in fee.

All business relating to the Western Lands was transacted by committees appointed by the claiming towns and by the General Court. In 1715, these towns (Hartford and Windsor,) took the initiatory steps toward exploring that portion of the western wilderness now embraced within our corporation limits, and purchasing whatever rights the natives possessed, or claimed to possess, to the soil. It would be interesting to know who was the first individual of the Anglo-Saxon race that ever visited the localities so cherished by us all. The earliest *record-evidence* on this point, is contained in an entry in the first Book of Records in our Town Clerk's office,* which is as follows:

"*The Town of Hartford, Dr.*

To John Marsh,

May 1715, For 5 days, man and horse, with expenses, in viewing the Land at the New Plantation,	£ 2	0	0

The Town of Hartford, Dr.

Jan. 22, 1715–'16, To 6 days journey to Woodbury, to *treat with the Indians about the Western Lands*, by Thomas Seymour,	£ 1	4	0
To expenses in the journey,	1	14	9
	£ 2	18	9

* The following is written on the first page of the book referred to—"This booke belonging to the Towne of Hartford, into which we, the Committee for Managing the affairs of the Western Grants, have entered our proceedings relating thereto, in conjunction with the Committee for the Towne of Windsor—as also an account of our disbursements therein." Dated June 17, 1718.

The Town of Hartford, Dr.

To Thomas Seymour, Committy,

	£	s.	d.
May 1716, By 2 quarts of Rum,	£0	2	6
Expenses at Farmington,		4	9
Expenses at Waterbury,		1	7
Paid Thomas Miner towards the Indian purchase,	7	10	0
Expenses at Woodbury	2	11	0
Expenses for a Pilot and protection,	1	10	0
Fastening horse-shoes at Waterbury,		2	0
Expenses at Waterbury,		1	8
Expenses to Col. Whiting for writing 40 deeds,	£ 1	10	0
" to Capt. Cooke for acknowledging 18 deeds,		18	0
" to Ensign Seymour,	1	0	0
" at Arnold's,	1	7	0
" by sending to Windsor,	0	4	0
August 4, 1718.—Sold 11 lots for	£49	10	0
Expenses for writing 20 deeds, to Mr. Fitch,		10	0
" to Capt. Cooke for acknowledging deeds,		7	0
" for making out a way,	2	0	0
" at Arnold's,		11	o
" to Tho's Seymour for perambulating north line,	1	6	4
" at Arnold's,	1	0	4
Feb. 10, 1818.—At a meeting of the Committees, then sold 16 lots reserved by Marsh for Hartford's part,	37	17	9
At same meeting, paid by John Marsh for expenses,		12	0
At same meeting, loss of money by mistake in acc't.		3	0
April 14, 1719.—A meeting of the Committees, expenses,		6	0
April 27.—At a meeting of the Committees, expenses,		7	."

By the earliest of these entries, we learn that Mr. John Marsh was sent out from Hartford "to view the lands of the new plantation," in May, 1715. He may, therefore, be regarded as emphatically the pioneer-explorer of this township. It is not improbable that an occasional hunter or adventurer had previously visited these hills, and carried hence an account of our beautiful lake and the rich alluvial meadows on its banks; but there is extant no written or traditionary evidence pointing to such an event. Mr. Marsh became an original proprietor and early settler of the town, and was one of its most important and useful men. He was the progenitor of all bearing his name in Litchfield—a numerous and respectable family. Mr. Thomas Seymour, of Hartford, appears in the record as the next explorer, and as the agent "to treat with the Indians" relative to the purchase of these lands. The subsequent items, though unimportant in themselves, are nevertheless deemed worthy of preservation, as they embrace all the information contained in our Town Books touching the action of the Committees relative to the lands in question, previous to the settlement.

The negotiations resulted in purchasing from the Indians all the lands in the original township of Bantam or Litchfield. The sum paid therefor in behalf of the Committees, though seemingly small, was doubtless satisfactory to the natives. Their estimate of land was founded mainly upon its value to them for hunting; and as they made a "reservation" for that purpose, the "fifteen pounds in hand received" was, we have reason to believe, to their "full satisfaction and contentment," as is expressed in the Deed—which was executed at Woodbury, March 2d, 1715–'16:

" *To all People to whom these Presents shall come*, GREETING:

KNOW YE that we, Chusquenoag, Corkscrew, Quiump, Magnash, Kehow, Sepunkum, Poni, Wonposet, Suckqunnokqueen, Toweecume, Mansumpansh, and Norkgnotonckquy, Indian Natives belonging to the Plantation of *Potatuck* within the Colony of Connecticut, for and in consideration of the sum of fifteen pounds money in hand received to our full satisfaction and contentment, have given, granted, bargained and sold, and by these presents do fully, freely and absolutely give, grant, bargain and confirm, unto Col. William Whiting, Mr. John Marsh and Mr. Thomas Seymour, a Committee for the town of Hartford; and Mr. John Eliot, Mr. Daniel Griswold and Mr. Samuel Rockwell, a Committee for the town of Windsor, for themselves and in behalf of the rest of the Inhabitants of the towns of Hartford and Windsor, a certain tract of Land, situate and lying north of Waterbury bounds, abutting southerly, partly on Waterbury and partly on Woodbury; from Waterbury River westward across a part of Waterbury bounds, and across at the north end of Waterbury bounds to Shepaug River, and so northerly in the middle of Shepaug River, to the sprains of Shepaug River below Mount Tom, thence running up the east branch of Shepaug River to a place where the said River runs out of Shepaug Pond, from thence to the north end of said Pond, then east to Waterbury River, then southerly as the River runs, to to the north end of Waterbury bounds upon the said River; which said Tract of Land thus described, To HAVE AND TO HOLD, to the said Col. William Whiting, Mr. John Marsh and Mr. Thomas Seymour, Mr. John Eliot, Mr. Daniel Griswold aud Mr. Samuel Rockwell, Committees of the Towns of Hartford and Windsor as aforesaid, in behalf of themselves and the rest of the Inhabitants of said Towns, to them, their heirs and assigns, to use, occupy and improve, as their own proper right of Inheritance, for their comfort forever; together with all the privileges, appurtenances and conditions to the same be longing, or in any wise appertaining. *And Further*, we, the said Chusquenoag, Corkscrew, Quiump, Magnash, Kehow, Sepunkum, Poni, Wonposet, Suckqunnokqueen, Toweecumo, Mansumpansh and Norkgnotonckquy, owners and proprietors of the above granted Land, do, for ourselves and our heirs, to and with the above said William Whiting, John Marsh, Thomas Seymour, John Eliot, Daniel Griswold and Samuel Rockwell, Committees as aforesaid, them, their heirs and assigns, covenant and engage, that we have good right and lawful authority to sell the above granted land; And Futher, at the desire and request of the aforesaid Committees, and at their own proper cost and charge, will give a more ample deed.

And for a more full confirmation hereof, we have set our hands and seals, this second day of March, in the second year of His Majesties Reign, A. D. 1715.

Memorandum.—Before the executing of this instrument, it is to be understood, that the grantors above named have reserved to themselves a piece of ground sufficient for their hunting houses, near a mountain called Mount Tom."

This document is subscribed by the Indians named in the beginning of the deed—the last one excepted. As the "uncouth scrawls" used by them for signatures, are meaningless, and were undoubtedly drawn quite at random by the aboriginal signers, no attempt will here be made to imitate them. The names of the *witnesses* subscribed to the deed are, Weroamaug, Wognacug, Tonhocks, John Mitchell, and Joseph Minor. It was "acknowledged" before Mr. Minor, the Indian Interpreter, as follows:

"The Indians that subscribed and sealed the above said deed, appeared personally in Woodbury, the day of the date thereof, and acknowledged the said deed to be their free and voluntary act and deed
Before me, JOHN MINOR."

In 1718, a Company was organized for the settlement of Bantam. The township, which contained about 44,800 acres, was divided into sixty rights or shares—three of which were reserved for pious uses, viz., one share to the first minister and his heirs forever; one, for the *use* of the first minister and his *successors* in the pastoral office; and one, for the support of Schools. Purchasers having been found for the remaining fifty-seven rights, deeds of conveyance were made by the Committees, confirming the entire plantation to the new proprietors. These deeds are dated, April 29, 1719—fifty-five of which are recorded on the Litchfield Land Records. The consideration for forty-eight shares, was £229 10 0, in bills of credit; for seven shares, the sum of £31 4 0 was paid. Mr. John Marsh purchased the two remaining shares, but the price paid therefor does not appear. The average cost of the land to the first purchasers, did not exceed one penny and three farthings per acre.

The subjoined list contains the names of all the "original proprietors" of the township:

John Marsh,* (2 Rights,)	from Hartford.
Samuel Sedgwick, Jr,	"
Nathaniel Goodwin,	"
Timothy Seymour,	"
Paul Peck, Jr.,*	"
Joseph Mason,*	"
Nathaniel Messenger,	"
Benjamin Webster,*	"
Joshua Garrett,*	"
Samuel Forward,	Windsor.
Thomas Griswold, Jr.,	"
Jacob Gibbs,*	"
Joseph Birge,*	"
Benjamin Hosford,*	"
John Hart,	Farmington.
Timothy Stanley,	"
John Bird,*	"
Joseph Bird,*	"
Samuel Lewis,	"
Ebenezer Woodruff,	"
Samuel Root,	"
Nathaniel Winchell,	"
Hezekiah Winchell,	"
Joseph Gillett,*	Colchester.
Jonathan Buck,	New Milford.
William Goodrich, Jr.*	Wethersfield.
John Stoddard,*	Wethersfield.
Ezekiel Buck,*	"
Jacob Griswold,*	"
John Buel,* (2 Rights,)	Lebanon.
Edward Culver,	"
Hezekiah Culver,*	"
Thomas Lee,*	"
Eleazer Strong,*	"
Supply Strong,*	"
Caleb Chapel, (2 Rights,)	"
Thomas Treadway,*	"
John Caulkins,	"
Ezekiel Sanford, (2 Rights,)	Stratford.
Nathan Mitchell,*	"
Thomas Pier,*	"
John Mann,	"
Joseph Peet,	"
Samuel Somers,	"
Nath'l Smith,* (2 Rights,)	Taunton, Ms.
John Collins,	"
Ephraim French,	"
Josiah Walker,*	Woodbury.
Samuel Orton,*	"
Joseph Waller,*	"
Isaac Judson,	"

Those proprietors whose names are here designated by a star (*) became *settlers* in the town. The Rights of a few others were settled upon by the *sons* of the first purchasers; others sold out their interest to persons who became permanent residents; while a few forfeited their shares by neglecting to comply with the terms of the purchase.

The title thus acquired was soon after confirmed by the following Act of the Legislature:

"AT a General Assembly holden at Hartford, May, A. D. 1719:

UPON the Petition of Lieut. JOHN MARSH, of Hartford, and Deacon JOHN BUEL, of Lebanon, with many others, praying liberty, under Committees appointed by the Towns of Hartford and Windsor, to settle a Town westward of Farmington, at a place called BANTAM.

This Assembly do grant liberty and full power, unto the said John

Marsh and John Buel and partners settlers, being in the whole fifty-seven in number, to settle a town at said Bantam: the said town to be divided into sixty Rights, three whereof to be improved for pious uses in said town. And the other fifty-seven shall, as soon as may conveniently be, settled upon by the undertakers, or, upon their failure, by others that may be admitted. Said town to be in length, east and west, eight miles, three-quarters and twenty-eight rods, and in breadth seven miles and an half—being bounded eastward by Mattatuck River, westward the bigger part upon the most western branch of the Shepaug River and partly upon the wilderness, north upon the wilderness, and south by Waterbury bounds and a west line from Waterbury corner unto Shepaug River; said town to be known by the name of LITCHFIELD, and to have the following figure for a a brand for their horse hind, viz. 9. And the same powers and privileges that other towns in this Colony do enjoy, are hereby granted to said town."

As this chapter may be regarded simply as an *introduction* to the subject-matter of the volume, a brief reference to the origin and meaning of the names by which this locality *was* and *is* known, will not be out of place here.

The *earliest* designation applied to this particular portion of the Western Lands, was *Bantam*—and the name is still borne by our principal Lake and one of our largest Rivers. Historians have generally concurred in calling this the Indian or Aboriginal name of the place. There appears to be good reason, however, to doubt the correctness of such a conclusion. Impressed with the belief that the word had a trans-Atlantic origin, I have occasionally asked the opinion of such friends as I knew to be familiar with the construction of languages, and likely to be much better informed on the subject than myself. In November, 1856, the Hon. Charles W. Bradley, LL. D., formerly Secretary of State, and now an American Consul in China, thus responded to my enquiry and suggestion:

"As to the name "Bantam," I fully agree with you that it hath a very un-Indian look and sound, nor have I ever regarded it as belonging to any of our native dialects. I have no idea how it got there. The only place of that name, within my ken, is near my late residence (Singapore,) where, in the Island of Java, is a town, once the capital of a District of the same designation, containing 3,428 square miles. Bantam is in lat. 6° S. long. 106° 13′ E—forty-seven miles W. from Batavia."

Prof. W. G. Peck, of Columbia College, New York, in October last, wrote:

"You will remember our conversation about the word *Bantam*, and that I took the ground that it was not of Indian origin. In looking over an old History of Java, the other day, I came across the fact that an expedition was fitted out in 1601, consisting of four ships belonging to the then newly-formed "East India Company;" and that the expedition sailed under Captain Lancaster in 1602, touching first at Acheen and then at *Bantam* in Java. Captain Lancaster, during the latter year, brought home a letter from the "King of Bantam" to Queen Elizabeth. From all this, you will see that the Java Bantam was in existence and had a king, eighteen years before the landing of the Pilgrims—and I don't know how much earlier. Bantam was occupied by the Dutch in the sixteenth century, and was a place of much consequence. In the Portuguese writings of Jono de Barras, (Lisbon 1777,) the place is called "Bintam or Bantam." I am unable to ascertain whether the word is Dutch or Javanese; at any rate, it is quite clear that the name is not of Connecticut origin."

The English and Danes had factories at Bantam previous to 1682, at which date they were taken by the Dutch. The harbor was long a favorite rendezvous for British shipping in the East. Of course the name was a familiar one in the English colonies at the time of the exploration of these Western Lands. *Why* it was transferred to this locality, must remain a matter of conjecture; perhaps it was because, like the Bantam of the old world, this was a wild and almost unknown region, inhabited by a race of barbarians; perhaps, as has been suggested by a distinguished antiquarian scholar, the name may have first been given by the settlers on the Connecticut to an Indian sachem residing in this vicinity, and, at a subsequent date, the country may have been named from *him*. At all events, it appears to have been the first designation by which this township was ever known to the Anglo-Saxon race; and as such, is worthy of being retained and cherished.

The Town, as we have seen, was first called LITCHFIELD in the act of incorporation, passed during the May Session, 1719, and was so named from the ancient city of LICHFIELD, Staffordshire, England—the *t* being added, probably by the legislative clerk, and has ever since been retained. It was with a sort of hallowed, home-sick feeling, that, in July 1855, the author of this volume (then on his way from London to North Wales,) made a brief stop at this famous ecclesiastieal emporium. Long before reaching the Lichfield Station, the spires of the noble Cathedral attracted the attention and elicited the remarks of the numerous strangers on the train. It is hardly to be presumed that *this* place received the name it bears, on account of any supposed resemblance of its *location* to that of the city whence its name is derived. The English Lichfield, it is true, stands upon elevated ground, and is surrounded by rural beauties which are rarely surpassed even in the British Islands; but the city cannot be said to stand on a *hill*, and the face of the surrounding country is materially different from the scenes upon which we are accustomed to look. With the same broad meadows, pastures and cultivated fields, interspersed with patches of wood-land, they lack the lake, and forest, and mountain scenery, which forms a principal attraction of our landscapes. Lichfield is said to have been erected into a bishopric as early as A. D. 656—the first bishop bearing the name of Diuma. The first cathedral was completed about the year 700, in the time of Bishop Hedda. The founder of the *present* edifice is stated to have been Roger de Clinton, who came to the see in 1138; though, from the style of architecture, it is believed that much of the building was erected during the thirteenth and fourteenth centuries. At the commencement of the civil wars, the Close of Lichfield was fortified by the royalists, and the command entrusted to Lord Chesterfield. In March, 1643, the garrison was attacked by the parliamentary forces under Lord Brooke, one of the Patentees of Connecticut, who is said to have made a vow that if he should succeed he would level the cathedral with the ground. A day or two after, however, his lordship was shot dead, as he walked along the street below, by a gentleman stationed on the great tower of the church. The garrison soon surrendered to the puritan army, who, if we are to believe Dugdale, demolished all the monuments, pulled down the curious carved work, battered in the costly windows, destroyed the records, stabled their horses in the aisles, and "every day hunted a cat throughout the church, delighting themselves in the echo from the goodly vaulted roof." These were strange pastimes, surely, for puritan soldiers; but doubtless the picture was somewhat overdrawn by the royal historian. The garrison was again captured by the royalists, and re-captured by the puritans. The cathedral suffered greatly from these successive sieges. It was estimated that not less than two thousand cannon-balls and fifteen hundred hand-grenades had been discharged against it. It was completely renovated by Bishop Hacket during the reign of Charles II. The city contains several churches, schools, and charitable institutions, and, in 1841, had a population of 14,754. Its streets are narrow, but well paved and well lighted; many of the buildings are handsome, and its general appearance is much above the average of English towns of its size. Its municipal officers are, a mayor, recorder, five aldermen, and eighteen Councilors. It is entitled to two members of parliament. In this place were born Garrick, Johnson, Lady Mary Wortley Montague, and other eminent characters.

As to the etymology of the word *Lichfield*, or *Litchfield*, Gorton in his "Topographical Dictionary of Great Britain and Ireland," (London, 1833, vol. ii, p. 564,) says—"Various derivations have been proposed of the name of this place; but it has generally been deduced from the term, Lich-field, signifying the *Field of the Dead*—thus denominated, according to some ecclesiastical historians, on account of the great number of Christians having suffered martyrdom here during the Dioclesian persecution in the beginning of the fourth century." In confirmation of this derivation, it may be added, that a field in the neighborhood, bearing the name of *Christian Field*, is still pointed out as the place where a thousand Christians were slaughtered at one time. This definition also corresponds with that given by the great lexicographer, Dr. Johnson, who was a native of Lichfield. In Saxon times, this town formed a portion of the extensive and powerful kingdom of Mercia, which was christianized upon its conquest by Oswy, King of Northumberland.

Our Litchfield (Connecticut) was the first place on this continent to bear the name. There are now seven other Litchfields in the United States, (all spelt with the *t*,) viz., one in each of the following States—Maine, New Hampshire, New York, Pennsylvania, Ohio, Michigan and Kentucky. These towns, with perhaps a single exception, were settled by Connecticut people. In Ohio, there is a post office named *Bantam*.

CHAPTER II.

INCIDENTS OF THE FIRST SETTLEMENT.

THE settlement of Litchfield was commenced by Capt. Jacob Griswold, from Windsor, Ezekiel Buck, from Wethersfield, and John Peck, from Hartford, all of whom removed their families into the township during the summer of 1720. In the course of this and the following year, several other families —chiefly from Hartford, Lebanon, Wethersfield and Windsor— erected log houses on their home-lots, and moved into them.

The record of what appears to have been the first Town Meeting, is *without date*. Dea. John Buel and Nathaniel Smith were appointed a Committee to hire a minister, and "to make and gather a rate, to pay him for his services amongst us." This Committee employed Mr. TIMOTHY COLLINS, of Guilford, a young licentiate who had graduated at Yale College in 1718. At the next Meeting, held November 6, 1721, it was voted, "that Mr. Collins be forthwith called to a settlement in this place in the work of the ministry;" and it was stipulated that he should receive fifty-seven pounds per year for four years—and thereafter, as follows, viz., "the fifth year, sixty pounds; the sixth year, seventy pounds; the seventh year, eighty pounds—and so to continue at eighty pounds per year" so long as he should remain in the pastoral office in this town. It was also agreed to pay him one hundred pounds previous to the 1st day of July, 1722, and to furnish him with fire-wood. Mr. Collins accepted the terms proposed, in a letter bearing date, "Litchfield, Dec. 12, 1721," and immediately entered upon his labors—though he was not ordained until the 19th of June, 1723.* In addition to his salary, as above

*Messrs. Nathaniel Smith, Eleazer Strong and Samuel Culver, were appointed a committee "to provide accommodations, at the town's cost, for the Elders and Messengers that shall be in attendance."

stated, Mr. Collins received in fee one-sixtieth part of all the lands of the township, together with the *use* for life of another sixtieth part.

The first meeting of the Inhabitants for the choice of *Town Officers*, was held Dec. 12, 1721, and resulted as follows:

John Marsh, *Town Clerk.*

John Buel,
Nathaniel Hosford, } *Selectmen.*
John Marsh,

William Goodrich, *Constable and Collector.*

Benjamin Gibbs and Thomas Lee, *Surveyors.*

Eleazer Strong and Samuel Root, *Fence Viewers.*

Daniel Culver, *Hayward.*

Joseph Bird, *Collector of Minister's Rate.*

The only person "admitted an inhabitant" at this meeting, was Mr. Joseph Kilbourn, from Wethersfield, who had recently purchased one-thirtieth part of the township—being the original Rights of Messrs. Mann and Peet.

On the 6th of February, 1721–'2, Messrs. Buel and Marsh were voted "the use of the stream of Bantam River and thirty acres of land," on condition that they would erect a *Grist Mill* and keep the same in order; and Messrs. Jacob Griswold, William Goodrich and Benjamin Gibbs were designated to lay out the land for their use.

On the 8th of the ensuing May, Messrs. Buel, Marsh, Smith and Hosford, were appointed a Committee, and fully empowered by the town, to negotiate a settlement of the boundary line between Litchfield and Waterbury, with a Committee appointed by the proprietors of the latter town. At the same time, Messrs. Buel and Marsh were directed to petition the General Assembly, on the town's behalf, "for liberty to set up a church and society in Litchfield."

It had been one of the conditions of the several deeds of conveyance to the original proprietors, that the grantees or their sons should build a tenantable house on each home-lot, or division, not less than sixteen feet square, and personally inhabit the same by the last day of May, 1721, and for three years ensuing; and no one was permitted "to leave or dispose of his share for five years thereafter, without the consent of the first planters." This was a wise provision, growing out of the dependent and exposed condition of a settlement in the wilderness. Not only was each individual purchaser expected to encourage the settlement by his personal presence and labors, but his assistance in planning and executing the various projects designed for the promotion of the public welfare, was deemed indispensable. His proprietorship in these "western lands" was no sinecure, resorted to for purposes of speculation. He must bear his full share of the burthens and perils incident to the life of a pioneer. For divers reasons, several of the first purchasers, as has been intimated, failed to comply with these terms. On the 8th of June, 1722, in general Town Meeting, it was voted that the following persons had "forfeited their Rights to Lands in Litchfield by not performing what they were obliged to in the articles of the settlement mentioned in the Grand Deed," viz., Timothy Seymour, Timothy Stanley, Isaac Judson, Jacob Gibbs, John Stoddard, Nathaniel Smith, Paul Peck, John Hart, Philip Bump, Nathaniel Woodruff, Thomas Griswold, John Baldwin and one of Ezekiel Sandford's Rights. Messrs. John Buel, Nathaniel Smith and John Marsh, were appointed a Committee to negotiate with the above-named individuals, with power to "prosecute the forfeiture to effect" in case the claimants should neglect or refuse to agree to the terms which might be offered them. Probably a compromise was effected with most of the delinquents. Some of them became active and useful men in the town.

In October of this year, the freemen, by a formal vote, expressed their desire to be annexed to Hartford County. They also voted that the tax for the support of the minister and for building the meeting-house, should be laid "one half on the Rights, and the other on heads and stock."

The second annual Town Meeting was held, December 17, 1722. The following Town Officers for the year ensuing were chosen:

[Nathaniel Hosford, *Moderator.*]
John Marsh, *Town Clerk.*

NATHANIEL HOSFORD, }
JOHN STODDARD, } *Selectmen.*
JOSEPH KILBOURN, }

JACOB GRISWOLD, *Constable.*

ELEAZER STRONG, *Grand Juror.*

JOHN BALDWIN and JOSEPH BIRGE, *Fence Viewers.*

NEHEMIAH ALLEN and THOMAS LEE, *Listers.*

JOSEPH HARRIS, *Collector.*

NATHAN MITCHELL, *Leather Sealer.*

At an adjourned meeting held on the 26th of December, it was ordered that the "town stock of powder and lead should be procured by a rate raised upon the Rights." A tax of one hundred and sixty pounds was laid towards building the meeting-house: and a subsequent vote provided for the raising of forty-three pounds more to be applied to the same object, and for the maintenance of the ministry. Messrs. Kilbourn, Stoddard, Hosford and Marsh, were appointed a Committee "to manage the affair of building the meeting-honse." The erection of a place of public worship appears to have been regarded by the town as the *one* great work to be accomplished. The votes in reference to it are frequent. One of them, passed April 19, 1723, describes the dimensions and style of the edifice as follows: It shall be "45 feet in length, 25 feet in breadth and 20 feet between joints; to be shingled and clapboarded, the lower floor laid, the seats and pulpit made, the walls sealed up the girts, all the windows made and glazed; the house well underpined, with all needful doors; all said work to be well and sufficiently done, according to the discretion of the com mittee appointed for the work; all of which work is to be finished within the space of *three years* ensuing the date hereof."* The *location* of the building is described as "northward of William Goodrich's, towards Mr. Collins's house"—or about midway between the present Mansion House corner and the Luke Lewis house.

In the earliest records, our present North street was called

* It is not improbable that the edifice was so far completed within the time specified as to be *used* for public worship; but as late as Dec. 24, 1731, we find an appropriation of £25 "towards *finishing* the meeting-house," and a committee was at the same time appointed to attend to the work. Dec. 27. it was voted "to get a cushion or pillow for the pulpit, to be made with plush, and stufft."

Town street, and was laid out twelve rods wide; that now called South street, was laid out eight rods wide, and was named Town Hill street; Gallows Lane was twenty-eight rods wide, and was called Middle street; the present East and West streets were twenty rods wide, and called Meeting House street—the first meeting-house standing in the center; the street running south from the present residence of Colonel Odell's, was then called South Griswold street, and was four rods wide; that running north from Dr. Eliada Osborn's, was called North Griswold street, and was eight rods wide; Prospect street was called North street, and was originally twenty rods wide, but soon reduced to seventeen.

The subject of Highways was also one of special importance, and engrossed much of the attention of the inhabitants in their Town Meetings. On the 26th of December, 1722, it was voted to lay out a highway from Bantam River to the Chestnut Hill home-lots, "in the range *where the foot-path now is*," as the record expresses it. On the following day, it was voted "to lay out a highway from John Marsh's home-lot [on Chestnut Hill,] to the south bounds; and the highway by Mr. Collins's house, to be continued to the north bounds; and the highway running east, to be extended to the east bounds; and west, or south-west, from Thomas Pier's, according to the best skill of the Committee; and the highway running north from Pier's, to be continued to the north bounds."

The proprietor of each Right was entitled, as a part of his division of lands, to a Home Lot of fifteen acres in the "town plat" or village. The choice of the Home Lots was decided by chance. The first choice fell to Nathaniel Winchell, who selected the lot on the south corner of South-street and Gallows Lane. John Marsh drew the second choice, and, singularly enough to us, selected the lot at the southern extremity of the village, bordering on Bantam River—on which the dwelling-house of Mrs. Frederick Prescott now stands. Timothy Seymour drew the third choice, and fixed the location of his lot on the north side of West-street, where Mr. Lyman J. Smith now lives. Numbers four, five and six, (drawn by Messrs. John Bird, Samuel Orton and Samuel Forward,) selected lots on the east side of South-street, adjoining each other, and lying immediately north of the lot of John Marsh on Bantam River. The Mansion House corner was selected by William Goodrich, who drew number twenty; Nathaniel Smith drew the twenty-fifth choice, and selected the Oliver Goodwin corner; the thirty-third choice fell to Samuel Lewis, who selected the County House corner, which he soon after transferred to Joseph Kilbourn, the purchaser of his Right. For his first "twenty acre division," Mr. Kilbourn selected the lot on the north corner of North and Prospect streets, now occupied in part by Dr. Richards' "Elm Park Collegiate Institute." The north-east corner of North and East streets, together with the lot adjoining on the north, was laid out to the Rev. Mr. Collins; the next lot north was for the benefit of Mr. Collins and his successors in the ministry; adjoining which, still further north, was the home-lot laid out on the School Right. The fifty-seventh (or last) choice was drawn by Ezekiel Sanford, who chose the lot in South-street now owned and occupied by A. C. Smith, Esq.—one of the most eligible sites in the village.

It is probable that the work of laying out these Home Lots was commenced in 1720, and that the first settlers, in compliance with the stipulation contained in their several deeds, erected tenements thereon. In May, 1722, Messrs. Hezekiah Culver and Thomas Lee were appointed to *complete* the work; but it would seem that they failed to attend to the business, for, in the following December, Messrs. John Stoddard, John Bird and Jacob Griswold, were appointed on a Committee for the same purpose. More than two-thirds of the Home Lots were located within our present borough limits; the remainder, farther west on West street and South Griswold street, and south-east on Chestnut Hill.

Two or three incidents connected with pioneering in the era of which we are speaking, will form a fitting close to this chapter.

"In May, 1722," says Mr. Morris, "Capt. Jacob Griswold being at work alone in the field about one mile west of the present Court House, two Indians suddenly rushed upon him from the woods, took him, pinioned his arms, and carried him off. They traveled in a northerly direction, and the same day arrived in some part of the township now called Canaan, then a wilderness. The Indians kindled a fire, and, after binding their prisoner hand and foot, lay down to sleep. Griswold fortunately disengaged his hands and feet, and though his arms were tied, he seized their guns, and made his escape into the woods. After traveling a short distance, he sat down and waited until the dawn of day. Although his arms were still pinioned, he carried both the guns. The savages awoke in the morning, and, finding their prisoner gone, immediately pursued him. They soon overtook him, and kept in sight of him the greater part of the day, while he was making his way homeward. When they came near, he turned and pointed one of the pieces at them; they then fell back. In this manner he traveled till near sunset, when he reached an eminence in an open field about one mile north-west of the center. He then discharged one of his guns, which immediately summoned the people to his assistance. The Indians fled, and Griswold safely returned to his family."

The following interesting narrative from "Travels in New England and New York," by Timothy Dwight, S. T. D., LL. D., President of Yale College, (vol. i. pp. 113—118,) has been often re-published in this country and in Europe. With characteristic caution, he remarks—"This story may be *circumstantially* erroneous; in *substance* I believe it to be true."

"NOT many years after the County of Litchfield began to be settled by the English, a strange Indian came one day into an Inn in the Town of Litchfield, in the dusk of the evening, and requested the hostess to furnish him with some drink and supper. At the same time, he observed, that he could pay for neither, as he had had no success in hunting; but promised payment as soon as he should meet with better fortune. The hostess refused him both the drink and the supper; called him a lazy, drunken, good for nothing fellow; and told him that she did not work so hard, herself, to throw away her earnings upon such creatures as he was. A man who sat by, and observed that the Indian, then turning about to leave so inhospitable a place, showed by his countenance that he was suffering very severely from want and weariness, directed the hostess to supply him what he wished, and engaged to pay the bill himself. She did so. When the Indian had finished his supper, he turned to his benefactor, thanked him, and assured him that he should remember his kindness, and whenever he was able, would faithfully recompense it. For the present, he observed, he could only reward him with a story; which, if the hostess would give him leave, he wished to tell. The hostess, whose complacency had been recalled by the prospect of payment, consented. The Indian, addressing himself to his benefactor, said—"I suppose you read the Bible." The man assented. "Well," said the Indian, "the Bible say, God made the world; and then he took him and looked on him, and say, 'It's all very good.' Then he made light; and took him and looked on him, and say, 'It's all very good.' Then he mode dry land and water, and sun and moon, and grass and trees; and took him and looked on him, and say, 'It's all very good.' Then he made beasts, and birds, and fishes; and took him and looked on him, and say, 'It's all very good.' Then he made man; and took him and looked on him, and say, 'It's all very good.' Then he made woman; and took him and looked on him, and he no dare say one such word." The Indian, having told his story, withdrew.

Some years after, the man who had befriended him had occasion to go some distance into the wilderness, between Litchfield, then a frontier settlement, and Albany, where he was taken prisoner by an Indian scout, and carried to Canada. When he arrived at the principal settlement of the tribe, on the southern border of the St. Lawrence, it was proposed by some of the captors that he should be put to death. During the consultation, an old Indian woman demanded that he should be given up to her; that she might adopt him in the place of a son whom she had lost in the war. He was accordingly given to her, and lived through the succeeding winter in her family, experiencing the customary effects of savage hospitality. The following summer, as he was at work in the forest alone, an unknown Indian came up to him, and asked him to meet him at a place which he pointed out, on a given day. The prisoner agreed to the proposal, but not without some apprehensions that mischief was intended him. During the interval, these apprehensions increased to such a degree as to dissuade him effectually from fulfilling his engagement. Soon after, the same Indian found him at his work again, and very gravely reproved him for not performing his promise. The man apologized, awkwardly enough, but in the best manner in his power. The Indian told him that he should be satisfied, if he would meet him at the same place on a future day, which he named. The man promised to meet him, and fulfilled his promise. When he arrived at the spot, he found the Indian provided with two muskets, ammunition for them, and knapsacks. The Indian ordered him to take one of each, and follow him. The direction of their march was to the south. The man followed, without the least knowledge of what he was to do or whither he was going; but concluded that if the Indian intended him harm, he would have dispatched him at the beginning, and that at the worst he was as safe where he was, as he could be in any other place. Within a short time, therefore, his fears subsided, although the Indian observed a profound and mysterious silence concerning the object of the expedition. In the day time, they shot such game as came in their way, and at night kindled a fire, by which they slept. After a tedious journey of many days, they came one morning to the top of an eminence, presenting a prospect of a cultivated country, in which was a number of houses. The Indian asked his companion whether he knew the place. He replied eagerly that it was Litchfield. His guide then, after reminding him that he had so many years before relieved the wants of a famishing Indian, at an Inn in that town, subjoined, "I that Indian; now I pay you; go home." Having said this, he bade him adieu; and the man joyfully returned to his own house."

The Rev. James Hamilton, D. D., F. L. S., of London, England, author of "The Royal Preacher," and other works, in a Lecture from the text, "Cast thy bread upon the waters," &c., gives the substance of this story, which he commences as follows: "Dr. Dwight, an American, tells how, when the country *near Albany* was newly settled, an Indian came to an inn in Litchfield," &c. (See Royal Preacher, pp. 275–'7.) Ignorance of our local geography, is of course excusable in a foreigner. The incidents of the narrative certainly afford an apt illustration of the truth of the text.

In August, 1723, (as near as can now be ascertained,) Mr. Joseph Harris, one of the most respectable citizens of the town, while at work alone in the woods about a mile and a half west of the village, was attacked by a party of Indians, shot, and scalped. As he did not return home when expected, the alarm was given, and search was immediately made for him, which was continued until the darkness of the night checked all further exertions. In the morning, his body was found leaning against the trunk of a tree. Harris was killed near the north end of the West Plain, a few rods south or south-east of the present residence of Mr. Myron Osborn. He was interred in the West Burying-Ground, where, in 1830, a monument was erected to his memory by voluntary contribution.*

These events effectually alarmed the settlers, and led to those measures of self-defense which are detailed with some degree of minuteness in the next chapter.

* The date of Harris's death given on his monument is 1721. Gibbs and Morris both place the event in "August 1722." These dates are of course impossible—as he was chosen Collector in December of the latter year.

CHAPTER III.

ALARMS AND MEASURES OF DEFENSE.

COULD we go back one hundred and thirty-six years, and, from some elevated stand-point, look down upon Litchfield as it was in the beginning of the year 1723, what a contrast to its present appearance would the scene present! Here and there, like dots on the surface of the landscape, little openings had been made in the primeval forests by the axes of the settlers. Forty or fifty log-cabins were scattered over the site now occupied by this village and its immediate vicinity. A temporary palisade stood where our Court House now stands, and four others were erected in more remote parts of the town, for the protection of the laborers at the clearings: all soon to give place to stronger and more permanent structures. The howl of the wild beast and the yell of the savage, daily and nightly reminded the people of the dangers by which they were surrounded. The little hamlet was quite beyond the bounds of civilization—the nearest white settlements being those at New Milford on the south-west and at Woodbury on the south, both some fifteen miles distant. An almost unbroken wilderness stretched westward to the Dutch settlements on the Hudson, and northward two hundred and fifty miles to the French villages in Canada. The Indians, still at war with the English, prowled on the frontiers like ravenous wolves eager for their prey. Their yells at the war-dance, an ominous sound, were heard on the distant hills, and at midnight their signal-fires on Mount Tom lit up the surrounding country with their baleful gleam. Without mails or newspapers, and with no regular means of communication with their friends in the older towns, they seemed indeed shut out from the world, and dependent upon their own little circle for intellectual and social enjoyment. Is it to be wondered at, that some of the first proprietors should have fled from scenes so uninviting and hazardous, even at the risk of forfeiting the lands which they had purchased?

In the autumn of 1722, a war had broken out between the Province of Massachusetts and the Eastern Indians, and in a short time its direful influences were felt in Connecticut—some of which have already been adverted to. The savages on our borders, many of whom had previously manifested a peaceable and conciliatory spirit, gave evidence that their professions of friendship were not to be relied upon. In the spring of 1723, the Committee of War, in Hartford, sent a military corps to keep garrison at Litchfield. At this time, there were about sixty male adults in the town, a large proportion of whom had families. The following are the names of those who are regarded as "first settlers"—or persons who became residents of the town during the first three years of the settlement:

Nehemiah Allen, from	Coventry.	Joseph Kilbourn,	Wethersfield.
Joseph Birge,	Windsor.	Thomas Lee,	Lebanon.
Joseph Bird,	Farmington.	John Marsh,	Hartford.
John Bird,	"	Joseph Mason,	"
Samuel Beebe,	Danbury.	Nathan Mitchell,	Stratford.
John Baldwin,	Stratford.	Samuel Orton,	Woodbury.
Ezekiel Buck,	Wethersfield.	Edward Phelps,	Windsor.
John Buel,	Lebanon.	Thomas Pier,	Stratford.
Daniel Culver,	"	Paul Peck, Jr.	Hartford.
Samuel Culver,	"	John Peck,	"
Hezekiah Culver,	"	John Stoddard,	Wethersfield.
Timothy Collins,	Guilford.	Eleazer Strong,	Lebanon.
John Catlin,	Hartford.	Supply Strong,	"
James Church,	"	Joseph Sanford,	Stratford,
Joseph Gillett,	Colchester.	Lemuel Sanford,	"
Abraham Goodwin.	Hartford.	Nathaniel Smith,	Taunton, Ms.
Joshua Garritt,	"	John Smith,	"
William Goodrich,	Wethersfield.	Samuel Smedley,	Woodbury.
Jacob Griswold,	"	Thomas Treadway,	Lebanon.
John Gay,	Dedham, Ms.	Benjamin Webster,	Hartford.
Benjamin Gibbs,	Windsor.	Josiah Walker,	Woodbury.
Jacob Gibbs,	"	Joseph Waller.	"
Benjamin Hosford,	"	Nathaniel Woodruff,	Farmington.
Joseph Harris,	Middletown.		

Such was the apprehension of danger from the Indians, during this period, that while one portion of the men were felling the forests, plowing, planting or reaping, others, with their muskets in hand, were stationed in their vicinity to "keep guard." In August of this year, (1723,) a meeting of the

Householders of Litchfield was held " to consider of and agree upon some certain places to fortify or make Garrisons for the safety and pseservation of the inhabitants of said town." At this meeting it was resolved that four Forts or Garrisons should be erected in different sections of the town. The names of the persons designated to build these Forts, are here inserted, as the list is supposed to embrace ALL the *proprietors* of the township at that date.

"For building the West Fort—Thomas Pier, Jacob Griswold, Ezekiel Buck, Nathan Mitchell Joseph Birge, Daniel Judson, John Stoddard, Daniel Culver, Timothy Seymour, Hezekiah Culver, Thomas Treadway, Lemuel Sanford, John Baldwin, Samuel Beebe and Joshua Boardman.

" For the North Garrison—Thomas Lee, Lieut. John Buel, John Buel, Joseph Kilbourn, Joseph Kilbourn, (Jr.,) Nathaniel Smith, William Goodrich, Eleazer Strong, Samuel Root, Samuel Somers, Josiah Walker, Nehemiah Allen and Supply Strong.

"For the East Garrison—Nathaniel Hosford, Benjamin Hosford, Paul Peck, Edward Phelps, Samuel Culver, Joshua Garrett, John Caulkins, Joseph Gillett, Joseph Mason, Benjamin Webster, John Gay and Thomas Griswold.

" For the South Garrison—John Marsh, John Peck, Benjamin Gibbs, Jacob Gibbs, Samuel Orton, John Bird, Joseph Harris, Abraham Goodwin, Widow Allen, Joseph Bird, Joseph Waller, Nathaniel Woodruff and Samuel Smedley."

On the 1st of April, 1724, Mr. John Marsh was chosen Agent of the town " to represent their state to the General Assembly concerning the settlement and continuing of their inhabitants in times of war and danger."

In May, the subject of the Indian disturbances in this quarter occupied much of the time and attention of the Council of War and of the Legislature. The Indians on the western lands were ordered to repair immediately to their respective places of residence, and not to go into the woods without Englishmen in company with them, " nor to be seen, contrary to this order, anywhere north of the road leading from Hartford to Farmington, Waterbury, and so on to New Milford." They were warned to submit to this order on pain of being looked upon as enemies, and treated accordingly. Two hundred men from Hartford, Wethersfield and Windsor, were directed to hold themselves in readiness to march at the shortest notice; and sixty more from each of the counties of New Haven, Fairfield and New London, with their proper officers, were called for to supply the garrisons at Litchfield and New Milford, when the soldiers then at those posts should be withdrawn. Friendly Indians were to be employed in scouting with the English, and £20 each were to be paid for the scalps of the "enemy Indians." An effective scout was to be kept marching in the woods north of Litchfield, between Simsbury, Westfield and Sackett's Farm, [or Sharon.] The thirty-two men, sent on a scout from Litchfield, were directed to be drawn off in ten days. It was also

"Resolved, That orders be forthwith sent to Major Eells, that he impress thirty.two able-bodied men, with a Lieutenant, and send them to Litchfield to be improved in garrisoning and scouting, as may be thought most advantageous by the said Lieutenant and the commissioned officers in Litchfield—and to continue in said service until they shall be released by further orders; and that Major Burr send orders to detail nine effective men, with a Sergeant, to march to New Milford, to be employed in scouting for the protection of the frontier; and a scout of six men are to be employed at Simsbury, for the discovery of the enemy in that quarter;—and all the aforesaid scouts *are directed to take dogs with them into the service* of scouting; and that the scout now out from Windsor, be drawn off on Tuesday next; and the scout now at Litchfield to draw off upon the present appointed scouts arriving there."

"The summer of 1724," says Mr. Woodruff, "was a period of excitement and alarm. The war between the English and the French was then prevailing, and the latter used great efforts to incite the northern Indians to attack the frontier settlements of the whites." The Hon. Noah A. Phelps, in his History of Simsbury, remarks—"The conduct of the Indians at the north and west, during this year, and *especially their hostile move-*

ments in the vicinity of Litchfield, induced the government to take such precautionary measures as the occasion demanded, in order to furnish protection to the weak and exposed settlements. A line of scouts was established, extending from Litchfield to Turkey Hills, curving around the most northerly and westerly settlements in Simsbury. On the 14th of June, 1724, Capt. Richard Case, of Simsbury, was directed to employ ten men on this scouting party, to rendezvous at Litchfield. The men employed in this service were Serg't. Jonathan Holcomb, John Hill, Nathaniel Holcomb, Joseph Mills, William Buell, Samuel Pettibone, Joseph Wilcoxon, Benjamin Humphrey, Nathaniel Westover and Charles Humphrey—all belonging to Simsbury. They continued in the service till October."

Among the papers on file in the office of the Secretary of State, is the following memorandum made by Gov. Talcott:

"A brief account of the minutes of the Council of War Book, of men sent into the service this summer, from May 24, to October 6, 1724:

"After the Assembly rose, ten men were sent to Litchfield, till June 24.

June 25—Four men sent to Litchfield from Hartford.

June 30—Major Burr sent ten men, and Major Eles ten men, to New Milford and Litchfield.

July 27—Six men sent from Woodbury to keep garrison at Shepaug twenty days.

July 30—Major Burr sent fifteen men, and Major Eles fifteen men, to New Milford, Shepaug and Litchfield.

August 18—Fifteen men were improved in scouts under the command of Sergt Joseph Churchill,* at Litchfield and New Milford; have orders sent to the 5th instant of October to draw off and disband.

October, 1724 JOSEPH TALCOTT."

The Assembly, at the October Session, voted "that the garrisons of soldiers at New Milford, Shepaug and Litchfield, be forthwith drawn off and disbanded; and that Captain Joseph Minor, of Woodbury, give notice thereof to the officers under whose command said soldiers are, that they be drawn off accordingly, by sending a copy of this to said officers."

* Sergt. Joseph Churchill, of Wethersfield, presented a Memorial to the General Assembly, in May, 1725, stating that during the preceding summer he had been employed in His Majesty's service for fifteen weeks at Litchfield, but had received no pay for Sundays. He therefore asks pay for fifteen Sundays. [Granted by the Lower House; lost in the Upper House.]

By our Town Records it appears that on the 15th of October, 1724, a Memorial to the General Assembly was agreed upon, and ordered to be signed by John Marsh, in the name of the town, and sent to New Haven by the hand of Mr. Timothy Collins, to be delivered to the Court. This Memorial is not on record, but is fortunately presevel among the files in the Secretary's Office in Hartford. It is an impressive and interesting document, and eloquently details the trials and perils encountered by our fathers amid these now peaceful scenes. It here appears in print for the first time:

"At a Meeting of the Inhabitants of the Town of Litchfield, October the 15th, 1824—

"A Memorial of the distressed state of the Inhabitants of the Town of Litchfield, which we humbly lay before the Honorable General Assembly now sitting in New Haven:

May it please your Honors to hear us in a few things. Inasmuch as there was a prospect of the war's moving into these parts the last year, the Governor and Council—moved with paternal regards for our safety—ordered Garrisons forthwith to be erected in this town. In obedience thereto, laying aside all other business, we engaged in that work, and built our fortifications without any assistance from abroad, whereby our seed-time in some measure was lost, and consequently our harvest this year small. The seat of the war in this colony (in the whole course of the concluding summer,) being in this town, notwithstanding the special care taken of us by the Honorable Committee of War, and the great expense the colony has been at for our security, yet the circumstances of our town remain very difficult in several respects. The danger and charge of laboring abroad is so great, that a considerable part of our improvable lands remote from the town lie unimproved, whereby we are greatly impoverished, so that many of our inhabitants are rendered incapable of paying their taxes which have been granted for the settling and maintaining of our ministry and building a meeting-house, (which we are yet destitute of,) whereby that great work seems to be under a fatal necessity of being neglected.

Many of our Inhabitants are drawn off, which renders us very weak and unable to defend ourselves from the common enemy, and the duties of Watching and Warding are become very heavy.

By reason of the late war, our lands are become of little value, so that they who are desirous of selling, to subsist their families and defray public charges which necessarily arise in a new place, are unable to do it. Your humble petitioners therefore pray this Honorable Court would be pleased to take thought of our difficult circumstances, and spread the garment of pity over our present distress, which moves us to beg relief in several respects:

1. That our deserting proprietors, who do not personally inhabit,

may be ordered to settle themselves or others upon their Rights, which will not only be an encouragement to those that tarry, and render our burden more tolerable, but prevent much charge to the colony.

2. That our Inhabitants may be under some wages, that they may be capable of subsisting in the town, and not labor under the difficulty of war and famine together.

3. That some addition be made to the price of billeting soldiers, especially for this town, where the provision, at least a greater part of it, hath been fetched near twenty miles for the billeting of soldiers this year

4. That some act be made concerning Fortified Houses, that the people may have free liberty of the use of said Houses as there is occasion.

5. That there may be an explanation of the Act of the Governor and Council, made the last summer, which obliges every proprietor of a home lot to attend the military, by himself or some other person in his room, as the law directs, in case a person hath fifty pounds in the public list; for many of our deserters have put off their home lots and some of their lands, so that many of them have not a whole Right or a home lot in this place, and so escape execution upon that act.

As to the Indians hunting in our woods, we submit to your Honors' ordering that affair as in your wisdom you shall think best for us.

All of which we humbly recommend to the consideration of this Honorable Assembly, and ourselves your servants desiring Heaven's blessing to rest upon you, and that God Almighty may be with you, to direct in all weighty affairs which are before you, and make you rich blessings in your day and generation, your humble petitioners shall, as in duty bound, ever pray. JOHN MARSH,

In the name and by desire of the rest."

On this Memorial, a Committee of Conference was appointed by the two branches of the Legislature, consisting of Samuel Eells and Matthew Allyn, Esquires, on the part of the Upper House, and Capt. John Fitch, Capt. David Goodrich and Mr. George Clark, on the part of the Lower House. The result of their deliberations was embodied in the following enactment, which passed both Houses at the October Session, 1724:

"Upon the Memorial of the Inhabitants of the Town of Litchfield—*Be it Enacted and Ordained*, by the Governor, Assistants and Deputies in General Court assembled, and by authority of the same,

That whosoever hath or ought to have been an Inhabitant, and is a Proprietor of Lands within the said Town of Litchfield, or have deserted and left said Town since difficulties have arisen there on the account of an Enemy, and shall neglect, for the space of one month after the rising of this Assembly, to rèturn to the said Town and there abide, or send some man in their room and stead to perform and do the necessary duties of Watching and Warding, and the like, during the continuance of the difficulties of the war, shall lose and forfeit all their right and estate in and upon any and all of the Lands aforesaid, and their estate, right and interest therein, unto the Corporation of Connecticut. *And Further, it is Provided*, That if any other man, being now a Proprietor and Inhabitant, or a Proprietor and ought to have been an Inhabitant in said Town, shall hereafter, during the continuance of fear and danger of the enemy, desert and leave the said Town, or neglect to repair thither and there personally abide, without constantly providing some other sufficient person in his room and stead, there to perform all duties as before mentioned in the case of those who have already deserted, shall likewise forfeit their estates in and to all the lands in the Town aforesaid, unto this Corporation. *And Further, it is Provided*, That upon complaint made to the Committee of War, at Hartford, of or against any such deserter, upon their satisfaction of the truth thereof, the said Committee shall declare the forfeiture; and the said Committee are empowered to admit any other person who shall go and abide there in the room of the deserter and perform the necessary duties as aforesaid, and he shall hereafter receive a grant from this Court of the estate escheated as aforesaid for his confirmation therein.

And it is Further Ordered, That five shillings per week shall be allowed for billeting soldiers in Litchfield for the summer last past."

On the 18th of January, 1724–'5, a meeting of the inhabitants of the town was held, on which occasion it was voted that a Committee should be chosen "to consider of and make application to the Council of War in behalf of the Town, for what they judge needful for the peace and safety of the Town in this time of trouble and danger." Rev. Timothy Collins, Mr. Nathaniel Hosford, Lieut. John Buel, Ensign Nathaniel Smith, Sergt. John Stoddard, Mr. Joseph Bird and Mr. John Marsh, were appointed said Committee.

At a Town Meeting held on the 10th of May, 1725, "it was voted and agreed, that there shall forthwith be erected one good and substantial Mount, or place convenient for sentinels to stand in for the better discovering of the enemy and for the safety of said sentinels when upon their watch or ward; that is to say, one Mount at each of the four Forts that were first agreed upon and are already built in said Town, which Mounts shall be built at the Town's cost, by order and at the discretion of such men as the Town shall appoint to oversee and carry on the above said work. At the same Meeting, *Voted*, That Joseph Kilbourn, shall take the care of building the Mount at the North Fort, and Samuel Culver shall take the care of building the Mount at the East Fort, and Jacob Griswold at the West Fort, and Joseph Bird at the South Fort."

During the Legislative Session then next ensuing, the Committee already named presented the following Memorial, viz.:

"To the Honorable Governor, Assistants and Representatives, in General Court convened—

The Petition of the Inhabitants of the Town of Litchfield humbly sheweth: That whereas your Petitioners, notwithstanding all that this Honorable Court hath done for us, which we accept with all thankfulness, remain under great trouble by reason of the war, which hath so much hindered us in our husbandy, which hindrance yet remains upon us, and hath already greatly shortened our crops. If the war continues, we shall scarcely be able to raise our bread-corn or support ourselves in this place, without some relief, either by putting our Inhabitants under some pay from the Government, or by some other way as your Honors in your wisdom shall think best for the whole of the Inhabitants; and that something be further done concerning our non-residents, by reason of whose absence we are great sufferers; and that some act be made concerning liberty in garrison-houses; and that some money be granted for finishing our Garrisons, which we are very unable to do ourselves. All which your humble Petitioners submit to your Honors' great wisdom; and that you may be made a rich and lasting blessing in your day and generation, your Petitioners shall, as in duty bound, ever pray.

Dated at Litchfield the 25th day of May, A. D, 1725.

JOHN MARSH, NATHANIEL HOSFORD, TIMOTHY COLLINS, JOHN BUEL, JOSEPH BIRD,	Committee or Agents Town of Litchfield."

The Upper House appointed His Honor the Deputy Governor and Major Wolcott a Committee on the Litchfield Memorial; Major John Burr and Messrs. Seymour and Leete were appointed a similar Committee on the part of the Lower House. The following Resolutions, which soon after passed both Houses, probably emanated from them:

"This Assembly, taking into consideration the difficulties of the Town of Litchfield in this time of trouble with the Indians, and that sundry persons claiming Rights in said Town are not resident in the same, have therefore Resolved:

1. That each person claiming a Right or Rights in said Town, that shall not be constantly residing in said Town, shall pay and forfeit, towards defraying the public charges in defending the same, the sum of £30 per annum for each Right he claims, and so *pro rata* for any time he shall be absent without allowance from Capt. Marsh, John

Buel and Nathaniel Hosford, or any two of them ; and by the same rule of proportion for part Rights. And if any such claimer shall neglect payment of the said forfeiture at the time and to the Committee hereafter appointed in this Act, the said Committee are hereby fully empowered to sell so much of the Lands in Litchfield claimed by such non-resident person, as will answer the sum so forfeited ; and all sales and alienations made of such Lands by the Committee, shall be good for the holding the same to the grantees and their heirs forever.

And this Assembly appoint Major Roger Wolcott, Capt. Nathaniel Stanley, Esq., and Mr. Thomas Seymour, a Committee to take account of all forfeitures that shall arise by force of this act, and upon the non-payment of the same, to make sale of the Lands as aforesaid.

And it is Further Ordered, That all such forfeitures shall be paid to the said Committee at the State House in Hartford, on the first Monday in June, which will be in the year 1726 ; and the said Committee are to deliver all such sum or sums as they shall receive by force of this act, unto the Treasurer of this Colony, taking his receipt for the same—the said Committee to make their accounts with the Assembly in October, provided nevertheless that the Right of Joseph Harris is saved from any forfeiture by force of this act. And it is further provided, that if any such claimer shall keep an able-bodied soldier in said Litchfield, who shall attend duty as the Inhabitants do, such claimer shall be excused for his non-residence during such time.

2. *And it is Further Enacted,* That all houses that are fortified in said Town, shall be free for the use of the people and soldiers in the garrison.

3. That the Inhabitants of said Town shall be allowed five shillings and six pence per week for billeting soldiers.

4. That Mounts shall be built in the Forts that are already made in said Town, at the public cost of the Colony ; and Capt. Marsh, John Buel and Nathaniel Hosford, or any two of them, are appointed to build the same, keeping fair accounts of their doings herein, and lay the same before the Committee for the War, who are directed to give orders to the Treasurer to pay what shall be justly due to them for their services.

5. That all able-bodied young men that are dwellers in said Town and are eighteen years old and upwards, and have no right to any Lands in said Town, and shall constantly reside therein until October next, and do duty with the Inhabitants, shall be allowed three shillings per week out of the Public Treasury, until October next, unless the Committee for the War in Hartford shall order to the contrary for part of said time.

6. That every able-bodied man that is fit for service to the acceptance of the commissioned officers, that hath a Right in said Town, and shall constantly reside therein and do his duty according to the command of the captain until October next, shall be allowed out of the Treasury eighteen pence per week, unless the Committee for the War shall order to the contrary for part of the time."

In consequence of the provision of the 4th Resolution, it was

"*Voted*, That the persons appointed by the Town to take the care of building the Mounts at the Forts, shall proceed no farther by virtue of their orders from the Town, that so the Mounts may be built at the charge of the Colony."

At the same Legislative Session, Messrs. Nathaniel Watson, of Windsor, and Matthew Woodruff, of Farmington, each presented a petition for a bounty for having shot an Indian during the preceding summer, while in the King's service at Litchfield. The statements of Messrs. Samuel Beebe, Shubael Griswold and Joseph Pinney, on the subject, are on file in Hartford. The following is from Mr. Beebe:

"SAMUEL BEEBE, of lawful age, testifieth and saith—That he heard Matthew Woodruff say that he thought he had not struck the Indian that he shot at, but thought he had overshot him. The next morning we went out to the place where we had the fight, and then said Watson went to the place where he stood when he shot at the Indian, and then directed a man to the spot where the Indian stood that he shot at, and there was the blood found very plentiful; and those that were there, followed the blood to the place where we did think the said Indian did die, and further. The Indian that said Watson shot at, was about six or seven rods from the place where the Indian stood that Woodruff shot at. SAMUEL BEEBE.

Litchfield, May the 24, 1725."

The annexed Petition is also copied from the colonial files:

"To the Honorable JOSEPH TALCOTT, Governor of His Majesty's Colony of Connecticut—Whereas, When your humble Petitioners were impressed to come up to Litchfield to keep garrison, we were encouraged by our officers to come, because it was but for a little while we should be continued here, just till the Inhabitants could get their seed into the ground. That business being over, and our necessity to be at home being very great, we humbly pray your Honor to dismiss or exchange us by the beginning of June; whereby your Honor will greatly oblige your Humble Petioners. JOSEPH ROSE,

Litchfield, May 23, 1725. In behalf of the rest."

During the summer of 1725, the war with the Eastern Indians still continued, though it does not appear that the people of Litchfield suffered in consequence, except by being kept in a state of suspense and anxiety. At the October session of the Legislature, it was voted that "forasmuch as the continuance of the unhappy war between Massachusetts and the Eastern Indians is likely to endanger our frontiers, and the county of Hampshire, this Assembly empowers the Governor and the Committee of War at Hartford, to impress and send forth such forces as they shall think needful to defend our own frontiers;

and in case of a threatened attack upon Hampshire county, a force may be sent to aid them, but they are not compelled to keep garrison there."

It is not until a year later, (October, 1726,) that the records give indication that any immediate danger was apprehended by the people of this town. At this date, " upon news that the Indian enemy were coming down upon our frontiers," it was resolved " that there be forthwith thirty effective men raised in the towns of New Haven and Wallingford, to march to Litchfield, to be under the direction and command of Capt. John Marsh, of Litchfield, for the defense of said town—twenty of whom shall be raised in New Haven, and ten in Wallingford; and that a Sergeant march with them directly from each of said towns; and that the Major of the county make out his orders to the Captain in said town accordingly."

Twenty effective men were at the same time ordered immediately to be raised in Milford, and marched to New Milford, to be under the command of Capt. Stephen Nobles, for the defense of that town.

Captains John Marsh and Stephen Nobles were directed at once to " send forth small scouts, to call, and, in the name of the Assembly, to command, all the friendly Indians to retire to their respective towns or places where they belong, and not to be seen in the woods except with Englishmen." The friend, ly Indians were to be employed for the defense of the frontiers- and for scouting—and were to be paid eighteen pence per day while engaged in the latter service, and twelve pence per day for warding and keeping garrison in towns. Five men were directed to be sent from Woodbury for the defense of Shepaug until the danger should be over. Captains Minor and Preston were directed to order their Lieutenants to see to it that the men were forthwith sent. These men were placed under the command of Lieut. Ephraim Warner.

Though Litchfield had been nominally incorporated, " with all the powers and privileges of the other towns in this colony," in 1719, she was yet without a Patent, or Town Charter. It appears to have been regarded by the settlers as a matter of importance as well as of etiquette, that the town should be more fully recognized and protected, by letters patent under the great colonial seal. Accordingly, in May, 1723, John Marsh was appointed by his fellow-townsmen an Agent to apply to the General Assembly for this purpose—who presented to that body the following Petition:

"To the Honorable Governor, Council and Representatives, in General Court assembled at Hartford, May 9th, A. D. 1723. The Petition of JOHN MARSH, Agent for the Town of Litchfield, humbly sheweth:

That this Honorable Assembly did give and grant to the Inhabitants of said town of Litchfield, all that land lying north of the town of Waterbury, and to begin at Waterbury north-west corner, and from thence to run in a west line to Shepaug river and to bound east on Waterbury river, and west by said Shepaug, and to run north seven miles and a half; as more at large by the record of said grant may appear.

That the Inhabitants of said Litchfield, for great and valuable considerations, have made a purchase of the said Lands of the towns of Hartford and Windsor, who had a claim thereto by virtue of a grant anciently made by this Assembly to them.

That the Inhabitants aforesaid have, through many fatigues, perils and dangers, removed themselves and families thither, and undergone the great hardships of settling a new town; the which your Honors will easily conceive to be attended with, since it is so remote a settlement and a frontier to the government. So that if the blessing of Heaven shall rest upon them, as it hath hitherto seemed to smile upon the undertaking, there is a prospect that they in a short time may become numerous, and succeed in some measure proportionable to the views they first had therein.

That the Inhabitants, excited by an observation made on the unhappy disputes that have oft arisen in towns by a long delay of settling and ascertaining their bounds, and determining the property of the Lands within, and being desirous in time to secure themselves from such uncomfortable and almost undoing disputes, have procured their lines to be run and necessary monuments to be made therein, on the north and south of said Litchfield, the procuring whereof (our present low circumstances considered, we being in our infancy,) must needs be very burthensome.

The said Inhabitants, by their Agent aforesaid, do therefore humbly pray this Honorable Assembly to give them a more particular grant of the said town, and confirmation thereof, by a *Patent* under the seal of the Government, in due form, and your Honors' humble petitioners shall, as in duty bound, ever pray. JOHN MARSH."

No sooner was this application known, than Woodbury sent in a remonstrance, particularly objecting to the southern bounds of Litchfield, as claimed by her. A Patent, however, was drawn up in due form, bearing date, May 19, 1724. For some cause, (probably on account of the continued remonstrances of Woodbury,) the instrument was not officially granted to the parties applying therefor, until several years subsequent to its date. In May, 1731, Messrs. John Bird and Benjamin Hosford, "Agents for the Proprietors of the Town of Litchfield," presented a Memorial to the Legislature, stating that they are yet without a Patent, and praying that "the difficulty and contention and impoverishing lawsuits, because of an unsettled line, may be prevented by a Patent according to our purchase and grant," as is therein expressed. The Legislature, in response, gave directions that the proprietors of Woodbury should be notified of the application, and warned to appear before the Assembly, and show cause, if any they had, why the memorial should not be granted. As nothing further is found relating to the matter, it is presumed that the petition was this time successful. A copy of the Patent is here given, viz.:

"THE Governor and Company of the English Colony of Connecticut in New England, to all to whom these Presents shall come, GREETING:

KNOW YE, THAT the said Governor and Company, by virtue of the power granted unto them by our late sovereign, King Charles the Second, of blessed memory, in and by His Majesty's Patent, under the great seal of England, dated the twenty-third day of April, in the fourteenth year of His Majesty's reign, and in pursuance thereof and in General Court assembled, according to charter, did, by their act, made May fourteenth, Anno Domini, 1719, upon the humble petition of Lieut. John Marsh, of Hartford, within the said Colony, and Dea. John Buell, of Lebanon, grant unto the said John Marsh and John Buell, and partners, settlers, being in the whole fifty-seven in number, liberty to settle a town westward of Farmington, in the county of Hartford, at a place called *Bantam*, which town was to be in length east and west, eight miles, three quarters, and twenty-eight rods, and in breadth, seven miles and an half—to be bounded east on Mattatuck river, west part on Shepaug river and part on the wilderness, north by the wilderness, and south by Waterbury bounds and a west line from Waterbury corner to the said Shepaug river. And Ordered, that the said town should be called by the name of LITCHFIED, as more fully appears by the said act. The said Governor and Company, by virtue of the aforesaid power, and by their special act bearing even date with these presents, for divers good causes and considerations them hereunto moving, have given, granted, and by these presents, for themselves, their heirs and successors, do fully, clearly and absolutely give, grant, ratify and confirm, unto the said John Marsh and John Buell, and the rest of the said partners, settlers of said tract of land [in their actual, full and peaceable possession and seizin being] and to their heirs and assigns, and such as shall legally succeed and represent them, forever, [in such proportions as they, the said partners and settlers, or any of them, respectively, have right in and are lawfully possessed of the same,] all the said tract of land now called and known by the name of Litchfield, in the county of Hartford aforesaid, be the same more or less, butted and bounded as followeth, viz: Beginning at the north east corner, at a tree with stones about it, standing in the crotch of Mattatuck river aforesaid, and running southerly by the side of said river until it meets with Waterbury bounds, where is a well known white oak tree standing about fifteen rods west of said Mattatuck river, anciently marked with IS: IN: From thence running west twenty three degrees thirty minutes south, to two white oak trees growing out of one root, with stones about them, and west one mile and a half to Waterbury north west corner bound mark; and from thence west five degrees thirty minutes north to Shepaug river, where is a tree and stones about it butting upon Waterbury township; then beginning at the first mentioned tree by Mattatuck river and running westward into the wilderness, to an oak tree marked and stones laid around it; then south to a crotch in the Shepaug river; and thence by the westermost branch of Shepaug river to Woodbury bounds. And also all and singular, the lands, trees, woods, underwoods, woodgrounds, uplands, arable lands, meadows, moors, marshes, pastures, ponds, waters, rivers, brooks, fishings, fowlings, huntings, mines, minerals, quarries, and precious stones, upon and within the said land. And all other rights, members, hereditaments, easements and commodities whatsoever, to the same belonging or in any wise appertaining, so butted and bounded as is herein before particularly expressed or mentioned, and the reversion or the reversions, remainder or remainders, rights, royalties, privileges, powers or jurisdictions whatsoever, of and in all and singular the said tract of land and premises hereby granted, and of and in any and every part and parcel thereof. And the rents, services and profits to the same incident, belonging or appertaining—*To Have and to Hold* all the said tract of land, and all and singular other the premises hereby given or granted, or mentioned, or intended to be granted, with all the privileges and appurtenances thereof, unto the said John Marsh and John Buell, and the rest of the partners, settlers of the same, their heirs and assigns, to their only proper use, benefit and behoof, forever; and to and for no other use, intent or purpose whatsoever. And the said Governor and Company, for themselves and their successors, have given and granted, and by these presents do give and grant, unto the said John Marsh and John Buell, and the rest of the partners, settlers of the tract of land herein before granted, their heirs and assigns; the said tract of land so butted and bounded as aforesaid, shall from time to time and at all times forever hereafter, be deemed, reputed, denominated, and be an entire town of itself, and shall be called and known by the name of LITCHFIELD, in the county of Hartford, and that the aforesaid partners, settlers and inhabitants thereof, shall and lawfully may from time to time and at all times, forever hereafter have, use, exercise and enjoy all such rights, powers, privileges, immunities and franchises, in and among themselves, as are given, granted, allowed, used, exercised and enjoyed, to, by, and amongst the proper inhabitants of other towns in this Colony, according to common approved custom and observance; and that the said tract of land and premises hereby granted as aforesaid, and appurtenances, shall remain, continue and be unto the said John Marsh and John Buell, and the rest of the partners, settlers, their heirs and assigns, in proportion aforesaid forever, a good, peaceable, pure, perfect, absolute and indefeasible estate of inheritance in fee simple, to be holden of His Majesty, his heirs and successors, as of His Majesty's Manor of East Greenwich in the County of Kent, in the Kingdom of England, in free and common soccage, and not in capite, nor by Knight's service—Yielding therefor, and paying unto our Sovereign Lord, King George, his heirs and successors forever, one fifth part of all ore of gold and silver which, from time to time and at all times forever hereafter, shall be there gotten, had or obtained, in lieu of all services, duties and demands whatsoever.

IN WITNESS WHEREOF, The said Governor and Company have caused the Seal of the said Colony to be hereunto affixed.

Dated at Hartford, May the 19*th day, Anno regni regis Decimo Georgii Mag'æ Britt'æ, Fran'æ, Hybern'æ, Annoque Domini, One Thousand Seven Hundred and Twenty-Four,* 1724.

G. SALTONSTALL, Governor.

By order of the Governor and Company in General Court assembled.

HEZ. WYLLIS, Secretary." [SEAL.]

CHAPTER IV.

MISCELLANEOUS EVENTS.

THE preceding Memorials and Resolves so vividly portray the hardships and dangers here experienced by our ancestors, in their efforts to subdue the wilderness and render it a fitting abode for civilized men, that any extended comments would be quite superfluous. Indeed, little can be known of their history during the period of which we have written, except what is gleaned from these plaintive yet manly expositions of their circumstances and feelings. It is difficult for *us*—surrounded as we are with the blessings of Peace snd Plenty—to realize that our predecessors amid these very scenes, were thus exposed to the combined evils of war and famine—bringing their food through the woods a distance of twenty miles; tilling their fields only when protected by an armed guard; men, women and children, from time to time flying in alarm to the garrisons for safety; and the whole adult male population of the town compelled, in turn, to keep public watch and ward through a succession of years; at the same time, clearing off the forests, hunting wild beasts, and fighting the common enemy! Is it not a matter of surprise as well as of gratitude, that during the entire continuance of the war on our frontiers, but one inhabitant of Litchfield fell a victim to savage violence?

The reader will have noted the interesting fact, that Roger Wolcott (afterwards Governor) was, even at this early period, actively engaged in devising measures for the protection and defense of this town—little imagining, probably, that here his descendants were destined to find homes so cherished, and to act so distinguished a part, during the succeeding century.

In a preceding chapter we have seen that the territory now embraced within the limits of this township, was covered by the Charter granted by Charles II. of England, in 1662, to the Governor and Company of the Colony of Connecticut; that in 1687, the colonial government conveyed it to the towns of Hartford and Windsor; that in 1716, committees appointed by these towns, purchased of the Indians all their right and interest therein; that in 1719, committees of these towns sold and conveyed these lands to John Marsh, John Buel, and their associates, in fee, for what was considered a fair equivolent. These latter gentlemen became the first individual owners of the specific tracts which were from time to time surveyed and laid out to them.

It would seem that for some years after the settlement of the township, Hartford and Windsor continued to exercise a kind of guardianship over the affairs of Litchfield. Thus, in February, 1722–'3, Messrs. Hosford and Buel were appointed to treat with the committees of these towns concerning the non-resident proprietors of Litchfield. At a town meeting held on the 1st of April, 1724, it was "voted that the committees of Hartford and Windsor choose inhabitants;" and in case these committees should select for residents any whom the authorities of this town should regard as "not wholesome," it was provided that the character of the new-comers should be judged by indifferent men, and if by them declared to be good inhabitants, then the cost was to be paid by Litchfield—otherwise, the cost was to be paid by the committees referred to.

Even during the prevalence of the Indian wars, though much of their time was necessarily engrossed in providing for the means of subsistence and defense, our fathers were not unmindful of the ordinary duties pertaining to them as public-spirited citizens. Divers matters of a miscellaneous character came up for consideration in their town meetings, some of which will be noted in this chapter.

The lowlands, south-west of the village—bordering upon Bantam River, the Little Pond, and Bantam Lake—are known on our early records as "Bantam Swamp, or the Flooded Lands." They cover about six hundred acres; and, having been nearly free from timber and brush at the time of the first settlement, they were regarded as very valuable on account of the grass. In the original allotment of lands to the first proprietors, each Right entitled the owner to four acres of meadow in this swamp. After all had thus received equal shares, a subsequent division of the balance was made.

As early as April 5, 1725, Lieut. John Buel and Nathaniel Hosford were "appointed to state the bounds of the Flooded Lands, in order to laying out the same; and if said Hosford and Buel cannot agree, then Joseph Kilbourn to be the third man to help in said work." At the same meeting, it was voted "that the clerk record no land laid out upon the Little Plain, until the difference concerning the same be issued." In order to understand the purport of the last record, it should be stated that a controversy had sprung up between Joseph Bird and Nathaniel Hosford, on one side, and the remaining proprietors on the other side—as to whether the "Little Plain" was a part of Bantam Swamp and ought to be laid out as such. The dispute waxed warm; and it was at last determined to appoint two arbitrators from out of town, who should have power to select a third. The gentlemen agreed upon by the contending parties, were, Capt. Joseph Hawley and Mr. Samuel Root, both of Farmington, who made choice of Ensign Nathaniel Wadsworth, also of Farmington, to assist them in the arbitration. They made the following Report—

"WE, the subscribers, having heard the pleas of both parties, and considered them with the reeords, concerning the land in controversy, are of opinion and do give it as our judgment, that the land called the *Little Plain* is no part of Bantam Swamp, nor ought to be laid out in lieu thereof; and that it is free to be laid out to make up the addition to the ten acre lots.

The charge of the arbitration is seventeen shillings; and we order that Lieut. Buel and John Bird pay the said charge—to Capt. Hawley seven shillings, to Ensign Wadsworth four shillings, and to Samuel Root six shillings.

JOSEPH HAWLEY,
NATH'L WADSWORTH.
SAMUEL ROOT."

Farmington, Feb. 25, 1725-'6.

At a town meeting held, Dec. 21, 1725, (Mr. John Buel, Moderator,) Messrs. Jacob Griswold, Benjamin Webster and John Marsh, were appointed a committee to *survey* Bantam Swamp. In November, 1726, a tax of ten shillings on each Right was laid, to be expended by a committee in "lowering the natural ponds for the draining of the swamp;" and Messrs. John Buel, James Church and Joseph Bird, were appointed said committee. The object intended, however, appears not to have been accomplished; for in March, 1731, and again in January, 1732, it was voted to make application to the Governor and Council for the same purpose. On the 30th of April, 1733, a vote was passed "to offer unto the Governor and Council Capt. Joseph Minor and Capt. William Preston, of Woodbury, and Dea. Nathaniel Baldwin, of Litchfield, as a committee for the proprietors of Bantam Swamp, in order to commissionate them to drain said Swamp," &c. Many years afterwards, by blasting away the rocks and erecting a dam on the outlet of Bantam Lake, the swamp was partially drained; but even now, during freshets or long rains, they are frequently overflowed.

As was the case with the settlers of the New England towns generally, the founders of Litchfield regarded the subject of *education* as a matter of primary importance. As stated elsewhere, one sixtieth part of the township (about seven hundred acres,) was originally set apart for the support of schools. In December, 1725, eight pounds were appropriated from the town treasury "for hiring school-masters and school-dames" to instruct the children in reading and writing for the year next ensuing; and a like sum was ordered to be raised by a tax upon the parents or guardians of the children, to be gathered by the town collector. Messrs. Marsh, Buel, Hosford and Goodrich, were chosen a school committee. Two years later, ten pounds were paid out of the public treasury for the same object, with the proviso that four pounds of this sum should be given for the support of a writing school, and the balance "for teaching of children by school dames"—from which we are to infer that the female teachers did not give instruction in *writing*. The first reference made by the records relative to *building a school house*, is contained in the doings of a town meeting held Dec. 23, 1731—(Mr. Joseph Kilbourn, Moderator)—which is as follows: "Voted to build a school house in ye center of ye town, on ye Meeting-House Green; and Joseph Kilbourn, Jr., Ebenezer Marsh and John Gay, were chosen a committee to carry on said work." At the same time it was voted to build the school house twenty feet square. The school committee were authorized to hire a school-master and set up a school during the succeeding fall and winter.

Messrs. Jacob Griswold and Benjamin Gibbs were appointed in December, 1727, to run the lines and set up monuments "between the School Lots and Pine Island."

The question as to how the School Lands should be disposed of to the best advantage, appears to have been very difficult to settle. On the 12th of March, 1729, it was voted to sell them for one thousand pounds; and Messrs. Marsh and Bird were designated to manage the sale. Some one, doubtless, called in question the right of the town to make such a sale; as, a week later, the inhabitants, in general town meeting convened, appointed Mr. Marsh their Agent to apply to the General Assembly "for *liberty* to make sale of the school lands in Litchfield." The application was unsuccessful; but the people soon found a way to evade the letter of the law. On the 29th of November, 1729, it was "voted that the School Right in Litchfield should be *leased out* for the maintenance of a school in said Litchfield for *nine hundred and ninety-nine years ensuing*." Messrs. Marsh, Buel, Hosford and Bird, were appointed a committee to lease the lands accordingly. As if apprehensive that even this lease might ultimately expire and thus give their descendants unnecessary trouble, with a far-reaching glance into futurity, they proceeded to bind their successors "in ye recognisance of ten thousand pounds lawful money, to *give a new lease of said Right* at the end of said term of nine hundred and ninety-nine years, *if there shall be occasion*"!

In pursuance of these votes, the committee appointed for that purpose, on the 15th of April, 1730, leased to sundry individuals the School Right for the time designated; the grantee paying twenty-seven pounds annually for eight years, for the support of the School; and the ninth year, paying to the selectmen four hundred and fifty pounds, to be forever kept for the support of a School in Litchfield. To the lease was annexed the following

"Postscript.—Before signing and sealing, the above-mentioned signers and sealers agreed, that whoever occupies and improves all the above land or lands, or any part of them, shall pay all rates or taxes that shall arise upon them or any part of them, during the whole term of the lease."

In the year 1767, it was "voted to divide the money for which the School Right was sold, between the old Society, the South Farms Society, and the Church of England, in proportion to the list of each part."

The subject of "seating the meeting-house," often came up for action in town meeting, and produced not a little commotion. In some of the old towns whence the Litchfield settlers came, the following order was observed in this matter, viz.: 1. Long public service. 2. Dignity of descent. 3. Rank in the Grand List. 4. Age. 5. Piety, &c. This order was in good degree discarded by our early Litchfield ancestors. Various methods were tried by them, but generally without any very satisfactory result. In December, 1735, the town appointed as a committee for this work, the following persons, viz., Sergt. Culver, Joseph Kilbourn, Jr., Ebenezer Marsh, John Gay and Supply Strong. At the same time this committee were thus instructed to act, to wit: "Every man's list for four years past shall be added together, and every man's age be reckoned at twenty shillings per year, to be added to his list; and for them that have not four lists, they shall be seated by the last list, or according to the discretion of the committee."

The committee proceeded according to these instructions, but the result did not suit. Their doings were ordered to be set aside; a *new* committee was appointed, with no other instructions than to act in accordance with their best judgment in the premises. Their action, for a wonder, was silently acquiesced in on this occasion.

In December, 1726, it was ordered that the people should be notified of the occurrence of each Town Meeting, "by a note set up on the sign-post and on the *grist-mill door*, seven days before the meeting; and said note shall specify the time and place and affairs of the meeting; and the *Grand Meeting* shall be on the 2d Tuesday in December annually." At a later date, notices of town meetings were directed to be "posted on all the grist-mill doors, and on the school-house door in South Farms."

In May, 1728, it was voted to petition the General Assembly for a tax upon all the undivided land in the town not already put in the list, of five shillings per hundred acres, each year for the space of four years. The prayer of the petitioners was readily granted, and in the following December, Messrs. Marsh and Buel were appointed to *lay the tax* "according to the grant made by the Assembly."

Our boundary lines have not unfrequently called for the action of the town. Naugatuck river on the east, and the Shepaug (in part) on the west, are "natural boundaries" which could not easily be mistaken. The north and south bounds, however, were for a long time not very clearly defined. In the words of the Patent, the town was bounded "north by *the wilderness*," and south by Woodbury and Waterbury, with no other *visible* bounds than marked trees and heaps of stones. In the Patent previously granted to Woodbury, that town is described as being "bounded north by the *commons*." It is fair to presume, that when the trees and stone-heaps disappeared, some doubts might arise as to the precise locality of the lines described.

It appears by the public records that as early as 1727, the accounts of Messrs. Joseph Bird, James Kilbourn and John Bird were adjusted "for meeting the Woodbury men, in order to perambulate." A year later, Messrs. Nathaniel Hosford and John Bird were chosen agents "to act in the controversy between Litchfield and Woodbury." In 1731, the gentlemen last named were re-appointed on a committee for a like purpose—or, as the record has it, "to enquire and make search what light can be had concerning our line against Woodbury." Subsequently, during the same year, it was voted in town meeting to "take some method to settle our south-west bounds according to our Grand Deed and Grant." At the same meeting, Messrs. Hosford and Bird were chosen "to carry on said affair, and trying to agree, and to agree, with Woodbury; and if they don't agree with them, to go to the General Court next, and endeavor to get a Patent according to our Deed and Grant." A tax of three shillings was laid on each undivided Right, to defray the expenses. Some eleven years after, (in

May, 1742,) the records inform us that this tax of three shillings on a Right had proved insufficient for the purpose intended, and a further tax of one shilling and six-pence on each Right *then* undivided, was laid for the furtherance of the same object. How the controversy with Woodbury was finally settled, does not appear. The only alteration of any consequence, *ever* made in our limits as originally defined, was in this south-west corner of the town. Litchfield, at this point, formerly ran down some distance below the junction of the Bantam with the Shepaug, embracing the beautiful valley south of Mount Tom, then and still known as "Davies' Hollow." Upon the incorporation of the town of Washington, in 1779, (which had previously been a part of Ancient Woodbury,) the Litchfield line was so altered as to run across the *top* of Mount Tom, thus ceding Davies' Hollow, and the lands adjacent, to Washington. Litchfield, in town meeting assembled, at first resolved to *oppose* this summary method of robbing her of a portion of her original domain, and appointed the Hon. Andrew Adams an Agent to appear before the General Assembly in her behalf. It was subsequently voted *not* to oppose the project; and, in stead, Colonel Adams was appointed to present a Petition to the Legislature that the town of Washington be cited to "regulate the line of the town." The line was soon after amicably agreed upon, and has not since been a subject of contention.

In December, 1753, Capt. Stoddard and Supply Strong were appointed a committee to "measure from the crotch of the Shepaug river to the north-west corner of the town, with Mr. Roger Sherman, County Surveyor."

There seems also to have been some uncertainty and dispute respecting our northern boundary, though the matter never assumed a serious aspect. At a town meeting in February, 1745-'6, Messrs. John Buel, Joseph Bird and Supply Strong, were appointed a committee "to settle the line between Litchfield and Goshen and Torrington." In May, 1754, Messrs. Ebenezer Marsh and Benjamin Webster "were appointed Agents to represent the town with respect to the north line, before the General Assembly at Hartford;" and in February, 1755, Captain Moses Stoddard and Messrs. Supply Strong and

Jonathan Kilbourn, were appointed "to go with the Surveyor of the County to the North Line of Litchfield."

The colonial files contain a statement in the hand-writing of the famous Roger Sherman, and bearing his signature, giving a minute account of the running of the north line of Litchfield, by him, as County Surveyor, in 1754; also several affidavits on the same subject from Edward Phelps, Moses Stoddard, Jonathan Kilbourn, Supply Strong, Ebenezer Buel, Thomas Catlin, John Bird, and others. As the bounds, however, were subsequently fully established in accordance with the claims of this town, and have not been a matter of controversy for the last eighty years, the publication of the evidence adduced can answer no good purpose.

The boundaries of South Farms were established and defined in 1767; those of Northfield in 1794; and those of Milton in 1795—at the time of the organization of these parishes.

It is an interesting fact, and one not generally known, that *the town of Goshen was organized at the house of Dea. John Buel in West-street*, in this village, which stood on the site now owned and occupied by Mr. Thomas Leverett Saltonstall. On the 27th of September, 1738, the proprietors of Goshen (originally called *New Bantam*,) met at the place designated, and elected Dea. Buel Moderator, and Capt. Joseph Bird, Clerk. They then adjourned to meet at the same place at 8 o'clock the next morning, when the organization of the town was completed. Dating from this day, the centennial anniversary of Goshen was celebrated on the 28th of September, 1838—on which occasion an interesting historical discourse was delivered by the Rev. Grant Powers. Several of the original proprietors of Goshen were residents of Litchfield.

Mr. Morris remarks—"Many years after the settlement of this town, deer, bears, and wild-turkeys, were numerous. Deer and bears were taken by hunters between the years 1760 and 1770, and turkeys at a later period. Wild-cats occasionally visit us, and destroy sheep and lambs. A small tract near the north-east part of the town, is rough and ledgy, and affords them a refuge from hunters and their dogs. Considerable mischief was done by them in the winter of 1811-'12."

Mr. Gibbs, the historian of the Administrations of Washington and Adams, (vol. i. p. 9,) writing of the boyhood of the younger Wolcott, (1765–'78,) draws the following picture of this town as it was seventy and eighty years ago:—" At a period much later than this, Litchfield was on the outskirts of New England civilization, and presented a very different aspect from its now venerable quiet. The pickets which guarded its first dwellings were not yet decayed. The Indian yet wandered through its broad streets, and hunters as wild as our present borderers, chased the deer and the panther on the shores of the lake. The manners of its inhabitants were as simple and primitive as those of their fathers a century back, in the older settlements on the Connecticut. Traveling was entirely on horseback, except in winter, and but a casual intercourse was carried on with the distant towns. Occasionally, and more frequently as they became more interesting, tidings reached them from Boston, and even from the old world."

There are persons yet living, who remember when bears and wolves were hunted in " Blue Swamp," and deer and wild-turkeys were frequently seen within two miles of the Court House;* when Indians, in companies of twenty or thirty, were accustomed to make their annual visits to this town, encamping on Pine Island or along the lake-shore—the men employing themselves in hunting and fishing, while the squaws made and peddled baskets and brooms. Foxes, minks, muskrats, rabbits, woodchucks and raccoons, are *now* frequently trapped within the limits of this township. Snipes, quails, partridges and wild-ducks, frequent our woods or lakes; while our waters abound in trout, suckers, eels, perch, roach, and pike or pickerel. The pickerel, however, is not a *native*. In April, 1779, the town voted, " on reqnest of Capt. John Marsh, that he might have the exclusive Pickerel Fishing in the Loon [or Cranberry] Pond, for the space of twenty years, provided he shall at his own expense procure Pickerel to breed and propa-

*Capt. Salmon Buel, (now in his 92d year,) has seen wild deer in the swamp between his present residence and the village. Mr. Amos Benton informs me that in 1774, (he then being a small child,) a bear passed but a few rods from him, while he was playing by the brook near his present residence. The alarm was given, and his father and some of the neighbors started in pursuit—but did not succeed in killing him.

gate therein, in a reasonable time." It seems, however, that no advantage was taken of this privilege; but in the winter of 1809, twenty-eight pickerel were brought from a pond in Southwick, Massachusetts, and put into Cranberry Pond. Their progeny has greatly increased, so that they are caught in abundance in the several lakes of the township. In Bantam Lake they often grow to a large size—sometimes weighing five and a half and even six pounds. They are familiarly termed by our fishermen, "Bantam Shad," and find a ready market in the village, as well as afford congenial sport to amateur anglers from city and country. By-Laws have from time to time been passed by the town for the protection of our "fisheries," by probibiting the drawing of seines and nets, which have had a good effect.

Of the Indians who inhabited this township previous to its settlement by the whites, comparatively little can now be gleaned. President Stiles, in his "Itinerary," tells us the Bantam Indians were on terms of allegiance with the Scatacooks, the Pootatucks, and Weatogues. Mr. Cothren supposes they were but a clan of the Pootatuck or Woodbury tribe. This seems not improbable, as the aboriginal names signed to the purchase-deed of Litchfield, (dated at Woodbury, March 2d, 1715–'16,) are all mentioned in the list of sachems, sagamores and principal men of that tribe. Some of them doubtless belonged in Bantam, and were familiar with the bounds of the territory disposed of. The fact, too, that a "reservation" was required for the hunting houses of the clan, favors such a supposition. Chusquenoag and Weroamaug (or Raumaug) whose names stand first on the deed—one as a grantor and the other as a witness—were Sachems of the Wyantenucks, who were the nearest neighbors of the Bantams on the west, and, (according to the same authority,) constituted another clan of the Pootatucks.

We have seen how much trouble was occasioned to the early settlers by the savages. It is by no means certain, however, that the murderers of Harris or the capturers of Griswold belonged to the Bantam clan. The Mohawks—a fierce, warlike, roving tribe—were a terror not only to the whites but to all the Indian tribes of Western Connecticut. Even in times of peace, they were accustomed to make their annual visits to the sea-side for purposes of fishing—subsisting, on their excursions, by plundering their weaker brethren along the route. With the fearful cry—" We are come, we are come, to suck your blood!" they rushed on from one hamlet or encampment to another, spreading terror before them, and leaving little but desolation behind them. When they made their appearance, the Connecticut Indians would raise the cry from hill to hill —" The Mohawks! the Mohawks!" and fly to some place of refuge, without attempting any defense. Sometimes they were pursued to the very threshold of their wigwams, and slain in the presence of their families. It is stated that in these and other cases of sudden alarm, all the tribes on the Housatonic, and between the Housatonic and the Naugatuck, could communicate with each other, from the Sound two hundred miles northward, in a few hours, by cries and rude telegraphic signals from a chain of " Guarding Heights" which they had established. One of these "Heights" was Mount Tom in Litchfield.* As the Bantam fishing-grounds were nearly in a direct line from the Mohawk country to the Sound at Milford, (which was long their favorite place of resort,) they would naturally enough pass this way. On the borders of our Great Lake they would encounter not only the native clans of the vicinity, but others who had come hither to fish and hunt. If there were warriors enough on the ground to make a stand against the intruding Mohawks, a fierce and bloody conflict would ensue. That such battles *have* been fought on the now quiet rural shores of our beautiful lake, and for a mile or two northward, is clearly indicated by the stone arrow-heads which are scattered in such profusion in the soil. It is true, they are found in other parts of the township, but nowhere in such abundance as in the locality described. The writer remembers, as one of the pastimes of his childhood, following in the furrow behind the plowman, on the West Plain, for the express purpose of picking up these interesting memorials of a by-gone race—then, of course, regarded simply as playthings. These arrow-

*Cothren's Hist. of Ancient Woodbury, p. 87.

heads are of various shapes and sizes, and are made of different kinds of flint—black, white, red, and yellow; showing them to have been manufactured by different and probably distant tribes. Divers *other* Indian relics have, in years past, been found in Litchfield, but, by reason of the want of some convenient place of deposit, they have generally been scattered and lost. Some of these, according to the accounts we have received, were of curious and skillful workmanship. Since the organization of "The Litchfield County Historical and Antiquarian Society," in 1856, quite a variety of stone hatchets, pestles, arrows, pipes, chisels and dishes, have found their way into its cabinet. In the autumn of 1834, a piece of "aboriginal sculpture" was found in this town, which is thus noticed by the *Enquirer* of October 2d, of that year:—"A discovery of a singular CARVED STONE IMAGE, or BUST, representing the head, neck and breast of a human figure, was made a few days since on the Bantam River, about forty or fifty rods above the mill-dam, half a mile east of this village. Some boys happened to discover near the banks, the head of the figure projecting above the ground, which so excited their curiosity that they immediately dug it out and conveyed it to the mill, where it is for the present deposited. The image, which is apparently that of a female, is carved from a rough block of the common granite, some part of which is considerably decayed and crumbly, yet must have required more patient and persevering labor than generally belongs to the character of the *natives*; and though in point of skill and taste, it falls something short of Grecian perfection, it is certainly 'pretty well for an Indian.' For what purpose it was intended—whether as an idol for worship, or the attempt of some fond admirer to preserve and immortalize the lovely features of his dusky fair one, or whether it was merely a contrivance of some long-sighted wag of old to set us Yankees a-guessing, or even whether it is one hundred or five hundred years old—all is unrevealed; though no doubt some tale is hanging thereby, if we could only find it out. All our American antiquities have this interesting peculiarity, that we know nothing of their history. We have not even the twilight of fabulous story to relieve our curiosity.

The Past is hidden in deeper obscurity than the Future." This curious relic is now preserved in the cabinet of Yale College.

Presuming our historians are correct in the opinion that the Pootatuck Tribe was spread over the present townships of Woodbury, Bethlem, Litchfield, New Milford and Washington, whatever relates to them can hardly prove uninteresting to my readers.

It has been asserted that the Pootatucks sometimes offered *human sacrifices* to appease or propitiate their gods. In proof of this, President Stiles in his "Itinerary" preserves an account of a great *powowing*, which took place at a village of this tribe, about the year 1720. Mr. De Forest gives the substance of Dr. Stiles' account, as follows: The scene was witnessed by a Mrs. Bennett, then a little girl; and after her death, was related by one of her children to the President. The ceremonies lasted three days, and were attended by five or six hundred Indians, many of whom came from distant towns, as Hartford and Farmington. While the Indians, excited by their wild rites and dark superstitions, were standing in a dense mass, a little girl, gaily dressed and ornamented, was led in among them by two squaws, her mother and aunt. As she entered the crowd, the Indians set up their "high powwows," howling, yelling, throwing themselves into strange postures, and making hideous grimaces. Many white people stood around gazing at the scene; but such was the excited state of the savages, that, although they feared for the child's safety, none of them dared to interfere, or to enter the crowd. After a while the two squaws emerged alone from the press, stripped of all their ornaments, and walked away, shedding tears and uttering mournful cries. The informant, deeply interested in the fate of one so near her own age, ran up to the two women, and asked them what they had done with the little girl. They would not tell her, and only replied that they should never see that little girl again. The other Indians also remained silent on the subject; but Mrs. Bennet believed, and she said that all the English then present believed, that the Indians had sacrificed her, and that they did at other times offer human sacrifices.

The Sachem whose residence and private domains were nearest to Litchfield, and with whom the early settlers of the town were most intimate, was Weroamaug, or Raumaug. His reservation in the parish of New Preston was adjacent to the reservation of the Bantam Indians, over whom his jurisdiction extended. He was a true friend of the whites, and in his last years professed to have become a convert to Christianity. The Rev. Daniel Boardman, who was ordained as the minister at New Milford, in 1716, became much interested in him. In a letter to a friend, he calls him "that distinguished sachem, whose great abilities and eminent virtues, joined with his extensive dominion, rendered him the most potent prince of that or any other day in this colony; and his name ought to be remembered by the faithful historian, as much as that of any crowned head since his was laid in the dust." During Raumaug's last illness, Mr. Boardman constantly attended him and endeavored to confirm his mind in the vital truths of the Christian faith. It was a sad place for the dying chieftain; for a majority of his people, and even his wife, were bitter opponents of the white man's religion, and used all their influence against it. One day when the good pastor was standing by the sachem's bedside, the latter asked him to pray, to which he assented. It happened that there was a sick child in the village, and a powow was in attendance, who had undertaken to cure it with his superstitious rites. As soon as the clergyman commenced his prayer, Raumaug's wife sent for the medicine-man and ordered him to commence his exercises at the door of the lodge. The powow at once set up a hideous shouting and howling, and Mr. Boardman prayed louder, so that the sick man might hear him above the uproar. Each raised his voice louder and louder as he went on, while the Indians gathered around, solicitous for the success of their prophet. The powow was determined to tire out the minister—and he, on the other hand, was quite as fully resolved not to be put to silence in the discharge of his duty by the blind worshiper of Satan. The invincible minister afterward gave it as his belief that he prayed full three hours, before he was permitted to come off conqueror. The powow having completely exhausted himself with his efforts, gave one unearthly yell, and then, taking to his heels, never stopped till he was cooling himself up to his neck in the Housatonic. Raumaug died about the year 1735—or, some fifteen years after the first settlement of Litchfield.

In consequence of the frequent alarms on account of the Indians, the settlement of the town was greatly retarded. Other Memorials, of a later date than those given in the chapter preceding this, complain of the difficulties which the settlers still encountered, and ask for legislative interference in their behalf. Indeed, for more than thirty years after the Garrisons were erected, they were resorted to with more or less frequency, by individuals and families, on account of apprehended danger. One of these Garrisons stood near the present residence of Mr. Holmes O. Morse, on Chestnut Hill, and was remembered by Mr. Elisha Mason, who died in this village no longer ago than May 1st, 1858. Another stood one mile west of the Court House, on the north side of West-street, opposite the homestead of Mr. Benjamin Kilbourn. Some of the remains of the last-mentioned fort were recently discovered.

Good penmanship and correct orthography were not universal accomplishments, even among Town Clerks, a century and a quarter since. As a general thing, in copying from records or files, I have not attempted to follow either the spelling or the punctuation of the original documents. In these respects the records are sometimes as quaint and peculiar as were the language and manners of the people themselves in a former age. Here is a specimen or two: "Voted that ye owners of shoolers sent to school for time to come shal find fire wood for ye schooll;" "Voted to ajurn this meeting to to morah Sun half an hour High at Night." These are by no means the *worst* cases to be found. A few other town votes are here *correctly* rendered, as curiosities in their way: Voted to appoint Lieut. Buel and Samuel Orton "to assist the Clerk in perusing the town votes and to conclude what shall be transcribed into the town book, and what not:" "Voted that sheep shall be free commoners;" "Voted that a Basin for Baptism be procured, and that the money be drawn out of the Town

Treasury to pay for the same;" Voted liberty to the Rev. Timothy Collins "to erect a Blacksmith's Shop joining to his fence the backside of the meeting-house;" Sergt. John Bird was "chosen *Quorister* to tune the Psalm in the public worship." Many other transactions of the town, equally primitive in their character, might be given—but these are sufficient to indicate the great change that a century has wrought in the nature of much of the business done at our town meetings.

It is a sad commentary on the frail tenure of human life, that, in every new settlement, no sooner have the pioneers erected their huts and commenced clearing up their lands, than it becomes necessary to provide a resting-place for the *dead.* The Burying Ground west of our village was set apart for that purpose by the first settlers of the place, and for many years was the *only* cemetery within the limits of the township. In this humble and now almost forsaken enclosure, rest side by side, sometimes in undistinguished graves, legislators, judges, mechanics, farmers, congressmen, paupers, merchants, maidens—parents and children—the lovely, the loving, and the beloved—pastor and people—the village patriarch and the infant of yesterday—pioneers, statesmen, peasants, officers, soldiers, slaves—the red warrior of the forest, and the beautiful-browed daughter of his Saxon successor—lawyers, and juries, and clients, and criminals—awaiting in hope or fear their final summons and destiny. Sweet be their slumbers, and glorious their awakening!

At the close of the first thirty years after the settlement of the town commenced, a large proportion of its founders had exchanged a life of labor and weariness for the repose of the grave. Generally, they reached a good old age, and, by the gradual decay of nature, passed gently and almost imperceptibly down the valley of years. Among these, were the two most conspicuous and useful men among the original proprietors of the township—JOHN MARSH and JOHN BUEL. A brief outline of the history of these men, will close this chapter.

JOHN MARSH had long been a prominent citizen of Hartford before he interested himself in the Western Lands; and from the time when he came out to "view the new plantation," in May, 1715, till about the year 1738, his name was intimately associated with the history of Litchfield. I need not recapitulate the many ways and times in which he was called upon by his fellow-citizens to serve them in public employments, as detailed on the preceding pages. He served this town in the various offices within her gift during the entire period of his residence here. While an inhabitant of Hartford, his native town, he was often a Representative in the Legislature, a Justice of the Peace, an Associate Judge of the County Court, and a member of the Council of War. He returned to Hartford in his old age, and died there. His remains lie interred in the old Burying Ground back of the Center Church. His children remained in this town, and his descendants here and elsewhere are very numerous.

JOHN BUEL was about fifty years of age when he became a resident of this town, and had previously filled the office of Deacon of the Church in Lebanon. That portion of our history which has already been given, affords a sufficient guarantee of the estimation in which he was held by his fellow-citizens. He was repeatedly elected to almost every office within their gift, besides being appointed on nearly all the most important committees. As a Deacon in the Church, Captain of the Militia, Selectman, Treasurer, Representative and Justice of the Peace, he discharged his duties efficiently and faithfully. A brief anecdote (as given by the Rev. Mr. Powers, in his Centennial Address at Goshen,) will serve to illustrate the bevolence of his character: In the winter of 1740–'41, a man came from Cornwall to purchase some grain for himself and family, who were in great need, and was directed to Deacon Buel. The stranger soon called, and made known his errand. The Deacon asked him if he had the *money* to pay for the grain. He answered affirmatively. "Well," said the Deacon, "I can show you where you can procure it." Going with the stragger to the door, he pointed out a certain house to him, saying, "There lives a man who will let you have grain for your money. I have some to spare, but I must keep it for those who *have no money*." Deacon Buel departed this life, April 6th, 1746, aged 75 years. His wife survived him twenty-two years. Both were interred in the West Burying Ground. The inscription on the tomb-stone of the latter is as follows: "Here lies the body of Mrs. Mary, wife of Dea. John Buel, Esq. She died November 4, 1768, aged 90—having had 13 Children, 101 Grand-Children, 247 Great-Grand-Children, and 49 Great-Great-Grand-Children; total 410. Three hundred and thirty-six survived her." The name of Buel has always been prominent in our local history.

Litchfield was peculiarly fortunate in the character of its early settlers. The proprietors seemed to know, instinctively, that the location of their settlement—so remote from all the elder towns of the colony, and apparently beyond the influences of civilization and religion—would naturally invite to its seclusion and consequent freedom from restraint, the vicious, the abandoned, and the fugitive from justice. Consequently, the utmost care was taken that none but persons of good character should settle among them. Mr. Woodruff says—"If a stranger made a purchase in the plantation, a proviso was sometimes *inserted in the deed*, that the Inhabitants should accept of the purchaser, and that he should 'run the risk of trouble from the Grand Committee.'" We have seen on another page the vote of the town on this subject. It is with pleasure, that a Son of Litchfield is able to say that the people of the town have ever borne and still bear the reputation of being distinguished for intelligence and virtue.

CHAPTER V.

EVENTS PRECEDING THE REVOLUTION.

THE first French War began in 1744, and closed with the signing of the Treaty of Aix la Chapelle, October 4, 1748. At this period, Litchfield was in a condition too weak and exposed to be expected to lend any efficient aid in such a contest. Indeed, it is not known that her soldiery were in any instance called upon to march any considerable distance from her own frontiers. Our records give no indication of any unusual excitement—the seat of the war being, in this instance, so far distant, that our people seem scarcely to have been conscious of its existence. The voters assembled in town meeting, went through with the ordinary routine of business, and adjourned, without intimating that the town or the colony was in any way interested in the fierce conflict that was then being waged between England and France.

Mr. Cothren informs us that in May, 1748, the inhabitants of Woodbury appointed Col. William Preston an Agent to prefer a Memorial to the General Assembly for the organization of a new county to be called the County of Woodbury, to embrace the towns of Woodbury, Waterbury, New Milford, Litchfield and New Fairfield, and as many of the northern towns as might choose to join them—with Woodbury for the county seat. The result need not be told.

At the October Session of the Legislature, A. D. 1751, the *County of Litchfield* was organized, and embraced seventeen towns, viz., Litchfield, Woodbury, New Milford, New Hartford, Harwinton, Barkhamsted, Colebrook, Canaan, Goshen, Cornwall, Hartland, Kent, Norfolk, Salisbury, Sharon, Torrington and Winchester. For some time much difference of opinion prevailed as to the location of the shire town. Litchfield, Goshen, Canaan and Cornwall, urged their respective claims with much zeal; but the most formidable contest was between Litchfield and Goshen. The latter was supposed to occupy the geographical center of the proposed county, and many persons had settled there in expectation that the seat of justice would be established in that town, among whom was Oliver Wolcott, afterwards Governor. To the sore disappointment of many of the contestants, *Litchfield* was ultimately named as the county seat in the act incorporating the new county. This was a most important event in the history of the town; and from this time onward, for several years, it rapidly improved in its appearance as well as in the number and character of its inhabitants. By a census taken in 1756, it was ascertained that its population was 1366. Oliver Wolcott was appointed first High Sheriff, and immediately thereupon took up his residence in this village. John Catlin, of Litchfield, was appointed County Treasurer; Isaac Baldwin, of Litchfield, County Clerk; William Preston, of Woodbury, Chief Judge; Thomas Chipman, of Salisbury, Samuel Canfield, of New Milford, John Williams, of Sharon, and Ebenezer Marsh, of Litchfield, Associate Judges; and Samuel Pettibone, of Goshen, King's Attorney.

Even after this county was thus formed, and its officers appointed, the town of Woodbury continued to manifest her dissatisfaction in various ways and at all reasonable times. Instead of being made the central and shire town of the new county, she was left quite in one corner. She first petitioned the Legislature, (in May and again in October, 1752,) to be re-annexed to the county of Fairfield. Twenty years later, an effort was again made to persuade the General Assembly to organize a county to be called Woodbury. On this occasion the town of Woodbury laid a rate of a penny and a half on the pound, in addition to the regular tax, to be applied toward erecting the *county buildings;* and, further, she generously offered the use of her *Town Hall* for a COURT HOUSE! The reader will not need to be informed, that these as well as more recent attempts to destroy the ancient landmarks of the County of Litchfield, have proved *unsuccessful.*

At a town meeting, held in December, 1753, liberty was voted to Isaac Hosford and others "to erect a house for their convenience on Sabbath Days, east of the meeting-house." In January 1759, liberty was granted to Mr. John Farnham to "set up a *Sabbath-Day House* in the highway a little north of the School House." Capt. Edward Phelps erected a similar house in the middle of East-street nearly opposite the present church-edifice of the First Congregational Society; and still another was remembered by the late Mr. Elisha Mason, which stood on or near the spot now occupied by the dwelling-house of Dr. Lewis in East-street. As they were among the "institutions" of the Olden Time, and are quite unknown in our day, a brief reference to their design in connection with one of the simple customs of our ancestors, can hardly require an apology. They were built by, and for the accommodation of, persons residing at a distance from church—their object being, to furnish the owners and their families, together with such friends as they might choose to invite, with a warm retreat, in winter, during the intermission between the forenoon and afternoon services on the Sabbath. We must bear in mind that in those days a stove, or any other means of warming a church, had never been seriously thought of. These houses generally consisted of two rooms, each about twelve feet square, with a chimney between them and a fire-place in each room; and in such cases were erected at the expense of two or more families. Dry fuel was kept in each room ready for kindling a fire. If the cold was extreme, the "hired man" or one of the sons might be sent forward in advance of the family, to get the room well warmed before their arrival. The family, after filling the ample saddlebags with refreshments, including a bottle of beer or cider, took an early start for the sanctuary. Calling first at their Sabbath-Day House, they deposited their luncheon, and having warmed themselves, and covered up the glowing embers, they were ready at the appointed moment to take their seats in the house of worship, there to shiver in the cold during the morning service. At noon, they returned to their room, with perhaps a few friends. The fire was re-kindled, the saddlebags were brought forth, and their contents placed upon a prophet's table, of which all partook. The frugal repast being ended, thanks were returned. The patriarch of the household then drew from his pocket the notes he had taken of the morning sermon, which were fully reviewed—all enjoying the utmost freedom in their remarks. Sometimes a well chosen chapter, or a page from some favorite author, was read, and the noon-service was not unfrequently closed with a prayer. All then returned to the house of God. Before starting for home at the close of the afternoon service, they once more repaired to their Sabbath House, gathered up the saddlebags, wrapped themselves thoroughly up, saw that the fire was left safe, and in due time all were snugly seated in the sleigh, and bound homeward.

By the Treaty of Utrecht that part of the old French dominion called Acadia, or Nova Scotia, was ceded to Great Britain. In 1749, three thousand seven hundred and sixty English adventurers, under the Hon. Edward Cornwallis, sailed for that country, and settled on the coast at a place which they named Halifax, in honor of the Earl of Halifax, one of the Lords of Trade and Plantations. During the following year, the French Governor of Canada sent an army of Frenchmen and Indians to reduce Nova Scotia. The expedition was successful—and Acadia was once more a French province. The French neutrals (many of whom had been driven off, or had been so persecuted that they were virtually compelled to leave,) now joyfully returned to their old homes, by special invitation of the government.

The sad story of the Acadians, or "French Neutrals," has often been told; but the subject is not likely to be exhausted, while sympathy for the innocent and sorrowing has a place in the human heart. The classic lyre of Longfellow and the historic pen of Bancroft have alike celebrated their wrongs; and a mere outline of the principal events in their history, must suffice for our present purpose. Acadia, or Nova Scotia, was early settled by the French Catholics, who soon surrounded themselves by many of the comforts and conveniences of civilized life. They erected respectable dwellings and churches, and cleared up and cultivated their lands. At length the

English took possession of the island, and the French were subjected to the grossest indignities by those who were bent upon obtaining possession of their houses and lands. They expressed their willingness to take the oath of allegiance to England, but refused to bear arms against their beloved France. Their oppressors now resolved to break up the settlements and disperse the people among the other English colonies in America. A proclamation was accordingly issued, ordering all the males of French descent, of ten years old and upwards, to appear at certain places designated, on the 5th of September, 1755. They obeyed the summons—little dreaming of the fate that awaited them. On their arrival, they were forthwith declared to be the king's prisoners, and were informed that their houses, lands and live-stock were confiscated to the crown, but that they were at liberty to take with them their money and household goods. On the 15th of the same month, one hundred and sixty-one men were driven, at the point of the bayonet, on board the vessel which was to convey them from their homes forever. During the autumn and early part of winter, seven thousand of these miserable exiles were thus forced on ship-board and scattered over the colonies, from New Hampshire to Georgia. Four hundred were sent to Connecticut; who, at an extra session of the Legislature convened on the 21st of January, 1756, were distributed among some fifty towns according to their grand lists. Husbands and wives, parents and children, brothers and sisters, were thus arbitrarily separated—their destination and destiny unknown to each other! Precisely the number that was ultimately allotted to Litchfield, I have not been able to ascertain. At least two of them are remembered by persons now living. One of the number (named Sybil Sharway or Shearaway) married Mr. Thomas Harrison, a prominent citizen of this town, in 1764, and her descendants are now among our most excellent and respected people. The Selectmen and Civil Authority of each town were directed to provide for the exiles, and take proper care of the sick and aged; and not to allow any one of them to leave the town without a written order or passport. It was further provided by the Legislature, that if any one should be found beyond the prescribed limits, he should thereafter be confined and not permitted to go at large.

It is not until January, 1759, that our town records make any allusion to these people. At this date it was " voted that the Selectmen may provide a house or some suitable place in the town, *for the maintenance of the French.*" In the County Treasurer's book, also, occurs the following entry, viz: " To paid John Newbree for keeping William Dunlap *and the French persons*, 54*s*. 6*d*., which the County allowed, and R. Sherman, Justice of the Quorum, drew an order dated April 25, 1760, as per order on file."

What is usually termed the *last* French War commenced in 1755 and continued eight years. In this great contest Litchfield was actively engaged. Indeed, the people of all the northern English colonies were required to exert themselves to their utmost capacity to repel the invasions of the French. During the preceding winter, Sir Thomas Robinson, one of the king's principal Secretaries of State, had addressed a letter to Connecticut in his majesty's name, containing the intelligence that troops were about to be sent from England to aid the colonies, and calling upon her to raise her quota of the balance of the forces that might be deemed requisite for the contemplated expedition against Crown Point. The Assembly was immediately called together; and it was resolved to raise one thousand men for the campaign, and the Governor was at the same time authorized, in case of emergency, to call out five hundred more. When the united forces of British, Provincials and Indians, reached Albany, their place of rendezvous, they constituted an army of over six thousand men—under the chief command of General William Johnson. The two Connecticut regiments were under the immediate command of General Phineas Lyman and Colonel Elizur Goodrich; the Indians being under guidance of the celebrated Mohawk Chief, Hendrick. In this campaign, the French were defeated in an important action near Lake George, though Colonel Williams, of one of the Massachusetts regiments, and the invincible Hendrick, were slain. Lieutenant-Colonel Whiting, who, by the fall of his superior, became the chief officer in the most fatal part of the engagement, eminently distinguished himself as a cool, brave and judicious commander. Seven hundred of the French were left dead on the field, and the brave Dieskau was fatally wounded and taken prisoner. For this victory Johnson was knighted. Before the battle was fought, however, he had sent an earnest requisition to Governor Fitch for more troops. In response to this call, the Legislature was convened in August, 1755; and it was resolved to raise two additional regiments, and send them forthwith into the field. Samuel Talcott and Elihu Chauncey were commissioned as Colonels of these regiments, and Drs. Timothy Collins of Litchfield, and Jonathan Marsh of Norwich, were appointed Physicians and Surgeons. These regiments, consisting of seven hundred and fifty men each, were on their march within a week after the alarm was given. Connecticut now had in the northern army not less than two thousand five hundred men. Though Crown Point was not taken, Great Britain and her Colonies were jubilant over the success of their arms.

I will not stop to detail the incidents of the disastrous campaigns of 1756 and 1757. Through the inefficiency of such British officers of Abercrombie, Loudoun and Webb, the finest army that had ever trodden the soil of America, was permitted to accomplish nothing. The capture of Crown Point had been abandoned, and an unsuccessful attack had been made upon Louisbourg. During these years, Connecticut kept constantly in the field a force of five thousand men. The campaign of 1758 opened with auguries of better success, under the auspices of Mr. Pitt, who had been elevated to the premiership. Connecticut at once resolved to raise five thousand men for the service, which was one quarter of all the troops called for from the northern colonies. The Connecticut troops were formed into four regiments, and Colonels Phineas Lyman, Nathan Whiting, Eliphalet Dyer and John Read, were appointed commanders. At the same time, Benjamin Hinman, of Woodbury, in this county, was commissioned as Lieutenant-Colonel of one of these regiments. Fourteen thousand regulars, and a considerable naval force, were sent over from England to co-operate with the provincials. A portion of these troops, under Lord Amherst and General Wolfe, together with the ships-of-the-line under Admiral Boscawen, were sent against Louisbourg; while the remainder of the provincials and regulars, under General Abercrombie and Lord Howe, went on an expedition against Crown Point and Ticonderoga. The Connecticut men were with *both* of these divisions of the army. The garrison at Louisbourg, with its two thousand five hundred regulars, six hundred militia, and vast quantity of military stores, was surrendered into the hands of the victorious English and provincials. Abercrombie's expedition, however, did not prove as successful. Having been twice repulsed, with the loss of Lord Howe, the commanding general ordered a retreat, in spite of the remonstrances of the provincial officers, who believed that victory was still within their reach. Colonel Whiting's Connecticut regiment was with Abercrombie; and the "orderly book" which he used in that unfortunate campaign, is still in the possession of his grandson, Major Jason Whiting, of Litchfield, and contains many interesting facts relating to the transactions of that branch of the army with which he was connected.

From this time till the close of the war, Connecticut continued to keep in the field not far from five thousand men. In the campaign of 1759–'60, Crown Point and Ticonderoga were captured by the English; and subsequently, Montreal and the whole of the French possessions in Canada were surrendered into their hands. In all the transactions of this memorable war, Litchfield contributed her full quota of men and means. Unfortunately, but a single list of the soldiers raised in this town, during the period referred to, has been preserved. The names of some of the Litchfield *officers* who received commissions between the years 1755 and 1763, are here given, as it is known that a part of them were in the war, viz., Solomon Buel, Captain, 1756; Ebenezer Marsh, Colonel, 1757; Isaac Baldwin, Captain, do.; Joshua Smith, Lieutenant, do,; Abner Baldwin, Ensign, do.; Archibald McNeile, Captain, 1758: Zebulon Gibbs, Ensign, do.; Stephen Smith, Lieutenant, 1760; Eli Catlin, Lieutenant, do.; Isaac Moss, Lieutenant, 1761; Josiah Smith, Lieutenant, do.; Asa Hopkins,

Lieutenant, do.; Gideon Harrison, Ensign, do.; David Landon, Ensign, do.; Lynde Lord, Ensign, 1762. Zebulon Gibbs (whose Narrative we give in the Appendix,) informs us that he was in the northern army from 1756 to 1762. In March, 1758, he was commissioned as Ensign in Captain Hurlbut's company, which was raised as a part of the force designed for the capture of Crown Point.

The following names are copied from "A Pay-Roll for Capt. Archibald McNeile's Company, in the Second Regiment of Connecticut Forces, for the year 1762,"—which is on file in the Secretary's Office, Hartford:

Archibald McNeile, Captain.
Isaac Moss, 1st Lieutenant,
Increase Moseley, 2d do.
Elisha Blinn, Ensign,
Thomas Catlin, Sergeant,
Nathaniel Taylor do.
Bezaleel Beebe, do.
Hezekiah Lee, do.
Arch'd McNeile, jr. do.
Roger Catlin, Corporal,
Wm. Drinkwater, do.
Nathan Stoddard, do.
James Lassly, do.
Daniel Barns, Drummer,
Jacob Bartholomew, do.
Charles Richards,
Samuel Warner,
Samuel Gipson,
Joseph Jones,
John Barrett,
John Barrett, jr.
William Forster,
Francis Mazuzan,
Thomas Wedge,
Reuben Smith,
Jeremiah Osborn,
Benjamin Landon,
Isaac Osborn,
Robert Coe,
Adam Mott,
Asahel Hinman,
Roswell Fuller,
Daniel Grant,
William Emons,
Moses Stoddard,
Gideon Smith,
Jonathan Smith,
Hezekiah Leach,
Adam Hurlbut,
Jeremiah Harris,
Eli Emons,
Alexander Waugh,
Orange Stoddard,
Ezekiel Shepard,
Ozias Hurlbut,
Daniel Harris,
John Collins,
Solomon Palmer,
Jonathan Phelps,
John Cogswell,
Mark Kenney,
Aaron Thrall,
Timothy Brown,
Roswell Dart,
William Bulford,
James Manville,

Benjamin Bissell,
David Nichols.
Ichabod Squire,
Comfort Jackson,
Elisha Walker,
Amos Brougton,
Nathaniel Lewis,
Levi Bonny,
Thomas Barker,
Samuel Drinkwater,
Asahel Gray,
Eliakim Gibbs,
Samuel Peet,
Ephraim Smedley,
Edmund Hawes,
Silas Tucker,
Robert Bell,
Thomas Sherwood,
Ephraim Knapp,
Titus Tyler,
Thomas Williams,
Justus Seelye,
James Francier,
George Peet,
Nathaniel Barnum,
Adonijah Roice,
Elisha Ingraham,
Daniel Hurlbut,
Ebenezer Blackman,
Domini Douglas,
Amos Tolls,
Thomas Ranny,
Daniel Hamilton,
Asahel Hodge,
Daniel Warner,
Titus Tolls,
John Ripner,
Caleb Nichols,
John Fryer,
Ebenezer Pickett,

It is not to be inferred that *all* the members of Captain McNeile's company belonged in Litchfield. Some in the list are recognized as residents of neighboring towns. Lieutenant Moseley, for instance, was a Woodbury man. He became an eminent lawyer, legislator and judge, in his native county, and afterwards removed to Vermont, and was there elevated to the bench of the Supreme Court.

The name of the late Colonel Beebe, of his town, will be noticed among the Sergeants of this company. At a still earlier date, he had been a member of Major Rogers celebrated corps of Rangers, and was engaged in one of the forest fights when the soldiers were dispersed by order of their commander, and each man was directed to fight, in true Indian style, from behind a tree. Beebe chanced to be stationed near Lieutenant Gaylord, who was also from Litchfield county. He had just spoken to Gaylord, and at the moment was looking him in the face for a reply, when he observed a sudden break of the skin in the forehead, and the Lieutenant instantly fell dead—a ball from the enemy having passed through his head.

The long succession of colonial wars, which had now terminated, had taxed the American people almost beyond precedent. The whole country was yet new, and but thinly settled. The farms were only partially cleared up, and the great mass of the population were poor and compelled to delve hard for the requisite food for the subsistence of themselves and families. Notwithstanding all this, a large proportion of the most efficient and able-bodied men were constantly being called off to fill the ranks of the army; while those who remained at home must support themselves, provide food and clothing for the soldiers, and pay the enormous taxes which war always brings in its train. If those who first enlisted, lived to return home, *they* or *others* were soon called upon again and again to enter the public service. This long experience and severe discipline, however, was, unwittingly to all, preparing officers, soldiers and citizens, for the severer and more important crisis which was then approaching.

The next great question which agitated the minds of our people, was that relating to the *Stamp Act*. The peace of 1763 had left Great Britain immensely in debt, and the eyes of her financiers were at once turned towards the American Colonies, as a field whence their future revenues might be materially augmented. The proposed impost was at length laid, by an act of parliament, "upon every skin, or piece of vellum, or parchment, or sheet or piece of paper," that should be thenceforth used in the colonies; and no deed, lease, bond, policy or mortgage, was legal, unless it bore the royal stamp. This act created great indignation on this side of the Atlantic. The Legislature of Connecticut protested against it, and finally agreed upon an address to parliament, which was sent to the colonial agent in London, with instructions "firmly to insist on the exclusive right of the colonies to tax themselves." The people everywhere were excited, and the measure was freely discussed and boldly denounced at the corners of the streets, in popular assemblies, and in town meetings. The more resolute and reckless of the populace formed themselves into secret organizations called "*The Sons of Liberty*," with the design of preventing the use of the stamped paper by a summary process, if necessary. In this town there was probs ably no difference of opinion on the main question at issue. On matters of minor importance, the people did not alway, agree. The *Connecticut Courant* of February 10th, 1766, contains a communication dated at Litchfield on the 1st of February of that year, which is as follows—" At the Desire of several of the Towns in this County, by their Agents chosen and sent here for that Purpose, a Meeting was called of the Free-born Sons of Liberty, to meet at the Court-House in this Town; and being assembled to the Number of about forty or fifty Persons- proceeded upon the Business for which they met. And notwithstanding the great Opposition they met with, from Col. E——r M——h and one S——n S——e,* (whereby the Meeting was much hindered,) yet they came to the Choice of five Gentlemen, who were to act as Agents, and are to join the Gentlemen from the other Towns in the County, who are to meet here, at a general County Meeting, to be held on the second Tuesday of February, 1766, at ten o'clock in the forenoon; when it is expected they will come to such Resolves as they shall think most Conducive to prevent the Thing we fear from ever taking Place among us. The Meeting would have been conducted with the utmost good Agreement and Dispatch, had it not been for the Gentlemen mentioned above, who employed all their Power to render it abortive, not only by consuming the Time in long and needless Speeches, (wherein Mr. M——h especially discovered to all present, an inexhaustible Fund of Knowledge, by several new-coined Words, unknown in the English Language before,) but they also opposed by their Votes almost every Motion that was made to forward it."

The *Courant* of February 24th, contains the doings of the convention referred to. In their declarations, the purest sentiments of patriotism and loyalty, are blended with a love of good order and a regard for the supremacy of the law, which are remarkable for those times. The people of Litchfield were no friends of mob-law, even when mobs were fashionable elsewhere. *Separation* from the mother-country, was a subject which had not then been breathed audibly, even if it had been thought of, by the most zealous patriot. Hence, while some of these sen-

* The names are thus left blank in the Courant.

timents, in the boldness and beauty of their expression, almost rival some of those which were ten years subsequently embodied in the Declaration of Independence, they are still made subservient to the condition of the people as faithful subjects of the king. The same *spirit* led them in due time to throw off the yoke of foreign despotism and to vindicate their rights as Freemen. In the article which is here given, the original copy is followed in *capitalizing* as well as in other respects:

"AT a Meeting of the Inhabitants of almost all the Towns in Litchfield County, convened by their Agents in Litchfield on the Second Tuesday in February, 1766, for the Purpose of giving the clearest Manifestation of their fixed and most ardent Desires to preserve, as far as in them lies, those inherent Rights and Privileges which essentially belong to them as a Free People, and which are founded upon the unalterable Basis of the British Constitution, and have been confirmed by the most solemn Sanctions—and of their readiness to promote (according to their Ability,) the public Peace and Happiness, which have been greatly disturbed by the most alarming Infringements upon their Rights—the following Sentiments were unanimously agreed in:

"I. That they entertain the highest Regard and Veneration for those just and virtuous Resolutions made by the Hon. House of Representatives of this Colony in October last, expressing the Duty and faithful Allegiance which they and the Inhabitants of this Colony owe to our rightful Sovereign, King George the Third—and those Rights and Privileges which essentially belong to His Majesty's Subjects in this Colony; and likewise those Sentiments respecting the unconstitutional Nature of an Act of the British Parliament for granting Stamp-Duties in the British Colonies.

"II. That they conceive, to keep up in their brightest View the first Principles and Origins of the English Government, and strictly to adhere to the primary Institutions of it, is the only sure Way to preserve the same, and consequently the Prerogative of the Crown, and the Civil Liberties of the Subject, inviolate.

"III. That they are not able to form a more perfect Idea of Allegiance to His Majesty, than what consists in an inflexible Attachment to the forementioned Principles.

"IV. That, in their Opinion, for any Power whatsoever to claim a Right to dispose of their Property without their Consent, given in a Constitutional Way, is, in Effect, to claim a Right to dispose of all their Property at Pleasure.

"V. That for innocent Subjects to be imminently exposed to certain Ruin, by the Execution of any penal Statute, is, they conceive, utterly irreconcilable with every just Idea of Freedom.

"VI. That God made Mankind free, (as being essential to their Happiness,) and as, by His Blessing, the Advantages of English Liberty have been handed down to them from their most virtuous and loyal Ancestors, so they will endeavor, by all reasonable Ways and Means within their Power, uprightly to preserve and faithfully to transmit the same to their Posterity.

"VII. That they really believe, without the least Shadow of a Doubt, that said Act, imposing Stamp-Duties, &c., is UNCONSTITUTIONAL, and therefore necessarily believe that the Observance thereof is not OBLIGATORY upon them.

"VIII. That any Office for distributing Stamped Papers in this Colony, appears odious and detestable to them, as being, in its Operation, utterly destructive of their most valuable Rights.

"IX. That if any Stamped Papers shall be imported into any Part of this Colony (which they most cordially wish might never be,) they hope the speediest public Notice thereof may be given, that the same may be preserved UNTOUCHED for His Majesty.

"X. That if any Person in this Colony has represented that the People in it might, under any possible circumstances, become willing to have the aforesaid Act executed upon them, or to have one Farthing of their Property taken from them, except by their own Consent, given as aforesaid, they are persuaded that such Representation must have been the Result of extreme stupid Ignorance, or dictated by a malignant, apostate Spirit.

"XI. That they will never suffer any Jealousies to arise in their Minds, that any Person in this Colony is unfriendly to its Civil Liberties, except upon the fullest, clearest, and most undeniable Evidence.

"XII. That it was never any Part of the Design of this Meeting to endeavor to bring about the least Alteration in the Legislative Body of this Colony.

"XIII. That whereas some very ignorant or dissolute Persons may, in this time of Perplexity, be disposed to commit Outrages against the Persons or Property of others, or to treat with Disrespect and Insult the civil Authority of this Colony: They do therefore hereby solemnly declare, that Nothing (except a Privation of their Liberties,) could or ought to fill their Minds with a deeper and more fixed Resentment than such Conduct—and that they will always be ready and willing to assist and support, to the utmost of their Ability, the public Magistrates, in preserving, in the greatest Purity, the Peace and good Order of the Public.

"XIV. That these their Sentiments of firm Allegiance to His Majesty, and their strong and unfailing Desires to preserve their Constitutional Rights and Privileges, and to promote the public Peace, good Order, and Happiness, be published in the Connecticut Courant, and that this Meeting be adjourned to the third Tuesday in March next, at ten o'clock in the forenoon, to be held at this place."

The Stamp-Act was followed by laying a tax upon divers other articles imported from England, which led to a combination known as "the non-importation agreement." This agreement was, however, shamefully violated by many of the New York merchants. The indignation of the people of Connecticut was in consequence fully aroused; and it was resolved that a General Convention of Delegates from all the towns in the colony, should be held in New Haven, on the 13th of September, 1770, "to take into consideration the perilous condition of the country, to provide for the growth and spread of home-manufactures, and to devise more thorough means for carrying out to the letter the non-importation agreement." A town meeting was held in Litchfield, on the 30th of August —Mr. Abraham Kilbourn presiding. At this meeting, Capt. John Osborn and Mr. Jedediah Strong were appointed Delegates to the Convention referred to.

The Legislature about this time, made special enactments providing for arming and disciplining the militia—*why*, they were scarcely themselves aware. Many of our most efficient officers of the French War now received advance commissions in the colonial regiments. These officers, by long service with the commanders in the Standing Army of England, had learned whatever was worth knowing in their system of military tactics, while they had failed to learn their inefficiency, procrastination, and punctilious regard for etiquette. They were now destined to turn the knowledge, thus acquired, to good account. Among those thus appointed, were, Oliver Wolcott, who had commanded a company in the northern army in 1748, and was now commissioned as Colonel; and Ebenezer Gay, a resident of Sharon but a native of this town, who was raised to the rank of Lieutenant-Colonel.

In the mean time, matters of local interest and importance were not neglected. The lands were laid out to the several proprietors, bridges were built, and by-laws were passed.

I have suggested that the establishment of Litchfield as the county seat, was an important event in the history of the town. Several wealthy and prominent gentlemen from a distance, soon after this event, settled in this village—among whom I may mention Elisha Sheldon, Lynde Lord, and Reynold Marvin, Esquires, all from Lyme, in the eastern part of the colony. Some of the finest mansions still standing on the Hill, were erected between 1752 and 1760, inclusive. The records give indications of the "march of improvement" in *other* respects. Liberty was granted to Joseph Pickett "to set up a *Barber's Shop* anywhere in the Highway except on the Meeting House Green." Lieutenant Stephen Smith, who had figured in the "late war," and was subsequently in the service at the North, received permission to set up a *Malt House* and *Distillery*. The first Court House was built on the public square, a little east of the Meeting-House ; but the town passed a vote forbidding the erection of a Jail and County House on the square —offering, however, a piece of land for that purpose in any other part of the town which might be selected.

In December, 1740, Messrs. Samuel Culver, Joseph Bird, Ebenezer Beebe and Moses Stoddard, were appointed " to view and lay out a suitable Highway through the north-westerly part of Litchfield leading to Cornwall ;" the same committee were also directed to lay out a road to the east part of Goshen —probably the highway which now connects with Goshen East Street. The principal highways leading to New Milford, Goshen, Woodbury and Harwinton, were all laid out previous to 1750.

In 1752, the Rev. Timothy Collins was dismissed from the pastoral office in this town ; and on the 4th of July 1753, Mr. Champion was settled in his stead. In 1762, a new meeting-house was erected on the Green, which stood sixty-seven years, when it was superceded by the present church-edifice of the First Society.

Benjn. Tallmadge

FROM A PENCIL SKETCH BY COL. TRUMBULL

CHAPTER VI.

THE REVOLUTIONARY ERA.

THE revolutionary spirit early began to manifest itself in Litchfield. A series of oppressive and retaliatory measures on the part of the British Parliament, served to test, to the fullest extent, the patience and patriotism of the people. In consequence of the destruction of the tea in the harbor of Boston, that Town was selected as a special object of ministerial vengeance; which, as a natural result, served to elicit the sympathy and co-operation of the friends of freedom throughout the country. The subjoined document evinces the spirit of the voters of this town on the occasion, and needs no explanation, except that Oliver Wolcott, Esq., was Moderator of the meeting from which it emanated:

"THE Inhabitants of Litchfield, in legal Town Meeting assembled, on the 17th day of August, A. D. 1774, taking into consideration the Distress to which the Poor of the Town of Boston may likely be reduced by the operation of an Act of the British Parliament for Blocking up their Port, and deeply commiserating the unhappiness of a brave and loyal People, who are thus eminently suffering in a General Cause, for vindicating what every virtuous American considers an essential Right of this Country, think it is their indispensable Duty to afford their unhappy distressed brethren of said Town of Boston, all reasonable Aid and Support. And this they are the more readily induced to do, not only as the Inhabitants of said Town are thus severely condemned for their reluctance to submit to an arbitrary, an unconsented to, and consequently unconstitutional Taxation, but the whole of the great and loyal Province of the Massachusetts Bay have been *condemned unheard*, in the loss of their Charter Privileges, by the heretofore unknown and unheard of exertions of Parliamentary Power, which they conceive is a Power claimed and exercised in such a manner as cannot fail of striking every unprejudiced mind with Horror and Amazement, as being subversive of all those inherent, essential and constitutional Rights and Privileges which the good people of this Colony have ever held sacred, and even dearer than Life itself, nor ever can wish to survive ; not only every idea of Property, but every emolument of civil life, being thereby rendered precarious and uncertain.

"In full confidence, therefore, that no Degree of Evil thus inflicted on said Town and Province, will ever induce them to give up or betray their own and the American Constitutional Rights and Privileges, especially as they cannot but entertain the most pleasing Expectations that the Committees of the several North American Provinces, who are soon to meet at Philadelphia, will in their wisdom be able to point out a Method of Conduct effectual for obtaining Redress of their grievances—a Method to which (when once agreed upon by said Committee) this Town will look upon it their duty strictly to attend. And in the mean time, earnestly recommend that *subscriptions be forthwith opened in this Town*, under the care of Reuben Smith, Esq., Capt. Lynde Lord, and Mr. William Stanton, who are hereby appointed a Committee to receive and forward to the Selectmen of Boston, for the use of the Poor in that place, all such Donations as shall be thereupon made for that purpose ; and also to correspond with the Committee of Correspondence there or elsewhere, as there may be occasion.

"We also take this opportunity publicly to return our thanks to the members of the Honorable House of Representatives of this Colony, for their patriotic and loyal Resolutions, passed and published in the last Assembly on the occasion, and order them to be entered at large on the Public Records of this Town, that succeeding ages may be faithfully furnished with authentic Credentials of our inflexible attachment to those inestimable Privileges which we and every honest American glory in esteeming our unalienable Birthright and Inheritance."

At the annual Town Meeting, held December 6, 1774, it was Voted, That the Honorable Oliver Wolcott, Esq., and Messrs. Jedediah Strong, Jacob Woodruff, John Marsh, John Osborn, Jehiel Parmelee, Abraham Bradley, Seth Bird, Archibald McNeile, Abraham Kilbourn, Nathan Garnsey, James Morris and Ebenezer Benton, be a Committee for the Purposes mentioned in the Eleventh Article of the Association Agreement of the Grand Continental Congress in Philadelphia, 5th of September last, and approved, adopted and recommended by the General Assembly of this Colony at their session in October last."

The "Eleventh Article of the Association Agreement," here referred to, provides for the appointment of "Committees of Inspection" in each city and town, "whose business it shall be attentively to observe the conduct of all persons touching this Association; and when it shall be made to appear that any person has violated its articles, they are to cause their names to be published in the Gazette, to the end that all such foes to the Rights of British America may be publicly known and universally contemned as the enemies of American Liberty, and thenceforth we break off all dealings with him or her." Committees of Inspection were also appointed at the annual Town Meeting in 1775 and 1776. In addition to the above, the following persons were appointed, viz., Messrs. Reuben Smith, Lynde Lord, Andrew Adams, Archibald McNeile, Jr., Moses Sanford, Tapping Reeve, Jonathan Mason, Caleb Gibbs, Nathaniel Woodruff, William Stanton and Nathaniel Goodwin.

The celebrated AARON BURR, (afterwards Vice President of the United States,) became intimately associated with Litchfield during this period. He graduated at Princeton College in October, 1772, and in the following June, his only sister, Sarah Burr, became the wife of Tapping Reeve, Esq., of this town. "In May, 1774," says his biographer, (Davis i, 46,) "he left the Rev. Mr. Bellamy's, and went to the house of his brother-in-law, Tapping Reeve, where his time was occupied in reading, principally history, but especially those portions of it which related to wars, battles and seiges, which tended to inflame his natural military ardor. The absorbing topics of taxation and the rights of the people were agitating the then

British Colonies from one extreme to the other. These subjects, therefore, could not pass unnoticed by a youth of the the enquiring mind and ardent feelings of Burr. Constitutional law, and the relative rights of the crown and the colonists, were examined with all the accumen which he possessed, and he became a whig from reflection and conviction, as well as from feeling." Burr remained in Litchfield on this occasion something over a year. The letters written by him while here, contain frequent allusions to local matters, and to individuals (especially the young ladies) residing in the place. In a communication to Matthias Ogden (dated at Litchfield, August 17, 1774,) he says—"Before I proceed further, let me tell you that, a few days ago, a mob of several hundred persons gathered at Barrington, and tore down the house of a man who was suspected of being unfriendly to the liberties of the people; broke up the court then sitting at that place, &c. As many of the rioters belonged to this colony, and the Supreme Court was then sitting at this place, the Sheriff was immediately despatched to apprehend the ring-leaders. He returned yesterday with eight prisoners, who were taken without resistance. But this minute, there are entering the town on horseback, with great regularity, about fifty men, armed each with a white club; and I observe others continually dropping in. I shall here leave a blank, to give you (perhaps in heroics,) a few sketches of my unexampled valor, should they proceed to hostilities; and, should they not, I can tell you what I would have done." After the "blank," the young hero adds—"The above-mentioned sneaks all gave bonds for their appearance, to stand a trial at the next court, for committing a riot."

While Burr remained at the house of Judge Reeve, he was startled by the news of the Battle of Lexington, which took place on the 19th of April, 1775. Immediately thereafter, he addressed a letter to his friend Ogden, urging him to come to Litchfield and make arrangements with him for joining the standard of their country. The Battle of Bunker Hill soon followed—(June 16th.) As Ogden could not come at once to Litchfield, Burr started for Elizabethtown, New Jersey, to assist his friend in arranging for a speedy trip to Cambridge, where the American army was then encamped. In July, they reached Cambridge; and in September, Burr enlisted as a private soldier in Arnold's expedition through the wilderness to Quebec. It may be added, that Litchfield was Colonel Burr's recognized *home* for some half dozen years.*

On the morning of the 10th of May, 1775, Colonel ETHAN ALLEN, a native of Litchfield, at the head of his brave Green Mountain Boys, surprized and captured the Fortress of Ticonderoga. Several of this little band of heroes were born and bred in this vicinity. Lieutenant Crampton, who entered the fort by the side of Allen, was also a native of this town, and had resided here during a large part of his life. On this occasion was captured the first British flag that fell into the hands of the Americans in the revolutionary contest! The magnitude and importance of this exploit will be better understood, when considered in connection with the vast amount of time, and treasure, and blood, which the fortress had cost the British Government. The day following the capture of Ticonderoga, the garrison at Crown Point, with all its military stores, were surrendered to Colonel Warner, a native of Roxbury, in this County.

* On the 27th of January, 1776, Judge Reeve wrote to Burr thus—"Amid the lamentations for the loss of a brave, enterprising General, [Montgomery,] your escape from such imminent danger, to which you have been exposed, has afforded us the greatest satisfaction. The news of the unfortunate attack upon Quebec arrived among us on the 13th of this month. I concealed it from your sister until the 18th, when she found it out; but, in less than half an hour, I received letters from Albany acquainting me that you were in safety, and had gained great honor by your intrepid conduct. * * It was happy for us that we did not know you were an aid-de-camp until we heard of your welfare; for we heard that Montgomery and his aids were killed, without knowing who his aids were. Your sister enjoys a middling state of health. She has many anxious hours on your account; but she tells me that, as she believes you may serve the country in the business in which you are now employed, she is contented that you should remain in the army. It must be an exalted public spirit, that could produce such an effect upon a sister as affectionate as yours."

For several months in 1781, Mrs. Theodocia Provost (the dashing young widow of Colonel Provost, of the British Army,) was a resident of Litchfield; and a few of her letters written from this place are preserved in Davis's Life of Burr, vol. i, pp. 224—227. She became the wife of Burr, July 2, 1782.

Aaron Burr became aid de-camp to General Washington, Attorney General of the State of New York, U. S. Senator, and, in 1801, was a candidate with Jefferson for the Presidency of the United States—the two receiving an equal number of electoral votes. After an exciting contest of several days in the U. S. House of Representatives, Jefferson was chosen President, and Burr Vice President.

In January, 1776, Captain Bezaleel Beebe, of Litchfield, received orders to enlist a company for the defense of New York. The tidings spread rapidly throughout the town, and awakened anew the enthusiasm of the whigs. A veteran who died within the last few years, stated that when the intelligence reached him, he *started on a run* for the Captain's headquarters, fearing the roll would be full before he could reach there. Captain Beebe's orders reached him on a Sunday, and by the following Saturday, the company had been raised, armed, and equipped, and were on their march toward Fairfield. The following paper, with the names attached, is inserted here for preservation:

"WE, the Subscribers, being convinced of the Necessity of a body of Forces to defeat certain Wicked Purposes formed by the instruments of Ministerial Tyranny, do solemnly engage ourselves and enlist as Private Soldiers, in a Regiment to be Commanded by Colonel ANDREW WARD, Jr., under the command of Major General LEE, for the Term of Eight Weeks at the utmost from the Day we March from Fairfield, which is the place of Rendezvous; the Honorable Major General Lee having given his Word and Honor that we shall not be Detained a single Day after said Term. Dated at Litchfield, 21st day of January, 1776."

Lieut. Jonathan Mason,
Briant Stoddard,
James Woodruff,
Oliver Woodruff,
Phineas Goodwin,
Zebulon Bissell,
Benjamin Taylor,
Moses Taylor,
Frederick Stanley,
James Crampton,
Caleb Munson,
Abraham Wadhams,
Martin Nash,
Oliver Griswold,
Zadock Gibbs, Jr.
Josiah Bartholomew, Jr.
Jesse Stanley,
Elisha Mayo,
Nathaniel Newell,
Sergt. Benjamin Bissell,
Elihu Harrison,
Roger N. Whittlesey,
Charles Woodruff, Jr.,
Joseph Sanford,
Stephen Brown,
William Patterson,
John Lyman,
Obed Stoddard,
T. Weed,
George Dear,
Jacob Gaylord,
Elihu Grant,
Abram Beach,
Ichabod Tuttle,
Chauncey Beach,
George Dear, Jr.
Adino Hale,
Allen Lucas,

Luman Bishop,
Asaph Benham,
Joseph Finney,
Zebedee Sturtevant,
Martin Curtiss,
Levi Swan.
Joel Barnes,
Peleg Holmes,
Alexander Sackett,
William Starr,
Heber Gilbert, Jr.
Zebulon Palmer,
Joseph Peters,
Truman Gilbert,
Heman Brown,
Luther Comstock,
Daniel Swan.

Those who have a knowledge of the leading men of Litchfield county from forty to seventy years ago, will recognize in the above list the names of many of her most prominent and influential citizens—men of wealth and enterprize, who, though surrounded by the endearments of domestic life, voluntarily enlisted as *private soldiers* in that dangers expedition. The roll as here given is not complete. About two-thirds of the persons named in the list belonged to this town; the remainder were from Goshen, Torrington and Warren. They were all enlisted from the 21st to the 25th of January, 1776. The names of a few additional members of this company may be gleaned from the following Appraisal:

"*Litchfield*, 26th January, 1776.

"WE, being requested to apprise the Arms belonging to Capt. Bezaleel Beebe's Company, in Col. Andrew Ward's Regiment, going on an expedition to New York under the command of General Charles Lee—we accordingly apprized the same, being first duly sworn, viz.,

Elihu Harrison's Gun, Bayonet and Cartridge Box, in his own hands. [*Figures omitted.*]
Roger N. Whittlesey's Gun in the hands of Briant Stoddard.
Joseph Sanford's Gun, Bayonet and Belt in his own hands.
Nathaniel Allen's Gun, Bayonet and Belt in his own hands.
Obed Stoddard's Gun, Bayonet, Cartridge box and belt.
Joshua Smith's Gun in his own hands.
Zebulon Bissell's Gun in his own hands.
James Woodruff's Gun carried by Stephen Brown.
Phineas Goodwin's Gun, bayonet and belt.
Whiting Stanley's Gun carried by James Crampton.
Oliver Woodruff's Gun carried by himself.
Hezekiah Agard's Gun carried by John Lyman.
Jedediah Strong's Gun, bayonet and belt carried by Wm Patterson.
Lieut. Jonathan Mason's Cartridge box.
Samuel Canfield's Gun carried by himself.
Noah Garnsey's Gun carried by T. Weed.

Sergt. Benjamin Bissell's Gun and Bayonet carried by himself.
Asa Osborn's Gun and Cartridge box carried by himself.
Jedediah Strong's Gun carried by Benjamin Taylor.
Jedediah Strong's Gun carried by Frederick Stanley.
Reuben Smith, Esq's, Gun, Bayonet, Case and Belt, carried by Capt. Beebe.
Capt John Osborn's Gun carried by Moses Taylor.

ABRAHAM BRADLEY, THOMAS CATLIN, OBED STODDER, } Appraisers on Oath.

In May, 1776, a regiment was ordered to be raised for the defense of the State, "to be subject to join the continental army, if so ordered by the Governor." Captain Beebe was appointed to the command of one of the companies of this regiment, with Jesse Cook for 1st lieutenant, and James Watson for 2d lieutenant. Lieut. Watson was soon transferred to another corps, and John Smith, of Litchfield, was commissioned in his place. The following is a complete list of the officers and soldiers of this company:

BEZALEEL BEEBE, Captain,	James Beach,
Jesse Cook, Lieutenant,	Asa Brooks,
John Smith, do.	Daniel Benedict,
Wait Beach, Ensign,	Samuel Baldwin,
Levi Peck, Sergeant,	Elisha Brownson,
Cotton Mather, do.	Benjamin Bissell,
Heber Stone, do.	Daniel Barns,
Solomon Goodwin, do.	Ebenezer Bacon,
Samuel Cole, Corporal,	Noah Beach,
Ezekiel Bissell, do.	Elisha Bissell,
Elijah Loomis, do.	Frederick Bigelow,
David Hall, do.	Hezekiah Bissell,
Joel Taylor, Drummer,	James Davis,
Epaphras Wadsworth, Fifer,	Friend Dickinson,
Nathaniel Allen,	Jesse Dickinson,
Cyrenius Austin,	Solomon Dickinson,
Enos Austin,	Ebenezer Dimon,
Joseph Austin,	Gershom Fay,
Andrew Austin,	Remembrance Filley,
Elihu Beach,	Joel Frost,
Barnias Beach,	John German,
Zebulon Bissell,	Phineas Goodwin,

Beriah Birge,
James Birge,
Noadiah Bancroft,
Ithamar Gibbs,
Moore Gibbs,
Samuel Gleason,
Isaac Hosford,
Abraham Haskins,
Amos Johnson,
Charles Kilbourn,
Henry HcIntire,
Thomas Mason,
Oliver Marshall,
Timothy Marsh,
Alexander McNiel,
Ebenezer Landon,
Remembrance Loomis,
James Little,
John Lyman,
Noah North,
David Olmsted,
Ethan Osborn,
John Parmeley,
Solomon Parmeley,
Joseph Goodwin,
Benjamin Gibbs,
Gershom Gibbs,
Henry Plumb,
Eliphaz Parsons,
Joseph Sanford,
Frederick Stanley,
Timothy Stanley,
Jared Stewart,
Joseph Spencer,
Daniel Smith,
Aaron Stoddard,
Ira Stone,
John Strong,
Peleg Sweet,
Stephen Taylor,
Joseph Taylor,
Samuel Vaill,
Jeremiah Weed,
John Weed,
Gideon Wilcoxson,
John Whiting,
Oliver Woodruff,

These names are copied from the account-book and billet-roll preserved among the papers of Col. Beebe. From various accounts and memoranda found in these papers, we are able to gather certain facts in the history of some of these soldiers. Thus—" August 9, To cash paid for *coffin* for Ira Stone;" Sept. 7, " Lieut. John Smith was discharged from the army in New York;" " John German was dismissed from my company by order of a General Court Martial, July 9, 1776;" " Aug. 9, James Beach *died* about 8 o'clock in the morning;" " Sept. the 5th, 10 o'clock at night, Samuel Gleason *died*;" in the account with Joel Taylor—"Paid one dollar to Zebulon Taylor to deliver to *the mother* of the above Joel Taylor, *deceased*, it being cash that was with him when he died;" " Sept. 27, 1777, Received of Capt. Beebe 22 shillings for mileage from Philadelphia to Litchfield. (Signed,) Abraham Haskins."

From the account of Gershom Gibbs—"Received of Capt. Beebe three dollars that *belonged to my husband and son*, which was part of the money sent to them whilst prisoners in New York. (Signed,) Tabitha Gibbs." From the account with Nathaniel Allen—"Sept 27, 1777, To cash left with Joseph Agard to be paid to *Mrs. Allen*, that was left with me when Mr. Allen *died*." From the account with Phineas Goodwin—"To back rations 16 days at Fort Washington," &c. The fate of some of these individuals, together with that of many others belonging to this company, will be more fully explained in the narrative which follows.

About the 1st of November, 1776, thirty-six *picked men*, (all of whose names are given in the preceding roll,) were placed under the command of Capt. Beebe and sent to Fort Washington to aid in its defense. This post, together with Fort Lee on the Jersey shore, commanded the mouth of the Hudson, and was hence regarded by the enemy as a tempting prize. In anticipation of an attack, the works had been strengthened and reinforced. At the critical time, the Fort and Harlem Heights were manned by two Pennsylvania Regiments commanded by Colonels Magraw and Shea, Rawlin's Riflemen from Maryland, some of the militia of the flying camp, and a few companies detailed from the Connecticut Regiments. On the 15th of November, Sir William Howe summoned Colonel Magraw, (who had the chief command of the garrison,) to surrender. That brave officer, acting under the immediate advice of Generals Putnam and Greene, responded, that he would defend himself to the last extremity. On the morning of the 16th the attack was commenced at four different points nearly at the same moment. The Hessians under Knyphausen assaulted the south side; the English Light Infantry, two battalions of Guards, the 33d Regiment, and a body of Grenadiers, commanded by General Matthews and Lord Cornwallis, attacked the east side; on the south, a feint was attempted by Colonel Sterling with the 42d Regiment; while Lord Percy, with a very strong corps, directed the assault upon the western flank of the fortress. The assailants were provided with excellent trains of artillery, which were brought to bear with effect. The attack was prosecuted with extraordinary energy and spirit, and the Americans continued to defend themselves until resistance became fruitless. During a recess in the fight, the garrison was again summoned to surrender; and, after a brief consultation with the officers, Magraw capitulated. The entire American force, amounting to two thousand six hundred men, surrendered as prisoners of war. During the seige, the enemy lost about twelve hundred, and the Americans about four hundred.

Gorton, the historian, informs us that "while the enemy were advancing to the attack, Generals Washington, Putnam and Greene, and Colonel Knox, with their aids, crossed the river and approached toward the Fort. They were warned of their danger, and, after much persuasion, were induced to return. The garrison, however, was watched with intense interest by Washington, who, from Fort Lee, could view several parts of the attack; and when he saw his men bayoneted, and in that way killed while begging for quarter, he cried with the tenderness of a child, denouncing the barbarity that was practiced."

The terms of the capitulation were regarded as liberal and honorable on the part of the victors, and highly favorable to the vanquished. The manner in which those terms were violated, and every principle of humanity set at naught, by the miscreants into whose hands the unfortunate prisoners were placed, is without a parallel in the history of the revolutionary struggle. Crowded, with hundreds of others, into the Sugar-House and on board the Prison-Ships, without air or water and for the first two days without food, contagion and death were the natural consequences. The dysentery, small-pox, and other terrible diseases, broke out among them, and very few of the whole number survived the terrible ordeal. On the 27th of December, 1776, an exchange of prisoners took place. Only eleven of Captain Beebe's Company were able to sail for Connecticut, viz., Marsh, Woodruff, R. Loomis, B. Beach, N. Beach, Marshall, Brownson, Bissell, Little, Benedict and Mason. Six of these died on their way home, viz., Bissell, Brownson, B. Beach, Marsh, Marshall and Loomis. The remainder of those who were living at that date, being too ill to be removed, were left behind—where all (except Sergeant Mather,) died within a few days, most of them with the small-pox. Here follow the names of these "picked men." The notes prefixed, appear to have been added by Captain Beebe at the different periods corresponding with the dates:

"*An Account of the Prisoners' Names and Places of Confinement.*

Sergt. Cotton Mather—returned home.
Sergt. David Hall—died of the small-pox on board the Grosvener, Dec. 11, 1776.
Elijah Loomis—died.
Gershom Gibbs—died on board the ship, Dec. 29, 1776.
Timothy Stanley—died on board the ship, Dec. 26, 1776.
Amos Johnson—died Dec. 26, 1776.
Timothy Marsh—died on his way home.
Barnias Beach—died on his way home.
Samuel Vaill—died on board the Grosvener, Dec. 27, 1776.
Nathaniel Allen—died of small-pox, Jan. 1, 1777.
Enos Austin—died of the small-pox, Dec. 4, 1776, in the evening.
Gideon Wilcoxson—died.
Thomas Mason—reached home.
Alexander McNiel—died.
Daniel Smith—died in New York, of small-pox, Jan. 1, 1777.
Noah Beach—reached home.
Daniel Benedict—reached home.
Isaac Gibbs—died Jan. 15, 1777.
Oliver Marshall—died on his way home.
Solomon Parmely—went on board the ship, and I fear he is drowned, as I cannot find him.
David Olmsted—died Jan. 4, 1777.
Jared Stuart—died Jan. 26, 1777, in the morning.
John Lyman—died Jan 26, 1777.
Elisha Brownson—died on his way home.

The above Prisoners are at Livingston's Sugar House.

Zebulon Bissell—died in Woodbury, on his way home.
Aaron Stoddard—died Jan. 12, 1777.
John Parmely—died Jan. 15, 1777.
Joel Taylor—died Jan. 9, 1777.
James Little—reached home.
Phineas Goodwin—died Jan. 5, 1777.

[*The above at the Church called the North Church.*

Oliver Woodruff—reached home.
Remembrance Loomis—died on his way home.
[*The above at Bridewell.*

The above Prisoners belong to Capt. Beebe's Company, Col. Bradley's Regiment.

Corporal Samuel Cole, Jeremiah Weed, Joseph Spencer, John Whiting,	Were either killed or made their escape from Fort Washington, on the 16th of November, 1776."

Probably no similar instance of mortality occurred during the entire war. Only *six* survivors out of a company of thirty-six hale and hearty young men, is a per-centage of loss rarely reached even in the most fatal engagements. But few, if any, of these men were slain in battle. They died miserable deaths, from cold, hunger, thirst, suffocation, disease, and the vilest cruelty from those to whom they had surrendered their arms on a solemn promise of fair and honorable treatment! Well might Ethan Allen (a professed infidel,) with clenched teeth, exclaim to Captain Beebe, as he did on one occasion—"I confess my faith in my own creed is shaken; there *ought* to be a hell for such infernal scoundrels as that Lowrie!"—referring to the officer in charge of the prisoners.

Captain Beebe, in consideration of his office, was allowed the limits of the city on his parol of honor, but was compelled to provide himself with food, lodging, and shelter. He was accustomed to visit his men daily, so long as any remained, and did whatever he was allowed to do, to alleviate their wretched condition. He was not exchanged with the other prisoners, but was detained within the "limits" for nearly a year, at his own expense. During much of this time, Colonel Allen was held in New York as a prisoner of war; and, before the remnant of the Litchfield soldiers were exchanged, these two gallant officers often met for consultation.

In June, 1776, the General Assembly ordered six battalions to be raised in this State and marched directly to New York, there to join the continental army. A company was raised in Litchfield for this service, of which Abraham Bradley was Captain, Tilley Blakesley, 1st Lieutenant, Thomas Catlin, 2d Lieutenant, and James Morris, Jr., Ensign.

Among the "Wolcott Papers" is preserved the following Deposition made on the 3d of May, 1777, before Andrew Adams, Esq., *J. P.*, by Lieutenant Thomas Catlin, of this town, (father of the late Dr. Abel Catlin,) who was an officer in the American army in New York in 1776. He avers, in substance, "That he was taken Prisoner by the British Troops on New York Island, September 15, 1776, and confined with a great number in close Gaol, eleven days; that he had no sustenance for forty-eight hours after he was taken; that for eleven whole days they had only about two days' allowance, and their pork was offensive to the smell. That forty-two were confined in one house, till Fort Washington was taken, when the house was crowded with other Prisoners; after which they were informed they should have two-thirds allowance—which consisted of very poor Irish Pork, Bread hard, mouldy and wormy, made of canail and dregs of flax-seed. The British Troops had good bread. Brackish water was given to the Prisoners, and he had seen $1 50 given for a common pail of water. Only between three and four pounds of Pork was given three men for three days. That for near three months, the private soldiers were confined in the Churches, and in one were eight hundred and fifty; that about the 25th of December, 1776, he and about two hundred and twenty-five others were put on board the Glasgow at New York to be carried to Connecticut for exchange. They were on board eleven days, and kept on black, coarse broken bread, and less pork than before. Twenty-eight died during these eleven days! They were treated with great cruelty, and had no fire for sick or well. They were crowded between decks, and many died through hardship, ill usage, hunger and cold."

This is *another* specimen of the treatment of our prisoners by the enemy. It is a source of gratification to every American to be able to say, that British prisoners in American hands, in the same contest, were treated more like gentlemen than like brutes.

"Before the revolution," says Mr. Gibbs, in his History of the Administrations of Washington and Adams, "a leaden equestrian statue of George III. stood in the Bowling Green in the city of New York. At the breaking out of the war, this was overthrown, and, lead being highly valuable, was sent to General Wolcott's at Litchfield for safe keeping; where, in process of time, it was cut up and run into bullets by his daughters and their friends."

In a paper read before the New York Historical Society, by the author above quoted, in October, 1844, he gives a curious and interesting history of this statue, from which the following extracts are made:

"ACCOUNT OF THE STATUE OF GEORGE III. FORMERLY STANDING ON THE BOWLING GREEN, NEW YORK.

"Most of the members are probably aware that an Equestrian Statue of King George III. stood upon the Bowling Green, in this city, prior to the Revolution, and was overthrown soon after its commencement. I believe, however, that its subsequent fate has never been recorded, and having in my possession a paper giving authentic information on the subject, I have supposed that the royal effigy might be worth a brief obituary.

Holt's (New York) Gazette, as quoted by Mr. Dunlap, gives the following notice of its erection:

'August 21st, 1770, being the birth-day of Prince Frederick, the father of George III., an elegant Equestrian Statue of his present Majesty, George III. was erected in the Bowling Green, near Fort George. On this occasion the members of his Majesty's Council, the City Corporation, the Corporation of the Chamber of Commerce, the Corporation of the Marine Society, and most of the gentlemen of the City and Army, waited on his Honor, the Lieutenant-Governor Colden, in the Fort, at his request; when his Majesty's and other loyal healths were drunk under a discharge of thirty-two pieces of cannon, from the Battery, accompanied with a band of music. This beautiful Statue is made of metal [Dunlap says, by way of parenthesis, 'the writer did not like to say *what* metal represented his royal majesty, the best of kings—*it was lead*,'] being the first equestrian one of his present Majesty, and is the workmanship of that celebrated statuary, Mr. Wilton of London.'

Symptoms of disloyalty, betokening revolution I suppose, soon manifested themselves in the rude treatment of the effigy, for on the 6th or February, 1773. an act was passed 'to prevent the defacing of statues which are erected in the city of New York.'

Upon the above account Mr. Dunlap observes—'This statue stood till sometime in 1776. I saw it in 1775. In 1776 it was thrown down, and tradition says converted into bullets to resist his gracious majesty's soldiers when sent to enforce the doctrine of 'the sovereignty of the British Parliament over the Colonies in all cases whatsoever' —the doctrine of Mr. Pitt, Lord Chatham, which he died in an effort to enforce. The pedestal stood until long after the Revolution. No fragment of the horse or his rider was ever seen after its overthrow, and so completely had the memory of the event been lost, that I have never found a person who could tell me on what occasion it was ordered, or when placed in the Bowling Green.'

Some cotemporary notices of the destruction of this effigy have been pointed out to me, which I will cite. The first is from a book of general orders issued by Washington, the original of which is in the possession of this Society. It is as follows:

'July 10.—Though the General doubts not the persons who pulled down and mutilated the statue in Broadway last night, acted in the public cause, yet it has so much the appearance of riot and want of order in the army, that he disapproves of the manner, and directs that in future these things shall be avoided by the soldiery and left to be executed by proper authority.'

The next is in a letter from Ebenezer Hazard to General Gates, dated July 12th, 1776, which will be found among the Gates Papers, and in the Society's Collection—and is as follows:

'The King of England's arms have been burned in Philadelphia, and his statue here has been pulled down to make musket balls of, so that his troops will probably have *melted majesty* fired at them.'

Another is in a letter from New York, of July 11, 1776, published in the New Hampshire Gazette of the 27th—

'Last Monday evening, the Equestrian Statue of George III., with tory pride and folly raised in the year 1770, was, by the Sons of Freedom, laid prostrate in the dust—the just desert of an ungrateful tyrant. The lead wherewith this monument is made, is to be run into bullets, to assimulate with the brains of our infatuated adversaries, who, to gain a peppercorn, have lost an empire. A gentleman who was present at the ominous fall of his leaden majesty, looking back to the original's hopeful beginning, pertinently exclaimed in the language of the angel to Lucifer—'If thou be'est he, but ah how fallen! how changed!' '

Mr. Stephens* (Incidents of Travel in Russia, etc., vol. ii, p. 23,) mentions having met with a curious memorial of its destruction, and at an out of the way place. This was a gaudy and flaring engraving in a black wooden frame, representing the scene of its destruction, which he found in a tavern at *Chioff, in Russia*. 'The grouping of picture,' he says, 'was rude and grotesque, the ringleader being a long negro stripped to his trowsers, and straining with all his might upon a rope, one end of which was fastened to the head of the statue and the other tied around his own waist, his white teeth and the whites of his eyes being particularly conspicuous on a heavy ground of black.' How this picture found its way to Russia, it would be difficult to imagine; it would certainly be not less a curiosity here than there.

The document I have mentioned gives an account of its remaining history in a shape which history seldom assumes, that of an *account*

* John L. Stephens, the celebrated traveler, was a graduate of the Litchfield Law School.

current. It is preserved among the papers of General (afterwards Governor) Wolcott, of Connecticnt. It is a statement of the number of cartridges made from the materials of the statue by the young ladies of Litchfield, and is in these words :

‘Mrs. Marvin,	3456 cartridges.	
" " on former account,	2602	
	——	6058
Ruth Marvin on former account,	6204	
Not sent to court house 449 packs,	5388	
	——	11,592
Laura, on former account,	4250	
Not sent to court house 344 packs,	4128	
	——	8378
Mary Ann, on former account,	5762	
Not sent to the court house 119 packs, out of which I let Col. Perley Howe have 3 packs,	5028	
	——	10,790
Frederick, on former account,	708	
Not sent to court house 19 packs,	228	
	——	936
		37,754
Mrs. Beach's two accounts,		2,002
Made by sundry persons,		2,182
Gave Litchfield Militia, on alarm,		50
Let the regiment of Col. Wigglesworth have		300
Cartridges, No.		42,288
Overcharged in Mrs. Beach's account,		200
		42,088’

The original document is in General Wolcott's hand writing, and is endorsed ‘ number of cartridges made.’ There is no date to it, nor is there mention made by him of the fact of their being made from the statue ; but a memorandum added by his son, the last Governor Wolcott, explains it as follows:

‘N. B. An equestrian statue of George the Third of Great Britain was erected in the city of New York, on the Bowling Green, at the lower end of Broadway. Most of the materials were lead, but richly gilded to resemble gold. At the beginning of the Revolution, this statue was overthrown. Lead then being scarce and dear, the statue was broken in pieces, and the metal transported to Litchfield as a place of safety. The ladies of the village converted the lead into cartridges, of which the preceding is an account. O. W.’

The Mrs. and Miss Marvin and Mrs. Beach, mentioned in the paper, belonged to families who yet reside in Litchfield ; the other persons named, were the two daughters and youngest son of General Wolcott.

Litchfield, it may be noticed, was, during the war, a place of great importance as a military depot. After the capture of New York by the British in 1776, all communication between New England and Pennsylvania was turned to the westward of the Highlands on the Hudson, and the troops and stores were usually passed through that village as a point on the most convenient route to the posts on the river yet in possession of the Americans. General Wolcott, who was a member of the Continental Congress, lived there; and, during the intervals of his congressional attendance, was constantly occupied in raising troops to supply the requisitions of Washington, Putnam and Gates. It appears from his letters that he returned to Connecticut shortly after the adoption of the Declaration of Independence, of which he was one of the signers, and it is probable that the statue was transported there at his instance, immediately after its destruction. Of its identity as the material for the cartridges above mentioned, there can be no doubt. The last Governor Wolcott, on graduating from Yale College in 1778, was appointed to an office in the Quarter Master's Department, under General Greene, and was posted at Litchfield in charge of the stores there. His opportunity for knowing the fact, as mentioned in his note, was therefore certain. The late Hon. Judge Wolcott, moreover, who figures in the account as 'Frederick,' and who was a boy at the time, informed me a few years ago that he well remembered the circumstance of the statue being sent there, and that a shed was erected for the occasion in an apple-orchard adjoining the house, where his father chopped it up with a wood axe, and the girls had a frolic in running the bullets and making them up into cartridges. I suppose the alarm of the militia, on which some were distributed, was Tryon's Invasion in 1777, when Danbury was burnt. On this occasion, fourteen men, *the last in Litchfield capable of bearing arms*, were started at midnight to aid in repulsing the enemy."

A few miscellaneous facts relating to Litchfield men are here introduced nearly in chronological order.

It should have been mentioned previously, that Captain David Welch, of Litchfield, commanded a company that was called into active service early in 1775, and in April of that year he was commissioned as Major in Colonel Hinman's regiment. He served throughout the war, and was an efficient and popular officer. During this year, also, Jedediah Strong was appointed a Commissary to purchase Horses for the Army; and Oliver Wolcott was chosen a member of the continental congress. Fisher Gay, of Farmington, (a native of this town,) was one of the Lieutenant-Colonels appointed and commissioned at the special session of the Legislature held in March.

In May, 1776, Amos Parmeley was allowed by the Assembly £14: 12: 1, lawful money, " for nursing his sick son, John, who was a soldier in Major Welch's company, General Wooster's regiment, in the northern army, in 1775." This is the John Parmeley who died in captivity in New York, in January, 1777. Jedediah Strong was appointed Commissary for the purchase of Clothing, and on a Committee to exchange bills of credit for specie.

On the 4th of July, OLIVER WOLCOTT *appended his name to the Declaration of Independence.* In October he was re-appointed a member of the continental congress.

Drs. Reuben Smith and Seth Bird were appointed by the Legislature, in October, on a committee "to examine all persons in this State that should be offered at Surgeons or Surgeons' Mates in the continental army or navy, and if found qualified, to give them certificates."

Andrew Adams was appointed, with others, to cause the arrest of all suspected persons, and those dangerous to the liberties of America.

In December, the Legislature appointed Tapping Reeve and Lynde Lord on a committee to "to rouse and animate the people," and endeavor to procure the enlistment of volunteers for Washington's army. A company was forthwith raised in Litchfield, and the following officers were commissioned—Nathaniel Goodwin, Captain; Alexander Waugh, Lieutenant; and Ozias Goodwin, Ensign. At the same session, Colonel Wolcott was promoted to the rank of Brigadier General, and given the command of the Fourth Brigade.

While General Wolcott was attending upon the sessions of Congress in Philadelphia, his principal Litchfield correspondents (aside from Mrs. Wolcott and his son Oliver,) were Samuel Lyman, Esq., and Dr. Reuben Smith—both, of course, true patriots. Mr. Lyman was accustomed to write upon family matters, and on public affairs *generally*; while Dr. Smith kept the General advised on subjects of local interest. We give the subjoined letter from Dr. Smith *entire*—with the simple suggestion, that considerable allowance must be made for the personal and political prejudices of the writer. His insinuation in regard to Major Welch, for instance, was alike ungenerous and uncalled for. If his active service on the field does not afford sufficient evidence of his zeal in the cause of Independence, we have yet a surer test of his patriotism in the fact that it was again and again *endorsed* by a majority of his fellow-townsmen, in electing him to various public offices—at times, too, when they would not tolerate the least suspicion of *toryism.* When Dr. Smith's letter was written, a feeling of coldness and despondency seemed to prevail among the patriots throughout the colonies. A re-action had succeeded the enthusiasm with which the Revolution was inaugurated. Frequent reverses had led some of the truest friends of freedom to fear as to the final result of the conflict in which they were engaged. In addition to this, the fact is not to be disguised that there had been from the first a formidable minority of the voters of this town who were bitter opponents of the "Great Rebellion," as they were wont to term it. These facts will serve to account for the temporary inactivity of the patriots in Litchfield, of which the Doctor complains.

"*Litchfield*, 17th April, 1777.

Hon'd Sir—Your favor of the 1st instant came to hand the 15th, and I now sit down to give you the desired information, though ignorant of any proper conveyance.

At the Town Council in January, John Marsh, 3d, and Daniel Rowe, were objected to as Innholders; upon which Captain John, who is this year one of the Selectmen, moved that Marsh might be called in, which was agreed to. He accordingly came in, and acknowledged the several charges in substance, and openly declared that in his opinion America had better settle the dispute on the best terms they could obtain from Great Britain; that the further we proceeded, the deeper we should get in the mire, (his own words,) and must finally submit. Captain John tried to help him out, by putting some questions which would admit of ambiguous answers; but the young man was too open and frank in his answers, and accordingly was left out, as was Rowe. Captain Seymour and David Stoddard were put in their room.

The latter end of January I joined the army under General Wooster, and retreating soon after in a stormy night, was over fatigued, fell sick, was carried up to Horseneck and there discharged, and returned home some time in February. Some soldiers having brought home the small pox, I found a number had ventured upon innoculation without making proper provision that it might not spread in the town. The people were much divided; some warmly engaged for innoculation, others as warmly opposed. Unhappily for me, I was chosen one of the Selectmen this year, (with Captain Marsh, Mr. Strong, Captain McNiele and Captain Osborn,) and was therefore under a necessity of interposing in the matter; and thought best, as it was against law, neither to encourage or oppose, but endeavor to bring it under proper regulations—in which, however, I failed of the wished for success, our counsels being very much divided. Several having taken it the natural way from those that were innoculated, Captain Marsh was engaged to crush innoculation wholly; and some people have been so unreasonable as to say Mr. Strong was both for and against it. Be that as it way, it served as a game. Both had like to have been losers.

I can't recollect that March produced anything very remarkable except the struggle about the small pox.

April is a month of great importance and expectation. Several appeared by the suffrages to be candidates for election at the Freemen's Meeting. Mr. Adams came in first; and, after many rounds, Mr. Strong just carried it against Captain Bradley. Captain John Marsh fell much short of the number I expected. Major Welch, who for some time has appeared a cool friend of the American cause, was observed to have nearly all the tory votes. So much for Deputies. The Constables for Litchfield were Lieutenant Mason, (since dead,) Alexander Catlin, Briant and David Stoddard. Lieutenant Mason was appointed in the winter service, was seized with a pleurisy at De-Lancey's Mills, (Westchester,) sent over to Rochelle, and when we retreated from Fort Independence, was removed to Mamrock, where he died the same day. His eldest son, who was with Captain Beebe at Fort Washington, came home about the same time in a very miserable condition, and is since dead. Captain Beebe and Lieutenant Jesse Grant still remain in captivity. It was said, after our success at Trenton and Princeton, that we were abundantly able to exchange all our prisoners; and certain it is, that we have numbers in hand, and yet our people are held prisoners. Is there not somewhere a neglect? May these partial ills be productive of universal good! Has my honored friend any bright prospects? Has he any cordial for one almost in the Nadir of Despondency? Public spirit and virtue exist with us only in idea. Almost every one is pursuing his private gain, to the entire neglect of the public good. Our proportion of the continental army, I believe, is not half completed. Men will not enlist, and if drafted only for six weeks, (as has lately been the case,) they will rather pay a fine of five pounds. Thirteen men were the other day drafted in Captain Marsh's company to go to Peekskill and to be held but six weeks after their arrival. Not one has gone or intends to go. This town met last week and voted £12 premium for every one that should enlist into the continental army for three years or during the war; but I cannot learn that one man has enlisted since. This day orders came to town from the Governor and Council of Safety to fill up the Eight Battalions immediately, by drafting men out of the militia and alarm companies, till the 1st of January; but it will not be done, as a fine of five pounds will excuse from going.

Our money is continually depreciating. This week, John Collins sold two yoke of oxen for £95, which might have been bought a twelve month past for £20 per yoke. Every necessary article is continually rising in price, which proves a fatal discouragement to men's engaging in the service; for if they go, their families (say they) must unavoidably suffer and starve, as their bounty and pay will not procure them the necessary support.

Monday, 28th April.—Finding no opportunity of forwarding the foregoing, direct, it has lain by until this time, and now send it to the Post Office in Hartford with the following addition:

Intelligence was brought to town last Saturday afternoon, that twenty-four Transports were come to a place called Compo, between Fairfield and Norwalk, and that the troops were landing. About two o'clock next morning, an Express came from New Milford, who informed that the troops landed to the number of three thousand, with some light field-pieces, and proceeded direct to Danbury, where they arrived without the least opposition on Saturday at two o'clock in the afternoon, took possession of our stores and the town, which was said to be in flames when the Express came away. The people with great spirit turned out immediately from all our towns, but I fear to little purpose; for if they fired the town Saturday afternoon, they will get on board their shipping before our people get down. Last night, advice was brought that the enemy was landing at New Haven on Saturday night, but I imagine it to be only a feint in order to prevent their retreat being cut off. We have heard nothing from Danbury since the departure of our people. The Tories are grown very insolent, but I believe they will not dare attempt anything openly with us.

Mrs. Wolcott and family are well. Oliver is gone to Danbury. My haste must apologize for abruptness, &c.

I am, Sir, Your Humble Servant,

REUBEN SMITH.

Hon. Oliver Wolcott, Philadelphia."

The last Governor Wolcott (then a student at Yale College,) was in Litchfield at the time of the alarm. Awakened at midnight by the summons to repair to the rendezvous of the militia, he armed himself; his mother, furnishing his knapsack with provisions and a blanket, hastened his departure, and dismissed him with the charge "to conduct like a good soldier." He, with the other volunteers from this town, participated in the skirmish at Wilton, as well as in the subsequent attacks during the retreat of the British from the burning of Danbury.

From another letter written by Dr. Smith to General Wolcott, (dated at Litchfield, May 12th, 1777,) we make the following extracts. It was penned, as will be observed, after the return of the Litchfield soldiers from the Danbury Alarm:

"Sunday morning, 27th April, about one o'clock, we were alarmed Our people turned out spiritedly; came up with the rear of the enemy about eleven the next day, a little below Wilton meeting-house, and pursued them aboard their ships. Paul Peck was killed in the last attack on the enemy. Levi Peck, (Thomas Peck's son,) was wounded in the shoulder about the same time. In Wilton, Ozias Goodwin was wounded in the arm, and Salmon Buel had one of his thighs broken, and the other shot through with the same ball.*

The infamous Daniel Griswold came into the western part of this town, the morning before the alarm, and was there concealed till Monday; and took off to join the ministerial army, David Kilbourn, Benjamin Kilbourn's son Charles, Isaac Kilbourn's son Abraham, and Samuel Kilbourn son of Giles Kilbourn, Jonathan Smith, Jr., and his brother Elisha, (who was enlisted in the light horse,) David Joy, Benjamin Doolittle, Josiah Stone, and John Davies' son David, and one John Beach of Woodbury who lived at Josiah Stone's.

The Wednesday following they were taken, (except Benjamin Doolittle and Charles Kilbourn, who it is said were killed in attempting to escape,)† and were carried to Derby, where they were tried by a Court Martial, and Griswold was sentenced to be hanged; which sentence was executed on the Monday following, at New Haven. The rest were pardoned, upon their enlisting into the continental army during the War.

Governor Franklin is confined in our Gaol, and a constant Guard is kept. We trust he will find it difficult to escape, should he attempt it. I understand he utterly denies the charge of dispensing Pardons and Protections."

Of Paul Peck, alluded to in the letter of Dr. Smith, it is said, "he was the most expert hunter of the time in which he lived. At the Danbury Alarm, he put his large gun in order, followed the enemy to Compo, on their retreat, and took a station behind a stone wall, where every shot told—until he was rushed upon by the enemy, who took his gun from him and dashed his brains out with it." He was killed, April 28, 1777, aged about seventy-five years.‡

---

* The Assembly allowed Mr. Buel £60 for his relief. He never fully recovered from the effects of his wounds. He was the father of Capt. Salmon Buel, who is still living.

† These men both *escaped*. Doolittle remained in Litchfield until some thirty years ago, when he removed West. Kilbourn settled in Canada. (See Biog. Sketches.)

‡ It is stated that Father Mills, the eccentric clergyman of Torringford, wishing on one occasion to illustrate the certain and irrevocable doom of the wicked, told of a timid Berkshire fox that started on a trip to the Sound. At first he was wary of every step, and frightened at the rustling of a leaf. But having safely passed the snares, and hunters, and hounds, that beset his way, he becames careless, proud and self-conceited. "He enters Fat Swamp at a jolly trot, head and tail up, looking defiance at the enemies he has left so far behind him. But Oh, the dreadful reverse:—In the midst of his haughty reverie, he is brought to a sudden and everlasting stop IN ONE OF PAUL PECK'S TRAPS."

Twenty or thirty prisoners of war, of various grades, were sometimes confined in the Litchfield Jail at once. The location being so far inland, and so distant from any navigable stream, it was thought they would be less liable to be discovered and rescued here, than at Hartford, New Haven or Boston. Among those confined here in 1776 and 1777, were Mr. Matthews, the English Mayor of New York, and Hon. William Franklin, the royal Governor of New Jersey. Franklin was a son of the famous Dr. Benjamin Franklin, and held the office of Governor from 1763 to 1776, when he was seized by the whigs and conveyed to Governor Trumbull, of Connecticut, by whose order he was for some time confined at Wallingford and Middletown. In April, 1777, the Council of Safety of this State received an order from Congress " to confine Governor Franklin without pen, ink or paper ; and directed him to be conveyed, under guard, by the Sheriff of Hartford county, to Litchfield Jail." In September, we find mention made in the records of the Council, of an order drawn in favor of Lynde Lord, Esq., of Litchfield, of £100 toward the expense of the guard placed over the Governor ; and on the 15th of January, 1778, another similar order was drawn in favor of Sheriff Lord.

Governor Franklin, after his release, went to England, and was pensioned for his sufferings and losses. He died in 1813, aged 86.

Under date of August 1, 1776, in the proceedings of the Council of War, occurs the following record as copied by Hinman, (Hist. Rev. p. 377) : " Letters from the Convention of New York sent by Mr. De Peyster, respecting the prisoners sent from New York to Litchfield Jail, were read ; and thereupon ordered, that the Mayor of New York should be brought to Hartford and there confined. Gilbert Forbes and William Forbes were directed to be confined in Litchfield jail, and the other ten to be taken to Norwich jail ; and warrants were ordered to be sent to the several jailers."

In the proceedings of the Council of Safety, under date of August 26, 1776, occurs the following memorandum, viz., " Last Monday, David Matthews, Mayor of the City of New

York, was brought from Litchfield, and on Friday was returned to Litchfield, to remain under the care of Captain Moses Seymour."

The first Pleasure Carriage ever brought into this town, was presented by Mayor Matthews to Mrs. Moses Seymour, whose husband, it will be seen, had the custody of the Mayor. The carriage was in use here as recently as 1818. The Mayor's traveling trunk is still in this town, in possession of one of Major Seymour's descendants.

Early in 1777, orders were issued for raising eight battalions in Connecticut for the continental service, "to serve for three years, or during the war." Ninety-two of the soldiers for these battalions were ordered to be raised in Litchfield. In April of this year, the town voted to pay out of the treasury to each soldier that should enlist for the full term specified, the sum of twelve pounds per annum, in addition to the pay they might receive from the State or General Governments. The Selectmen were at the same time directed to lay a tax for the purpose designated, and Messrs. Miles Bach, Leman Stone, Moses Barns and Stephen Bidwell, were appointed Collectors.

Before proceeding farther, it is proper to add, that at the period of which we are writing, Litchfield was the home of a remarkable number of educated and thinking men—some of whom were already distinguished, and others who were destined to act an important part in their country's history. Indeed, no town in the State could boast of a community more refined, intelligent and patrotic. Within our present borough limits resided, Oliver Wolcott, Andrew Adams, Reynold Marvin, Tapping Reeve, Isaac Baldwin, Samuel Lyman, Isaac Baldwin, Jr., Elisha Sheldon, John Pierce, Jr., Dr. Thomas Little, Lynde Lord, Rev. Timothy Collins, Rev. Judah Champion, Dr. Lemuel Hopkins, Dr. Reuben Smith, Moses Seymour, Timothy Skinner, Abraham Bradley, William Stanton, Ambrose Collins, Elijah Wadsworth, and Ephraim Kirby—all of whom, and many more, were conspicuous as public men and patriots. To this "goodly companie" were soon added, Oliver Wolcott, Jr., Ashbel Baldwin, Ezekiel Woodruff, Julius Deming, Uriah Tracy and Doct. Daniel Sheldon—who all became residents here before the close of the war. Sixteen of the gentlemen named, were graduated at Yale College, and one (Judge Reeve) at the College of New Jersey; three were members of the State Council; four were members of the national congress, or became such; seven were captains in the revolutionary army, and four rose to the rank of general officers; two became Chief Justices and two Governors of the State. Jedediah Strong, whose residence was just outside the limits stated, was a member of the State Council and of the continental Congress. Every section of the town, in fact, furnished its full proportion of able and faithful men both in public stations and in private life—some of whom have already been referred to. Among these were Dr. Seth Bird, Rev. George Beckwith, Colonel Beebe, Major Welch, Captains Morris, McNiel, Goodwin, Osborn, Stone, Waugh, Stoddard, Buel, &c.

The era was characterized by a rancor of party feeling which has rarely been equalled in the history of this or any other country. At times, the zeal of the patriots knew no bounds, and they naturally enough regarded all who differed from them relative to the kingly prerogative, as foes to liberty and inimical to the vital interests of the country. The gentlemen named above, belonged to the popular and triumphant party, and their memory is cherished by a grateful posterity. There were *others* in this town, as elsewhere throughout the land—honorable, influential and conscientious men—who, while they openly disapproved of many acts of the parliament, were yet warmly attached to the royal cause. They looked upon *revolution* as not only treason to their sovereign, but predestined to be ruinous to all who might engage in it; and they chose to suffer what they regarded as only temporary evils, rather than rush into the vortex of war for redress. Nor is all this a matter of surprise, when we consider the force of education. In the colonies, as in England, the people had been taught that, next to religion, *loyalty* was the cardinal virtue. "Fear God, and *honor the King*," was a precept which none but the infidel and traitor had ventured to gainsay. Some argued that any attempt at independence was rank *ingratitude* on our part. "In our weakness," said they, "were not the armies of England again and again sent over to protect us from the French and Indians?" The Episcopalians, or members of the Church of England, were drawn towards the mother country by still stronger and dearer ties. Their clergymen were ordained and set apart to the work of the ministry, by English Bishops; and their Book of Common Prayer taught them to pray for the King and Royal Family. Besides, Litchfield was still a "missionary station," under the direction and patronage of the "Venerable Society in England for Propagating the Gospel in Foreign Parts"—the Rector of St. Michael's Church receiving a portion of his annual salary directly from that Society. With *them*, independence not only involved a political separation from Great Britain, but a severance of an ecclesiastical bond of union which they had long regarded as indispensable to their prosperity, if not to their very existence as a church. Hence a large proportion of the Episcopalians in Litchfield were opposed to the Revolution. This fact, it is to be presumed, will hardly be called in question—and, for the reasons given, does not necessarily imply any lack of patriotism on their part. The late Rev. Isaac Jones, of this town, in his Centennial Discourse, in 1845, says—"In the War of the Revolution, churchmen were generally attached to the Gov erment of Great Britain, as were their ministers; but not all of them, however. The ministers derived their support from the Venerable Society, etc. For their adherence to the royal cause, they were troubled, and suffered much. So were they in this town." The late Rev. Truman Marsh, for thirty years Rector of St. Michael's, in 1845, thus wrote: "The writer of this sketch can remember when, in this village, he has been ridiculed and insulted when going to or returning from church on the Lord's day; when the windows of the church were broken; and in the place of broken panes of glass, wooden sliding windows were opened to let in the light of heaven to read the prayers of the Common Prayer Book. Thanks be to Heaven for the great change in public sentiment!"

In such a contest as that of which we are speaking, contentions, and strifes, and bitterness, are almost inevitably engen dered. In this town, friends, neighbors, and even households, became divided and estranged. Not unfrequently, the father took one side, and the sons the other—and brothers sometimes took opposite sides. "Natural affection" seemed for awhile to be regarded as a sentiment which ought not to be tolerated between *whig* and *tory*. This feeling reached its culminating point in the death of Daniel Griswold, already mentioned in the letters of Dr. Smith. Griswold is said to have been a young man of good character and great energy, and was not unpopular with a large class of whigs. Perhaps, by the bloody code of war, he ought to have suffered death as a traitor for enlisting soldiers for the king's service; though it is a fact beyond dispute, that there were among the king's troops, in that very contest, whole regiments of "Royal Americans," as they were styled. Many of the leading whigs of Litchfield were open in their condemnation of the action of the Court Martial in this instance, and the event probably did not advance the republican cause in this town.

CHAPTER VII.

THE REVOLUTIONARY ERA—CONTINUED.

From 1776 to 1780, Litchfield was a depot for military stores and provisions, which were guarded by a considerable military force. The depot for provisions stood on the premises now occupied in part by Dr. Buel's Private Lunatic Asylum, in North street, where a building was erected for that purpose sixty feet long and two stories high. On the site of the present Court House, was erected a building of similar dimensions as a depot for *other* military stores. A work-shop for the army, (which was also sixty feet in length and two stories high,) stood on the north side of East street, just west of the Burying Ground. The prisoners of war were generally kept in the Old Jail, which stood in East street, on the spot now occupied by the dwelling-house of Mr. Charles L. Perkins. At each of the places here designated, a military guard was stationed night and day—the roll being called, the soldiers drilled, and the guard set, at stated intervals, with as much precision as would have been observed by an army encamped in the vicinity of the enemy. The stores and provisions deposited here, were for much of the time under the general superintendence of Commissary William Richards, of Elizabethtown, N. J. Ashbel Baldwin, a native of this town, graduated at Yale College in 1776, and soon received the appointment of Quartermaster and was stationed here. He remained at this post between two and three years, when he received an honorable discharge, and was succeeded in office by Oliver Wolcott, Jr., who graduated in 1778.

On the 30th of June, 1777, Governor Trumbull wrote to General Wolcott, informing him that a team would be sent to Litchfield loaded with powder, lead and flints, and requesting him to send a team to Salisbury for a load of cannon-shot to be forwarded to Hartford by the returning teams. By a subsequent record of the Council of Safety, it appears that on this occasion, there were sent to Litchfield seventeen hundred pounds of gun-powder, two thousand pounds of lead, one thousand flints, and three hundred pounds of cannon-powder.

On the 23d of July following, an order was drawn on David Trumbull for £25: 5: 10, in favor of John and Daniel Dewey, "for carting powder and lead from Lebanon to Litchfield." Late in the autumn of this year, a large proportion of the military stores taken at the capture of Burgoyne were deposited here.

In August, General Wolcott wrote to the Governor and Council, stating that he had ordered all the effective men of Sheldon's Horse and Humphreys' regiment, (who had not been called to do duty under the recent act and were liable to be called out of the State,) to march immediately to Peekskill, well provided with arms, and with forty days' provisions. The General's course was approved, and an order was directed to be drawn on the State Treasurer, in his favor, for the sum of £1,000. About the same time, Sheriff Lord was directed to procure from the merchants of Litchfield county, for the use of the army, four hogsheads of rum, six hogsheads of sugar, and two thousand pounds of coffee, at a stipulated price. If the merchants refused to furnish the goods at the price named, the Sheriff was ordered *to take the articles wherever he could find them*, at the appraisal of two or three judicious freeholders, and to make return of his doings to the Council.

In September, Litchfield was established by the Council as the place of rendezvous for the Sixth Brigade, and Major Beebe was stationed here as the recruiting officer of the brigade.

On the 7th of October, a special town meeting was held, of which Jacob Woodruff, Esq., was Moderator. At this meeting it was voted that Messrs. Lynde Lord, Thomas Catlin, Caleb Gibbs, David Welch and Alexander Catlin, be a committee to purchase and provide shirts, frocks, overalls, stockings and shoes, for the non-commissioned officers and soldiers in the continental army belonging to this town—agreeable to a resolve of His Excellency the Governor and Council of Safety passed Sept. 12, 1777."

The Committee of Safety, at a session held December 4th, appointed one person in each county to see that the Clothing for the Army, demanded of the several towns, was forthwith provided by the Selectmen; and to furnish pack-horses, or other means of transportation, to convey the same to the Commissary at Middletown. Alexander Catlin, of this town, was appointed the member of this Committee for the county of Litchfield.

On the 10th of December, the following votes were passed in town meeting, viz.:

"1. Voted, That Messrs. David Welch, Nathaniel Woodruff, Archibald McNiel, Jr., Ebenezer Benton and Thomas Waugh, are hereby appointed a Committee to provide for the families of soldiers according to law and to the votes of the town.

"2. To pay the Committee a reasonable compensation for their time and trouble.

"3. That the Selectmen, together with Messrs. Tapping Reeve, Seth Bird, Andrew Adams, Samuel Lyman and Lynde Lord, be a Committee to prepare, state, and present for recovery, sundry matters and accounts for money supposed to be due the town.

"4. That the Selectmen be empowered and desired to distribute to the non-commissioned officers and soldiers in the continental army belonging to this town, and to the poor of the town, and to the families of such as have died in the service, whether continental or militia, or in captivity, and to such other families in this town as are not in circumstances to to supply themselves, forty-two bushels of SALT lately brought from Boston—in such proportion as they shall judge most suitable and right—at the rate of ten shillings per bushel; and the residue, to such as are able to purchase the same, at prime cost."

"At a meeting of the inhabitants of Litchfield, legally warned and convened on the sixth day of January, A. D. 1778, to take into consideration the Articles of Confederation and Perpetual Union between the States of New Hampshire, Massachusetts Bay, Rhode Island and Providence Plantations, Connecticut, New York, New Jersey, Pennsylvania, Delaware, Maryland, Virginia, North Carolina, South Carolina and Georgia, exhibited by the Selectmen pursuant to a requisition from His Excellency, the Governor—the said articles being distinctly and repeatedly read and considered:

"Voted unanimously, That the said Articles of Confederation be approved, and that the Representatives of this town be instructed to use their influence and votes in the General Assembly to invest the Delegates of this State with competent powers, in the name and behalf of this State, in continental congress, to subscribe and confirm the said Articles of Confederation and Perpetual Union between the States."

Andrew Adams, Esq., was Moderator of the preceding meeting.

At different dates during the continuance of the war, the following persons (in addition to those already named,) were appointed to furnish clothing, &c., for the soldiers in the public service from this town, and to provide for their families, viz., Capt. Joseph Vaill, Arthur Emons, Phineas Baldwin, 2d, Capt. Solomon Marsh, Lieut. David Stoddard, Judson Guiteau, Jonathan Wright, Timothy Skinner, Gad Farnham, Benjamin Webster, John Smith, Ebenezer Plumb, and John Marsh.

In March, 1780, the following inhabitants of this town were appointed Inspectors of Provisions for the Army, to wit, Mr. Asahel Strong, Capt. Miles Beach, Capt. Reuben Stone, Lieut. Thomas Catlin, Capt. Archibald McNiel, Jr., Ensign Jonathan Wright, Mr. Abel Camp, Jr., Lieut. Lemuel Harrison, Capt. Zebulon Taylor, Capt. Alexander Waugh, Mr. Edward Linsley and Mr. Levi Stone.

In the spring of 1780, in consequence of the distressed situation of the army that had wintered at Morristown, Washington appealed to Governor Trumbull for assistance, and he never appealed to him in vain. The following was related by the late George Washington Parke Custis to Charles Hosmer, Esq., of Hartford: A special messenger was despatched from Washington's head-quarters to Governor Trumbull, to ascertain whether he could rely on any supplies from Connecticut.

The messenger was detained but a short time, when Governor Trumbull placed a sealed letter in his hand directed to General Washington. The contents of the letter were unknown to the bearer, but he arrived safely in camp and delivered it to Washington. After the commander-in-chief had looked it over in the presence of Mr. Custis, he remarked in the words of the unbelieving Lord of Samaris—" If the Lord would make windows in heaven, might this thing be." He then read the letter aloud in the presence of Mr. Custis. Its purport was, that on a certain day, and at a certain hour of the day, he would receive at Newburgh, by a wagon-train from Hartford, 200 barrels of Flour, 100 barrels of Beef, and 100 barrels of Pork. It also contained a request that a guard might be sent to a place specified, for the protection of the train. Notwithstanding Washington's unbelief, he sent a horse guard, as requested. At the hour appointed, they saw the wagon-boys of Connecticut approaching with their train of provisions. This train passed through Litchfield on their way, where they obtained some additional supplies. When Washington received these provisions, he remarked to Mr. Custis—" No other man than Governor Trumbull could have procured them, and no other State than Connecticut would have furnished them." Accompanying the train, Colonel Henry Champion had a drove of cattle which were tolled across the Hudson by the side of small boats. Col. Champion (who held the office of Commissary-General,) was father of the Rev. Judah Champion and Mrs. Julius Deming, and the grandfather of Mrs. Asa Bacon, all of this town.

Early in the spring of 1780, a train of sleds loaded with provisions for the army, passed through Hartford and Litchfield on their way to Newburgh. Their progress was slow, and the teamsters (among whom were Eleazer Pinney and Ebenezer Nash of Ellington,) suffered incredible hardships on account of the unprecedented depth of snow and the unbroken state of the roads over which they passed. On arriving at the Hudson, they attempted to cross on the ice, when their teams broke through. The horse at the head of Mr. Nash's team, was detached from the oxen and floated under the ice. In due time, but not till after a desperate struggle, the oxen were all rescued from their perilous situation. The principal part of the stores were then drawn across the river on light sleds, with but a single horse attached to each. These supplies were so much needed by the army, that no risk was considered too great in conveying them speedily to Washington's camp.*

"At a legal Town Meeting, holden at Litchfield on Saturday the 8th day of July, A. D. 1780—the Hon. Oliver Wolcott, Moderator—it was voted, That to every able and effective man belonging to this town, to the number of fourteen, who shall voluntarily enlist himself into the Connecticut Battalions of Infantry of the Continental Army, for three years or during the war, this town will pay every such recruit such a sum in money, including the wages he shall receive from the State or the United States, as shall be sufficient to procure ten bushels of good merchantable Wheat for every month he shall so serve, the price of which Wheat shall be computed and the money paid to such recruit, or his assigns, in Litchfield, in every year, on the 1st day of January, during the time such recruit shall serve as aforesaid; and that this town will also pay as a Bounty to every such recruit, or his assigns, in Litchfield, on the 1st day of January of every year for so long a time as such recruit shall serve as aforesaid, at the rate of thirty bushels of good merchantable Wheat for one year's service, or the full value thereof in money—for the payment of which monies or wheat as aforesaid to such recruit or his assigns, in case he shall enlist himself into said Battalions by the 15th day of July instant, this town hereby becomes bound as aforesaid."

At the same Meeting, it was

"Voted, That whereas the Militia of this town are required by an order of Colonel Andrew Adams, grounded on an act or order of the Governor and Council of Safety made the 30th day of June, 1780, to furnish fourteen able and effective men to serve in the Connecticut Line of the Continental Army until the 31st day of December next, this town being anxious to give every necessary encouragement to the public service, hereby

*See No. XV, "South Windsor Sketches," in Hartford Times.

plight themselves to pay to every such recruit, or his assigns, as shall voluntarily enlist himself into said Battalions by the 10th day of July instant, to serve in said Battalions until the last day of December next, such sum in money as shall be sufficient, including the wages he shall receive from this State or the United States, to procure as much good merchantable Wheat as might be obtained by the monthly wages of forty shillings in the year 1774—Provided, nevertheless, that the Militia of this town not being called upon by virtue of said order to furnish more than fourteen able recruits to serve in said Battalions. This town will not consider themselves bound by the votes of this day to pay Bounties or Wages to more than fourteen such recruits; and in case a greater number shall enlist, the preference shall be given to such as shall enlist for three years or during the war—and of them, to such as shall first enlist. And the Colonel or Commanding Officer of this Regiment is desired to discharge any supernumerary recruits, agreeable to these votes.

"Voted, That a Rate or Tax of six-pence on the pound, on the list of 1779, be and the same is hereby laid, and made payable in Gold or Silver Coin or Bills of Credit of this State of the emissions of the present year, by the 1st day of September next."

Judson Gitteau, Timothy Skinner, Jonathan Wright and Ozias Lewis, were appointed to collect the said Tax.

"At a legal Town Meeting holden at the Meeting-House in the first society in Litchfield, on the 15th day of November, Anno Dom. 1780—Major David Welch, Moderator—is was

"Voted, That a Tax of one shilling upon the pound be laid upon the Polls and Rateable Estate contained in the Grand List of this town, given in the year 1779, to be collected and paid to the Town Treasurer by the 1st day of December next, in the Bills of Credit emitted by this State since the 1st day of January last, new Continental Money issued under the authority of this State, Gold and Silver, or old Continental Money after the rate of forty shillings in old Continental Money for one shilling Lawful Money, for purchasing Provisions and requisite Supplies for the Army, and to defray other necessary expenses of the town.

"Voted, That Messrs. Timothy Skinner, Seth Farnham, Theodore Catlin and Harris Hopkins, be Collectors of the said Tax accordingly.

"Provided, Nevertheless, that any person may pay any part of said Tax in Provisions required, and at the respective prices fixed in the Act of Assembly made at their session in October last, entitled 'An Act for Collecting and Storing a Quantity of Provisions for the use of the Continental Army and the Forces raised for the Defense of this State.'

"Voted, That Messrs. Timothy Skinner, Seth Farnham, Theodore Catlin and Harris Hopkins, be a Committee to purchase Provisions agreeable to said Act of Assembly.

"Voted, That Messrs. Miles Beach and Leman Stone be appointed to receive the Salt, procure Casks to contain said Provisions, to receive and inspect the same, see that it is good and merchantable and well put up, and mark and store the casks, and report to the Governor, agreeable to said Act of Assembly.

"Voted, That said Beach and Stone be also employed to purchase any of such Provisions as occasion may offer or opportunity present.

"Voted, That said Timothy Skinner, Seth Farnham, Theodore Catlin, Harris Hopkins, Miles Beach and Leman Stone, be also appointed to purchase the Clothing required for the Army, agreeable to directions to be given to them from time to time by the Selectmen."

December 26, 1780—Reuben Smith, Esq., Moderator—"Voted, That Timothy Skinner, Heber Stone, James Stoddard, Reuben Stone, David Welch and Zebulon Taylor, be a Committee to hire, at the cost of the town, the requisite number of recruits to complete the quota of this town in the Connecticut Line of the Army of the United States, for three years or during the war."

January 9, 1781.—Colonel Andrew Adams, Moderator.—"Voted, That whereas it is necessary that this town raise a number of soldiers to fill up their quota in the Army of the

United States, the town does promise and engage to each soldier that shall enlist into said service in either of the Connecticut Battalions, before the 1st day of February next, that they will make good to him his forty shillings per month, by such addition to the pay he shall receive from the State or the United States as shall make said pay sufficient to purchase as much Provisions as forty shillings would have done in 1774."

A tax of three pence on a pound was laid on the List of 1779, one half to be paid in Wheat Flour, Rye Flour, and Indian Corn. Captain Abraham Bradley and Leman Stone were appointed Receivers of the Flour and Corn.

Jan. 18, 1781.—It was voted to divide the town into classes for the purpose of procuring the requisite number of recruits; and the Selectmen, together with Captain Abraham Bradley, Captain John Osborn, Ensign Edward Phelps and Dr. Seth Bird, were appointed a Committee for that purpose.

March 26, 1781.—Nine Foot soldiers and two Horsemen are required of this town, in addition to those already in the field; and the necessary steps were taken to raise them.

July 9, 1781.—"Voted, That the men belonging to this town, lately detached for a term of three months by special order of the Captain General, agreeable to a resolve of His Excellency the Governor and Council of Safety of the 19th of June, founded on an earnest Requisition of His Excellency General Washington for eight hundred men, &c., have and receive out of the Town Treasury, by the 1st of January next, each the sum of twenty shillings in silver, or other equivolent, for each month he shall be in actual service agreeable to such detachment."

September 18, 1781.—"Captain Miles Beach was chosen Receiver of Clothing and Provisions on the 2*s*. 6*s*. tax payable in December next; and Leman Stone was chosen Receiver of such part of said tax as shall be delivered to him."

January 3, 1782.—"Voted, That the Town Treasurer be desired to procure the order or orders drawn by the Committee of Pay Table in favor of this town, for Bounties on raising recruits in the year 1781, now in his hands and office, to be exchanged for small orders to the same amount; and to deliver out thirty pounds thereof to each of the respective classes, taking proper receipts therefor."

February 25, 1782.—"Voted, to raise ten men for State Service or the Regiment of Guards for Horseneck, as required by Act of Assembly, by dividing the town into classes on the List of 1781."

Captain Abraham Bradley, Colonel Bezaleel Beebe and Captain Lynde Lord, were appointed a Committee for that purpose.

"Voted, That ten men be added to the above Committee, whose business it shall be to notify the respective classes to meet at the time and place by them appointed, to proceed in raising recruits as aforementioned, viz.,

For the 1st class, Ensign Edward Phelps.
" " 2d " Ozias Lewis.
" " 3d " Benjamin Peck, Jr.
" " 4th " Elihu Harrison.
" " 5th " Ephraim Smedley, Jr.
" " 6th " Leaming Bradley.
" " 7th " Ensign Jonathan Wright.
" " 8th " Lieutenant David Stoddard.
" " 9th " Captain Alexander Catlin.
" " 10th " Lieutenant Timothy Skinner.

"Voted, That each non-commissioned officer and soldier that is or shall be detached out of this town into actual service, the current year, shall receive twenty shillings per month for the time he shall thus continue in actual service on such draft, or procure a man to serve for him; and that the Selectmen draw orders on the Treasurer accordingly."

March 25, 1782.—"Stephen Stone, Elijah Griswold and Benjamin Kilbourn, having lately been assessed on examination by the Civil Authority and Selectmen, agreeable to law, *for each a son gone to the enemy*, and having requested a hearing in Town Meeting, and being heard accordingly, the question was proposed relative to said Stone in particular; and the town by vote did not discharge said Assessment. Whereupon, it being late, and other business requiring attention—adjourned till Thursday the 28th, at 10 o'clock P. M."

At an adjourned Meeting, the vote in the case of Stephen Stone was reconsidered, and he was released from his assessment. In the other cases mentioned, the assessment was confirmed.

April 2, 1782.—" Messrs. Timothy Skinner, Moses Seymour and Abraham Bradley, were appointed a Committee to make enquiry whether any of the Deserters from the Army belonging to this town, and not accounted as part of the quota of the town in the late returns of the army, have joined or are likely to join the army in consequence of the General's Proclamation; and whether this town is not overrated by a mistake in the Report of the Committee for ascertaining deficiences," &c.

" In Town Meeting, 16th October, 1783—Captain Moses Seymour, Moderator—it was Voted, That the present Selectmen adjust the claims of the non-commissioned officers and soldiers who lately served in the Eight Battalions of this State as part of the quota of this town and claim a grant of twenty shillings per month agreeable to a vote of this town passed April 15, 1777; and having by agreement with said claimants, or otherwise, ascertained the sum to them respectively due, to divide each man's sum into three equal parts, and give certificates thereof in behalf of the town, payable at three different periods, viz., on the 1st days of January, 1784, 1785 and 1786—the last to be on interest; which certificates shall be paid by the Treasurer according to the tenor of them, the one half of each in money, and the other half in provisions at the market price; and that the Selectmen for the time being make three Town Rates for that purpose, viz., in the years 1783, 1784 and 1785, to be collected by the Collectors of Town Rates for those years respectively, in December annually, and paid into the Town Treasnry and kept distinct from all other Town Rates or Monies, Orders and Accounts, whatsoever."

It will hardly be expected that I should here *detail* the particular acts and services of our citizens during the important period covered by this and the preceding chapter. A more appropriate place for this, is in the Biographical Sketches which will be found in another part of this volume. In general terms, it may be remarked, that through the entire war Litchfield was represented in the persons of one or more of her sons, on the Committee of Safety, in the Council of State, and in the Continental Congress. At the regular session of the Legislature in May, 1780, the Representatives from this town were Andrew Adams and Jedediah Strong; the former was chosen Speaker, and the latter Clerk, of the House. Major Moses Seymour commanded a Litchfield Company of Cavalry at the capture of Burgoyne. Colonel Beebe was, during the latter part of the war, chief in command of the troops raised for the defense of our sea-coast. General Wolcott, General David Smith and Colonel Tallmadge, were active and energetic officers from the commencement to the close of hostilities. Colonel Sheldon, commander of the celebrated corps of Cavalry known in history as "Sheldon's Regiment of Horse," had been for some twenty years a resident of Litchfield, and his troops were raised almost exclusively in this vicinity. Captains Seymour, Stanton and Wadsworth, of this town, commanded companies in this corps—Captain Stanton being at the same time Paymaster of the regiment. Colonel Tallmadge was one of Sheldon's most efficient Majors. This regiment was Washington's favorite corps, and continued to act under his immediate direction till the Treaty of Peace was signed—constituting at once his messengers, his body-guard, and his agents for the accomplishment of any enterprise, however desperate. Captain Morris, also of this town, commanded one of the companies of the "forlorn hope" at the Seige of Yorktown. Indeed, the citizens of Litchfield were found at the head of their battalions or in the ranks in nearly all the great battles of the Revolution, including those of Germantown, Trenton, Princeton, Long Island, and Stoney Point.

The following interesting incidents, (copied from Hollister's "History of Connecticut," vol. ii. pp. 390, 391,) will serve as an illustration of the character of the clergy of that period:

"When the whole country was in a state of alarm at the intelligence that Lord Cornwallis, with a large fleet and armament, was approaching the American coast, Colonel Tallmadge happened to pass through Litchfield with a regiment of cavalry. While there, he attended public worship with his troops on Sunday, at the old meeting-house that stood upon the village green. The occasion was deeply interesting and exciting. The Rev. Judah Champion, then the settled minister of the place—a man of great eloquence and of a high order of intellectual endowment—in view of the alarming crisis, thus invoked the sanction of Heaven :

"Oh Lord! we view with terror the approach of the enemies of thy holy religion. Wilt thou send storm and tempest, to toss them upon the sea and to overwelm them upon the mighty deep, or to scatter them to the uttermost parts of the earth. But, peradventure, should any escape thy vengeance, collect them together again, O Lord! as in the hollow of thy hand, and let thy lightnings play upon them! We beseach thee, moreover, that thou do gird up the loins of these thy servants, who are going forth to fight thy battles. Make them strong men, that "one shall chase a thousand, and two shall put ten thousand to flight." Hold before them the shield, with which thou wast wont in the old time to protect thy chosen people. Give them swift feet that they may pursue their enemies, and swords terrible as that of thy Destroying Angel, that they may cleave them down when they have overtaken them. Preserve these servants of thine, Almighty God! and bring them once more to their homes and friends, if thou canst do it consistantly with thine high purposes. If, on the other hand, thou hast decreed that they shall die in battle, let thy Spirit be present with them and breathe upon them, that they may go up as a sweet sacrifice into the courts of thy temple, where are habitations prepared for them from the foundations of the world."

In the course of the revolutionary struggle, Litchfield was visited by most of the principal officers of the army. In one of the letters from Colonel Adams to General Wolcott, dated at Litchfield, May 6, 1777, the writer says—"While I am writing, *a Prussian General has arrived in town* on his way to headquarters, said to have proper credentials." This is understood to have been Count Rochambeau, who came to this country early in the year 1777. General La·Fayette passed at least one night in this village, while *en route* toward the Hudson with a train loaded with provisions and stores for the French Army. On this occasion he lodged in the south front room of the Judge Reeve House in South street. On the evening of Saturday, August 23d, 1780, General WASHINGTON arrived here, on his way from Hartford to West Point, and was (according to Mr. Gibbs,) entertained at the hospitable mansion of General Wolcott, in South street. He spent the night in the village, and on the following morning proceeded westward, arriving at West Point about 11 o'clock on Monday morning. It was at this time that he discovered the treason of Benedict Arnold, who commanded at that post. Washington's suite, among whom were Hamilton and Meade, were with him on the occasion referred to.*

Nearly a year later, Washington again passed through this town, as appears from the following extract from his Diary:

" May 18, 1781.—Set out this day for an interview at Wethersfield, with the Count de Rochambeau and Admiral Barras. Reached Morgan's Tavern, forty-three miles from Fishkill Landing, after dining at Colonel Vanderberg's. 19th.—*Breakfasted at Litchfield*, dined at Farmington, and lodged at Wethersfield, at the house of Mr. Joseph Webb."

It is more than probable that the commander-in-chief was in Litchfield a *third* time. On the first visit above referred to, (if the dates given at the time, in the Hartford Courant, are correct,) he lodged here on a Saturday night, and took his departure for the Hudson on Sunday morning. Our venerable fellow-townsman, Captain Salmon Buel, well remembers to have seen Washington on one of his visits to this town, at which time he is very sure he *spent the night* at the Gould House, in North street, then occupied as a tavern by Mr. Samuel Sheldon. At all events, he went there in the *morning*, with about fifty of his school-fellows, for the purpose of seeing the renowned commander. A company of horse-guards were drawn up before the house, waiting for him; but, as he was not ready to start, the guards rode down North street, and for a considerable distance out West street—returning in a short time to the Gould House. The General now came out, mounted his horse, and the cavalcade proceeded down *South street*—perhaps te enable him to pay his respects to the Wolcotts. Captain Buel is certain this was not on a *Sunday* morning.

*See Gibbs' Adm's. of Washington and Adams, vol. i. p. 17; also, Hollister's Hist. of Conn, vol. ii. p. 387.

The late Rev. Truman Marsh informed George C. Woodruff, Esq., that in one of his visits to this town, Washington put up at the Kilbourn House, in North street, it then being an inn kept probably by Captain William Stanton. This house is still standing, between the Tallmadge Place and the residence of the late Dr. Samuel Buel.

Several incidents connected with Washington's visits to Litchfield have been preserved. " A ludicrous story is told on this subject," writes Judge Boardman, of New Milford. "While Washington was riding through the west part of Litchfield, at the head of his retinue, a man named Clemons sallied out with a square bottle of rum in his hand, and addressed him somewhat after this style—" Great and glorious Washington ! will you condescend to take a dram with such a poor dog as I am ?" The General, with his habitual dignified courtesy, took the bottle and put it to his lips, to the immense gratification of his enraptured admirer, who always believed he had drank with General Washington."

The following anecdote has been before published : A staid farmer residing in the upper part of Beach street—well known by the sobriquet of " Uncle App"—set out for the East Mill on horseback, with a load of grain. He was a true patriot, and loved the very name of Washington. On reaching the County House corner, he was informed that Washington had just left the village, and the procession was pointed out to him in the distance. In an instant, Uncle App's horse was seen dashing at full speed to the westward, the bags bounding at every jump, and the long skirts of the rider's overcoat streaming in the wind. Gaining the head of the procession, he confronted the leader face to face. " Are you General Washington ?" he eagerly asked. " I am, sir," was the reply. " *God Almighty bless your Excellency !*" was the emphatic response of the farmer, as he wheeled his horse—and the next moment he was quietly jogging toward the Mill.

I recently submitted this incident, as here given, to Captain Buel, who knew Uncle App intimately. He assures me that the story is correct except in one important particular, viz., that the officer with whom he had the interview was *not* General Washington, but one of his attendants—perhaps the Captain of the Guard; and that in fact he did not see Washington at all! If Captain B. is correct in this, (and he is not likely to be mistaken,) the event doubtless took place at the time referred to on page 130, when the Guard paraded through West street before Washington was ready to join them.

It is stated in the Appendix to the Rev. Isaac Jones' Centennial Discourse, preached in this town in 1845, that once when Washington passed through Litchfield, his soldiers, to evince their attachment to him, threw a shower of stones at the windows of the Episcopal church, which then stood about a west of the Court House. He promptly reproved them, saying—"I am a Churchman, and wish not to see the church dishonored and desecrated in this manner."

It is a well known fact that during the war which had now closed so auspiciously, the American Army received frequent and valuable accessions by desertions from the British ranks. Two English soldiers, named Robert Morris and Richard Morris, at one time applied for admission into the corps commanded by Captain Beebe of this town. They were accordingly enrolled as members of his company, and proved to be most excellent soldiers. It so happened that on one occasion they were about to engage in battle with the very regiment from which they had deserted. As a guard was to be left behind to protect the baggage, Captain Beebe, well knowing what their fate would be should they be taken prisoners, proposed that they should remain for that purpose. They begged to be excused from such an inglorious service—preferring to *fight*, and declaring that they did not intend to be taken. They *did* fight, and the English captain under whom they had formerly served, was among the prisoners who fell into the hands of the Americans. On the return of peace, Richard Morris settled in this town, and here for many years pursued his trade as a weaver. Being a bachelor, he built himself a little house, and lived entirely alone. In his latter years he became intemperate. He was found dead in his bed, August 24, 1806. The verdict of the Jury of Inquest was—"His death was occasioned by drinking too large a draft of spirituous liquor, taken intentionally from his own hand." The fatal bottle, containing about half a gill of brandy, lay on his breast, round the neck of which one hand was clasped, the other being plaeed on the bottom. John I. Gatta, a Hessian soldier, also became a permanent resident of Litchfield. He was a native of Hesse Castle, in Germany, and the only son of a wealthy baker, to which business he was also bred. With many others, he was pressed into the military service by order of the reigning Prince, who had stipulated to furnish soldiers to King George of England, at so much per head, to be employed against the colonies. Gatta was soon put to the work of baking for the troops. He seems to have resolved from the first never to fight against America; but an incident occurred before his arrival on our coast, which doubtless confirmed this resolution and hastened his desertion. He was a young man of spirit, and quite unaccustomed to the discipline which prevailed in the army. On being insulted by a subaltern officer, he suddenly raised a glass bottle which he held in his hand, filled with vinegar, and broke it over the head of the offender. For this breach of order, he was sentenced to receive five hundred lashes—which sentence was subseqaently executed, though he was accustomed to say the flogging "didn't hurt much." On a certain night, while the ship in which he was brought over was lying at anchor near New York, Gatta quietly lowered a small boat into the water, paddled himself ashore, enlisted into a New York regiment, and served his adopted country faithfully during the remainder of the war. As already stated, he settled in this town; and here, in 1791, he married Sarah, daughter of Mr. Oliver Collins and granddaughter of the Rev. Timothy Collins. His descendants are now among our most respected people. Mr. Gatta was a marked character, and somewhat eccentric. He had been so long in the service as to acquire habits of military precision and promptness, and a soldier's proverbial indifference to death. Said he—"When the Lord calls John I. Gatta, I shall answer, '*Here!*'" Alas!—he heard the roll-call long ago, which summoned him from a world of vicissitude and trial to the land unseen. He died in this town in 1837, aged 81 years.

Towards the close of life, he thought and talked much of his native land and of the friends of his youth; and sometimes told, with much emotion, how, after his impressment, his mother, having pleaded in vain for his release, followed the press-gang for a distance of twenty miles, that she might have the mournful satisfaction of bidding her son farewell!

John Glass, William Barrell, Henry Poulson, James Glass and Adam Tilford, all British soldiers in the revolution, became residents of this town, and some of them died here, leaving families.

Moses Seymour

CHAPTER VIII.

MEN OF THE REVOLUTION.

THE historic names of the Revolutionary Period most intimately associated with Litchfield, are those of Ethan Allen, Oliver Wolcott, Elisha Sheldon, Andrew Adams, Bezaleel Beebe, Moses Seymour, Jedediah Strong and Tapping Reeve. This chapter will be mainly devoted to brief biographical sketches of these eminent and useful men.

GENERAL ETHAN ALLEN, the Hero of Ticonderoga, was born in Litchfield, January 10, 1737–'8. He was the eldest child of his parents—Joseph and Mary (Baker) Allen—who, when Ethan was about two years old, removed to the adjoining town of Cornwall. The subject of this sketch spent his youth and early manhood in Cornwall and Salisbury; and about the year 1765, emigrated to the "New Hampshire Grants," as they were then called—a wild, mountainous region lying between Lake Champlain on the west and the Connecticut river on the east, and extending from the Massachusetts line northward to the Canadas. This territory was claimed alike by the governments of New Hampshire and New York—a fact which led to a fierce and long continued struggle between the settlers and Governor Tryon of the latter Province. The hardy and resolute pioneers banded themselves together under the name of the "Green Mountain Boys," chose Allen as their commander, and waged a war of extermination against all intruders from New York. This contest continued until the attention of both parties was diverted by the more important events which immediately preceded the Revolution. By this time, Allen was famous throughout the North. When, therefore, the seizure of the British Fortresses on Lake Champlain was secretly resolved upon by the whigs of Massachusetts and Connecticut, Colonel Allen was, by common consent, selected as the leader of the hazardous enterprize. In another part of this volume, I have referred to this subject, and can here only give it a passing notice. In the twilight of a peaceful May morning, in 1775, the hero, followed by a little band of trusty soldiers, entered the fortress of Ticonderoga, and thundered at the door of the commander, demanding the instant surrender of the garrison. "By what authority do you demand it?" asked Captain Delaplace, as he stood trembling before the giant apparition. "IN THE NAME OF THE GREAT JAHOVAH AND THE CONTINENTAL CONGRESS!" responded Allen, at the same time threatening the Captain with instant death if his demand was not forthwith complied with. There was no alternative. With a countenance and manner not to be mistaken, Allen stood with his drawn sword, ready to execute his threat. The garrison were at once surrendered as prisoners of war, and all the arms, ammunition, provisions, &c., contained in the fort, fell into the hands of Allen. The capture of Crown Point by Colonel Warner, on the following day, gave the whigs complete possession of Lake Champlain. Colonel Allen now visited the Provincial Congress of New York and the Continental Congress at Philadelphia, and was received with marked consideration by both of those illustrious bodies. He was admitted to the floor of each, and permitted to detail his plan for the conquest of Canada. His plan was approved, and he was commissioned as a Colonel in the Continental Army. In September following, he made an unsuccessful attack upon Montreal, was taken prisoner, carried to England, and confined in Pendennis Castle. As Ticonderoga had long been a famous place in that country, the renown of his exploit had preceded him thither. On his arrival at Falmouth, so great was the curiosity to see him that crowds of people thronged the highways, house-tops and rising grounds in the vicinity—the officers being compelled to force their way through the throng, for a mile, with drawn swords. He was dressed in a fawn-skin jacket, an underdress and breeches of sagatha, worsted stockings, coarse shoes, and a red worsted cap. On ship board he was treated with great severity, being a part of the time hand-cuffed and imprisoned in a dirty cell. When angry, his rage was terrible. Once, on being insulted by a petty officer, he twisted off, *with his teeth*, a ten-penny nail with which his shackles were fastened! During the spring of 1776, he was brought back to America—but was detained in New York as a prisoner of war, until May 6, 1778, when he was exchanged for Colonel Campbell. After repairing to headquarters, and offering his services to General Washington, Allen visited the Grants, (or Vermont,) were his arrival was announced by the discharge of cannon, and other demonstrations of joy. The newly organized State of Vermont appointed him to the office of Major-General and commander-in-chief of the State militia, and sent him as a special delegate to the National Congress. He was also elected a Representative to the Legislature—a post to which he was repeatedly re-elected.

Aside from several pamphlets which had their origin in the controversy with New York, Allen published a Narrative of his Captivity in a volume of 200 pages, and a theological work entitled "*The Oracles of Reason*," in which he attempts to subvert the doctrines of Christianity. His writings are bold, artful and egotistical, and, though sometimes crude and unpolished, evince talents of a high order.

The following anecdote (indicating that Allen in reality had very little faith in his own system of divinity,) is contained in a note to page 409, volume ii, of President Dwight's "Travels in New England and New York:"

"Dr. Elliot, who removed from Guilford in Connecticut, to Vermont, was well acquainted with Colonel Allen, and had made him a visit at a time when his daughter was very sick and near to death. He was introduced to the Library, where the Colonel read to him some of his writings with much self-complacency, and asked—"Is not that well done?" While they were thus employed, a messenger entered and informed Colonel Allen that his daughter was dying, and desired to him. He immediately went to her chamber, accompanied by Dr. Elliot, who was desirous of witnessing the interview. The

18

wife of Allen was a pious woman, and had instructed her daughter in the principles of Christianity. As soon as her father appeared at her bed-side, she said to him—'I am about to die; shall I believe in the principles you have taught me, or shall I believe in what my mother has taught me?' He became extremely agitated; his chin quivered; his whole frame shook—and after waiting a few moments, he replied—'*Believe what your mother has taught you.*'"

While Allen was on parole in New York, a British officer of honorable rank sent for him to call at his lodgings. On his arrival, the officer told him that his fidelity, though in a wrong cause, had won the good opinion of Lord Howe, who was disposed to show him favor. He, at the same time, held out to him brilliant prospects of promotion and money, and large tracts of land either in Connecticut or Vermont at the close of the war. Allen replied, that if by faithfulness he had recommended himself to General Howe, he should be loth by unfaithfulness to forfeit the General's good opinion; and as to the lands, he regarded the offer not unlike that made by Satan to Christ, who promised him "all he kingdoms of the world," when in fact "the old devil didn't own an acre!" The officer thereupon sent him away as incorrigable.

Jared Sparks, LL. D., (late President of Harvard College,) in his Biography of the subject of this sketch, says—"There is much to admire in the character of Ethan Allen. He was brave, generous and frank—true to his country, consistent and unyielding in his purposes, seeking at all times to promote the best good of mankind—a lover of social harmony, and a determined foe to the artifices of injustice and the encroachments of power. Few have suffered more in the cause of freedom, few have borne their sufferings with a firmer constancy or a loftier spirit. His courage, even when approaching to rashness, was calm and deliberate. No man probably ever possessed this attribute in a more remarkable degree. He was eccentric and ambitious, but these weaknesses, if such they were, never betrayed him into acts dishonorable, unworthy or selfish. So rigid was he in his patriotism, that, when it was discovered that one of his brothers had avowed tory principles and had been guilty of a correspondence with the enemy, he entered a public complaint against him in his own name, and petitioned the Court to confiscate his property in obedience to the law. His enemies never had cause to question his magnanimity, or his friends to regret confidence misplaced or expectations disappointed. He was kind, benevolent, humane and placable. In short, whatever may have been his peculiarities, and however these may have diminished the weight of his influence and the value of his public services, it must be allowed that he was a man of very considerable importance in the sphere of his activity, and that to no individual among her patriot founders is the State of Vermont more indebted for the basis of her free institutions and the achievement of her independence, than to ETHAN ALLEN."

This is certainly a high compliment, coming from the source it does. The theological writings of Allen, however, were not calculated to render him popular with the good people of New England. Preachers, poets and critics joined in a furious crusade against him, to all of which he affected the utmost contempt. Soon after the publication of his "Oracles," alluding to the anticipated attacks of the clergy, (in a letter to a friend,) he says—"I defy the whole artillery of hell-fire." The following piece of satire from the pen of Dr. Lemuel Hopkins, (himself for some years a resident of Litchfield,) is preserved in Dr. Elihu Hubbard Smith's "Collection of American Poetry," which was printed at Litchfield, by Collier & Adam, in 1792:

"Lo, Allen, 'scaped from British jails,
His tushes broke by biting nails,
Appears in hyperborean skies,
To tell the world the Bible lies.
See him on Green Hills north afar,
Glow like a self-enkindled star,
Prepared (with mob-collecting club,
Black from the forge of Beelzebub,
And grim with metaphysic scowl,
With quill just plucked from wing of owl,)
As rage or reason rise or sink,
To shed his blood, or shed his ink.
Behold, inspired from Vermont dens,
The seer of anti-Christ descends,
To feed new mobs with hell-born manna
In Gentile lands of Susquehanna;
And teach the Pennsylvania quaker
High blasphemies against his Maker.
Behold him move, ye staunch divines!

His tall head bustling through the pines;
All front he seems, like wall of brass,
And brays tremendous as an ass.
One hand is clenched to batter noses,
While t'other scrawls 'gainst Paul and Moses!"

On the 23d of June, 1762, Allen married Mary Bronson of Woodbury, who died in 1784. Their children were—Joseph, Loraina, Lucy, Mary Ann, and Pamela. Loraina died young, and was the subject of the anecdote just given.

General Allen died of apoplexy, on his estate at Colchester, Vermont, February 12, 1789, aged 51 years. A splendid monument, forty feet in height, (to be surmounted by a colossal statue of the hero,) has recently been erected to his memory at Burlington, by the Legislature of Vermont.

THE HONORABLE ELISHA SHELDON, a native of Lyme, and a graduate of Yale College in the class of 1730, became a resident of this village in 1753, and here spent the remainder of his life. He was an Associate Judge of the Court of Common Pleas for Litchfield County from 1754 to 1761; at which latter date he was elected a member of the Council, or Upper House, in which distinguished body he sat until his decease—a period of eighteen years. He was also chosen a Representative by the freemen of this town at ten semi-annual elections. Mr. Sheldon was equally conspicuous in the civil and ecclesiastical affairs of the town, and was often called upon to preside at our town meetings. He also, for a period of eighteen years, held the office of County Treasurer. An active patriot in the revolution, he was not unfrequently appointed by the Legislature, and by his fellow-citizens, on important committees, having for their object the advancement of the common cause. He died in the midst of the great contest. His remains rest in the West Burying-Ground, beneath a marble tablet, on which is inscribed the following epitaph: "This Monument is erected to the Memory of the Hon. ELISHA SHELDON, Esq., who departed this life September the first, Anno Domini 1779, in the 79th year of his age. A Gentleman of extensive genius and Liberal Education, called in early life to various public employments, both Civil and Military, all which he executed with punctuality and fidelity; much respected for his Generosity and Benevolence, and greatly lamented by his extensive Acquaintance. In early life he made a profession of the Christian Religion, and till his Death adorned it by a very Exemplary Conversation. 'Blessed are the Dead who die in the Lord.'"

The wife of Mr. Sheldon was Elizabeth Ely, by whom he had five children, viz., Lois, (m. Lynde Lord, Esq., Sheriff,) Mary, Thomas, Samuel, and Col. Elisha, (commander of the 2d Regiment of Light Dragoons in the Continental Army.)

THE HONORABLE OLIVER WOLCOTT, *LL. D.*, (son of His Excellency, the Hon. ROGER WOLCOTT, Governor and Chief Justice of Connecticut,) was born in Windsor, December 20, 1726, and was graduated at Yale College in 1745. In early manhood, he commanded a company of volunteers in the Northern Army, in the war against the French. Having pursued the usual course of medical studies, he established himself as a physician in Goshen, and was residing there at the date of the organization of the County of Litchfield, October, 1751. The Legislature appointed him the first High Sheriff of the new County, and he immediately took up his abode in this village, and continued to reside here until his decease, a period of forty-six years. He was thus but twenty-five years of age when he became a resident of Litchfield, and hence his fame, subsequently achieved, as really belongs to us as if he had been born in the town. In 1752, he erected the "Wolcott House" in South street, which is still one of the most desirable residences in the place, though more than a century has rolled by since its foundations were laid. With a commanding personal appearance, dignified manners, a clear and cultivated intellect, and a character for integrity far above the reach of suspicion, it is not to be wondered at that he became a favorite of the people with whom his lot was cast. Besides holding the office of Sheriff for over twenty years, he was chosen a Representative to the Legislature five times between the years 1764 and 1770, inclusive; a member of the Council or Upper House from 1771 to 1786; Judge of the Court of Probate for the District of Litchfield from 1772 to 1795; Judge of the Court of Common Pleas from 1773 to 1786; and member of the Continental Congress from 1775 to 1784, (except two years.)

He was one of that memorable band of patriots and sages who, on the 4th of July, 1776, affixed their names to the Declaration of Independence. In the early part of the war of the Revolution, Judge Wolcott was commissioned as a Brigadier General, and Congress appointed him a Commissioner on Indian Affairs for the Northern Department, with General Schuyler and others. In May, 1779, he was elected by the Legislature and commissioned by Governor Trumbull, as Major General of the Militia of Connecticut, to succeed General James Wadsworth, resigned. In these important and responsible stations, he rendered the country essential service. On the field, in the camp, at the rendezvous, in the apartments of the Commissary of Supplies—in fact, wherever he could render himself useful—he was found, ever prompt in planning and efficient in executing. At the same time he was an active member of the Committee of Safety; and, when at home, was equally zealous and conspicuous in the local affairs of the town—officiating as Moderator, Selectman, Committee-man, &c. Indeed, no man in the State, at this period, discharged so many and varied public duties. A considerable share of the reputation which Connecticut acquired for promptness in furnishing men and means for the army, is due to General Wolcott. Certainly, to no other individual in the western counties could Governor Trumbull or General Washington appeal for aid, with the certainty of success, as to him.

In 1786, he was elected to the office of Lieutenant-Governor of the State, and was annually re-elected for a period of ten years. In May, 1796, he was chosen Governor—the highest executive office in the gift of the people of his native State. To this distinguished position he was again elevated at the annual election in 1797. He was now seventy years of age. His naturally robust constitution began to feel the weight of care and responsibility which had been so long pressing upon it. He departed this life at his residence in Litchfield, December 1, 1797, aged 71 years. A sermon was preached at his funeral by the Rev. Azel Backus, D. D., which was published. Governor Wolcott had long been a professed disciple of Christ, and his faith in the efficacy of the great Atonement sustained him in the decisive hour. "With all the splendor of his station and his well-earned fame," says Dr. Backus, "he was not ashamed to pray in the expressive language of the Publican, 'God be merciful to me a sinner,' and to make the most feeling declarations of his own personal unworthiness. For several days before his death, the shattered remains of a once noble mind and vigorous body were devoted continually to God. His very breath appeared to be prayer, until, after many painful struggles, he fell asleep. O Death! in what a mortifying light doth thy power put the little glory of this diminutive world! To what insignificance do earthly honors dwindle, before the grandeur of eternity! Nevertheless, the death of such a character is a grievous loss, especially under the present threatening aspects of Divine Providence, and the perilous situation of the country. Such tried characters are the "salt of the earth," and the pillars of our national existence. The presence, firmness, counsels, prayers and example of such Fathers, should be esteemed the "chariots of Israel and the horsemen thereof." But God governs the world, and his will is done. Let it be the solemn care of each one of us, to make a profitable improvement of the frown of Heaven in this removal."

Joel Barlow, in his great national poem, *The Columbiad*, thus refers to his zeal and efforts in the cause of Independence:

> "Bold WOLCOTT urged the all-important cause,
> With steady hand the solemn scene he draws;
> Undaunted firmness with his wisdom joined,
> Nor kings nor worlds could warp his steadfast mind."

No resident of the town ever achieved a more honorable and wide spread fame, than OLIVER WOLCOTT—and no name in the historic annals of the Town and State in which his life was passed, is more earnestly and affectionately cherished, than his. His family have been and are distinguished—some for high political stations, others for enterprize and wealth, some as professional or literary men—and all, for their liberality, sterling moral qualities, and exalted social position. His mortal remains rest in our East Burying-Ground, surrounded by those of many of his descendants and kindred.

Governor Wolcott married Lorana Collins, of Guilford, in 1755; she died, April 19, 1794. Their children were, Oliver, (who died in infancy, and was interred in the West Burying-Ground;) Oliver, 2d, (see Biographical Notes;) Lorana, m. Hon. William Moseley, M. C., of Hartford; Mary Ann, m. Lieut. Gov. Goodrich, of Hartford; Frederick, (see Biographical Notes.) Ursula Wolcott, (a sister of Gov. W. next older than himself,) married Governor Matthew Griswold, and was the mother of Governor Roger Griswold. Thus, her father, brother, husband, son, and nephew, were all Governors of Connecticut!—a fact which cannot, probably, be said of any other lady who ever lived in the State or United States.

The Honorable ANDREW ADAMS, *LL. D.*, (a native of Stratford, and a graduate of Yale College in the class of 1760,) commenced the practice of law in Litchfield in 1774, and continued to reside here until his death, which took place in November, 1797. He rose rapidly in public esteem, and was chosen a Representative in October, 1776—a post to which he was nine times re-elected. A friend of the Revolution, he took a prominent part in its favor in our town meetings, and by his influence and efforts did much to promote the cause of the patriots in this vicinity. He rose to the rank of Colonel, and was for a short time in actual service in the war. In 1779, and again in 1780, he was Speaker of the House of Representatives—the other member from Litchfield, (the Hon. Jedediah Strong,) being at the same time Clerk of the House. Colonel Adams was a member of the Council of Safety two years, a member of the State Council nine years, a member of the Continental Congress three years, a Commissioner of the Northern Congresses at Hartford and Providence in 1780; an Associate Judge of the Superior Court four years, and Chief Justice from 1793 until his decease. He was also for a few years a Deacon of the First Church in this town.

The body of the subject of this sketch rests beneath a marble tablet in our West Burying-Ground. His epitaph is as follows: "In Memory of the Hon. Andrew Adams, Esq., Chief Judge of the Superior Court, who died November 27, 1797, in the 63d year of his age. Having filled many distinguished offices with great Ability and Dignity, he was promoted to the highest Judicial Office in the State, which he held for several years, in which his eminent Talents shone with uncommon Lustre, and were exerted to the great Advantage of the Public and the honor of the High Court in which he presided. He made an early Profession of Religion, and zealously sought to promote its true Interests. He lived the Life and died the Death of a Christian. His filial Piety and paternal tenderness are held in sweet Remembrance."

Mrs. Eunice Adams, his wife, died June 4, 1797, aged 53 years.

The "Litchfield Monitor" mentions it as a sad and singular coincidence, that Governor Wolcott and Chief Justice Adams, (the two highest official dignitaries of the State,) both residing in the same village and on the same street, should be lying apparently at the point of death at the same time. Governor Wolcott survived his distinguished neighbor about three days only.

The children of Judge Adams were—1. ANDREW, Jr., who m. Annis Canfield, of Sharon, and had two daughters, Cornelia, (wife of Dr. Tomlinson and mother of the Hon. Theodore E. Tomlinson, of New York city;) and Maria C., (wife of the late Hon. Henry F. Tallmadge. Andrew Adams, Jr., died in Litchfield in the year 1806. 2. SAMUEL, died also in L., unmarried. 3. ELIJAH, (see Biographical Notes.) 4. EUNICE, m. Mr. Masters. 5. POLLY, m. (perhaps) Nathaniel Lamson. 6. LYDIA, m. Elias Cowles, merchant, of Litchfield, afterward of New York; the Hon. Edward E. Cowles, late Judge of the Marine Court in that city, is their son.

COLONEL BEZALEEL BEEBE was born in Litchfield, April 28, 1741, and spent his life in his native town, except when absent in the service of his country. At the age of seventeen he enlisted as a soldier in the French War, and marched with Captain Evarts' company to Fort George, where he was for some time stationed. He was afterward a member of Major

*I have said that Judge Adams commenced the practice of law in Litchfield in 1774. The indications are, that he became a *resident* here some eight or ten years earlier than that date. *An* Andrew Adams of this town was a Commissioner on two estates at early as 1766; and was chosen a Lister in 1772 and 1773.

Rogers' celebrated corps of Rangers, an account of whose exploits was published in London by their heroic commander; and, with Rogers, he participated in the engagement which resulted in the capture of Major Israel Putnam. During much of the succeeding year, he was stationed at Fort Miller under Captain Whiting. In 1760, he enlisted in a company commanded by Captain McNeile, of Litchfield, and continued in the service for three years—having in the mean time been chosen one of the Sergeants of the company. On the 11th of July, 1764, he was married to Elizabeth, daughter of Captain John Marsh, of this town, and settled on the paternal homestead, north of Bantam Lake, which is still owned and occupied by his descendants. On the breaking out of the revolutionary contest, he was once more summoned to the field—having been commissioned as a Lieutenant in the first recruits raised for that service, April, 1775. He forthwith marched with his company to Boston, and thence, after a short detention, to Crown Point, where he was transferred to the Quartermaster's Department. From this time onward, he was in actual service (except while detained as a prisoner of war,) until the spring of 1781, at which time he applied for and received an honorable discharge, and once more returned home. As his distinguished public services have been frequently referred to in the preceding pages, it will not be expected that I should repeat them here. Suffice it to say, that he rose to the rank of Colonel in the Continental Army, and enjoyed in an eminent degree the confidence and respect of his superiors in office as well as of the soldiers under him. While chief commander of the coast guard of this State, he performed the duties and received the pay of a Brigadier General. A commanding figure, and a peculiar dignity of character and manner, united to an innate kindness of heart and a courage equal to any emergency, contributed to render him an efficient and popular officer.

He was chosen a member of the House of Representatives for the first time in the autumn of 1781, as a colleague of the Hon. Jedediah Strong, and was re-elected during the two succeeding years. In 1788, the Constitution of the United States was ratified, and the general government re-organized. In

1792, '93 and '95, Colonel Beebe was returned to the Legislature. He also served his fellow-citizens as a Selectman both before and after the war; and through life, was much employed by the Court of Probate in settling estates of persons deceased. He departed this life, May 24, 1824, aged 83—his widow surviving him about a year. Several of his revolutionary letters, to Governor Trumbull, General Silliman, etc., are preserved among the "Trumbull Papers" in the Library of the Mass. Hist. Soc., Boston.

Colonel Beebe had six children, viz., 1. SARAH, d. unm'd. 2. ELIZABETH, m. Joshua Garrett, of Litchfield. 3. REBECCA, m. Reuben Rockwell, Esq., of Colebrook, and had children, among whom are, the Hon. Julius Rockwell, late U. S. Senator from Massachusetts, the Hon. Reuben Rockwell, etc. 4. EBENEZER, Major United States Army. 5. JAMES, settled in Winchester, Conn., where he was three times elected a Representatives, besides being twice chosen Senator for the 15th District. In 1837, he was a member of the Corporation of Yale College. He now resides in Hartford, Trumbull co., Ohio. 6. WILLIAM, settled on the homestead in Litchfield where he still resides; besides being seven times a Representative, he was a Senator in 1845; he has also been President of the Litchfield Mutual Fire Insurance Company, President of the Litchfield County Foreign Mission Society, &c.

THE HONORABLE JEDEDIAH STRONG was born in Litchfield, November 7th, 1738, and here spent his entire life. He graduated at Yale College in 1761, and, with a single exception, he was the first native of the town who ever received a collegiate degree. He first studied divinity, but, being early elected to office, he abandoned the sacred profession for the more congenial pursuits of pettifogger and politician. With in fact little to recommend him to the good opinion of his fellow-townsmen, he acquired and long maintained a political ascendency second only to that of Wolcott and Adams. An imperious will and an affectation of power, and a happy faculty of being at the same time "all things to all men," no doubt contributed to the result. A diminutive figure, a limping gait, and an unpleasant countenance, were, however, in some measure atoned for by a certain degree of promptness and tact in the discharge of public business. He was a good penman, familar with legal forms, and, though his style was verbose and complicated, he was much employed, both at home and abroad, in drafting, compiling and recording the official transactions of public bodies. He was a Representative at about thirty regular sessions of the Legislature—at fourteen of which he was Clerk of the House. In May, 1773, he was appointed (with Roger Sherman, Eliphalet Dyer, Matthew Griswold and William Samuel Johnson,) a commissioner to wait on Governor Penn at Philadelphia, to negotiate relative to the lands west of the Delaware. In May, 1779, he was appointed a Delegate to the Continental Congress, in place of the Hon. Stephen Titus Hosmer, resigned; and was re-appointed in the October following. He was also an Associate Judge of the County Court for eleven years, a member of the Council of Safety, a member of the State Council, and a Delegate to and Secretary of the Convention which ratified the Constitution of the United States. He was a Lister six years, a Selectman thirteen years, and Town Clerk sixteen years. The first wife of Judge Strong was Ruth Patterson, who died leaving an only daughter, Ida Strong. In 1788, he married Susannah, daughter of the Hon. George Wyllys, Secretary of State, Hartford. The sequel is told in the following extract from The Monitor, bearing date July 26, 1790:

"Last Saturday se'nnight, the Hon. JEDEDIAH STRONG, Esq., a member of the Council of State, and one of the Judges of the County Court in Litchfield, was arrested upon complaint of his wife, and brought before Tapping Reeve, Esq., for trial. The delinquent requested an adjournment that he might procure counsel, and the Court adjourned to Monday last. At the time of trial, the concourse of people made it necessary to adjourn to the Court House, where, after full enquiry, it appeared in evidence that the accused had often imposed unreasonable restraints upon his wife, and withheld from her the comforts and conveniences of life; that he had beat her, pulled her hair, kicked her out of bed, and spit in her face times without number. Whereupon the Judge, after summing up the testimony in a very eloquent and masterly manner, pronounced sentence that the delinquent should become bound with sureties for his good behavior toward all mankind, and especially toward his wife, in the penal sum of One Thousand Pounds, and to appear and answer the charges against him at the next County Court. Nothing could be more satisfactory than this sentence, among his acquaintances in Litchfield and elsewhere, who have long known the infamy of his private character, while his hypocrisy and intrigues have imposed upon the good people of the State at large."

Several subsequent articles appeared in the Monitor, both for and against Judge Strong. The trial for divorce came on in New Haven, before the Council of State, of which the Judge was himself a member, and resulted in granting the prayer of the petitioner. From this time his career was *downward.* He became a drunkard and a beggar, and the town assisted in his support. But notwithstanding his degradation, he seems to have retained to the very last an earnest affection for his daughter. He left a long Will in her favor, which may be found on our Probate Records. It is written in his peculiar style, and is a curiosity—bearing date, March 31, 1801. It is mainly occupied with pious reflections and counsels addressed to his daughter. "And finally," he adds, "that worldly wealth or earthly estate which it hath pleased the Universal Proprietor to commit to my temporary care and stewardship on the sublunary, probationary theater, (or the remnant fragments after so much spoliation of Envy, Covetousness, Oppression, or whatever mistake in extreme career of permitted human vicissitude,) my most mature and deliberate option and volition is, that disposition be made as follows : I recommend, give and bequeath, to my beloved daughter, Ida Strong, my Bibles and inferior Orthodox Treatises on Religion and Morality, or relative or appertaining to Vital Piety or Practical Godliness, and all other Books, Pamphlets or Manuscripts, except Romances, if any be left extant, which I have long since, (though not soon enough,) intentionally consigned or destined to deserved oblivion in native shades of chaos." The amount of his "worldly wealth," as per inventory, was $96 66; while as an offset to this, claims against him to the amount of a few hundred dollars, were sent in. His executors were Captain Thomas Collier (editor of the Monitor,) and Ida Strong.—

Judge Strong died August 21, 1802, aged 64, and was interred in our West Burying-Ground. No stone marks his grave, and the precise place of his sepulture is unknown. His daughter Ida died in Rupert, Vermont, in 1804.

COLONEL BENJAMIN TALLMADGE was born at Brookhaven, L. I., February 25, 1754. His father, who bore the same name, was the pastor of the church in that place; and his mother was a daughter of the Rev. John Smith, pastor of the church at White Plains. The subject of this sketch graduated at Yale College in 1773. While superintendent of the High School at Wethersfield, in this State, he received a Lieutenant's commission, with the appointment of Adjutant of the Regiment—both commission and warrant bearing date June 20, 1776. In these capacities he joined the army, and continued in actual service until the close of the war. On the 15th of December, of the year last named, he received a Captain's commission in (Sheldon's) 2d Regiment of Light Dragoons. As this commission came from General Washington himself, the honor was conspicuous and highly appreciated. He was promoted to the rank of Major, April 7, 1777, and took his station as a field officer of the regiment. A separate detachment for special services was committed to him several times in the course of the war, on which occasions he received his orders directly from the commander-in-chief. On the opening of the spring campaign, 1777, General Washington, foreseeing that General Howe meditated some decisive blow, directed that all recruits should be sent forward to headquarters as fast as they were collected. He also sent a particular order to Colonel Sheldon (who was at his winter quarters in Wethersfield,) to send on all the effective men of his regiment. Having about men and horses enough for four companies, they were placed in the best possible order, and the command given to Major Tallmadge. His own company were all mounted on dapple gray horses, which, with black straps and black bear-skin holster covers, looked superbly. On his route to Washington's encampment at Middlebrook, New Jersey, he passed with his troops through Farmington, Litchfield,*

* May not this have been the time when Father Champion gave utterance to the remarkable prayer inserted on page 129?

poor girl at his side, begging him to protect her. Without a moment for reflection, he told her to mount behind him, which she did—and in this way they rode at full speed to Germantown, about three miles.

After taking part in the Battle of Monmouth, and in the defense of Norwalk, (Conn.,) Major Tallmadge planned and executed an expedition against the enemy at Lloyd's Neck, on Long Island. Here was a strongly fortified post, manned by about five hundred troops—in the rear of which post a large band of marauders were encamped. For the purpose of breaking up this band of freebooters, he embarked at Shipan Point, near Stamford, September 5, 1779, at 8 o'clock in the evening, taking with him about one hundred and twenty men. The attack was so unexpected, that nearly the whole party were captured. Having destroyed the boats and huts of the enemy, the party re-embarked, with their prisoners, and before daylight landed on the Connecticut shore, without the loss of a man.

In the autumn of 1780, Major T. was stationed on the lines in Westchester county. Returning from below to the regiment, then near Northcastle, on the evening of September 23d, he was informed that a prisoner had that day been brought in, by the name of John Anderson. On enquiry, he learned the particulars of his capture by three militia-men, Paulding, Van Wert and Williams. He further ascertained that Lieutenant-Colonel Jameson, (who, in the absence of Colonel Sheldon, then had command of the dragoons,) had sent the prisoner to General Arnold's headquarters, accompanied by a letter of information respecting his capture. At the respectful but earnest solicitations of Major Tallmadge, Anderson was brought back to Northcastle, but Jameson persisted in sending the letter forward to General Arnold. The observation of the Major soon led him to the conclusion that the prisoner had been *bred to arms*, and communicated his suspicions to Lieut.-Colonel Jameson—requesting him to notice his gait, especially as he turned on his heel to retrace his course across the room.—The Major remained with him almost constantly, and became deeply interested in his new acquaintance. After dinner on poor girl at his side, begging him to protect her. Without a moment for reflection, he told her to mount behind him, which she did—and in this way they rode at full speed to Germantown, about three miles.

After taking part in the Battle of Monmouth, and in the defense of Norwalk, (Conn.,) Major Tallmadge planned and executed an expedition against the enemy at Lloyd's Neck, on Long Island. Here was a strongly fortified post, manned by about five hundred troops—in the rear of which post a large band of marauders were encamped. For the purpose of breaking up this band of freebooters, he embarked at Shipan Point, near Stamford, September 5, 1779, at 8 o'clock in the evening, taking with him about one hundred and twenty men. The attack was so unexpected, that nearly the whole party were captured. Having destroyed the boats and huts of the enemy, the party re-embarked, with their prisoners, and before daylight landed on the Connecticut shore, without the loss of a man.

In the autumn of 1780, Major T. was stationed on the lines in Westchester county. Returning from below to the regiment, then near Northcastle, on the evening of September 23d, he was informed that a prisoner had that day been brought in, by the name of John Anderson. On enquiry, he learned the particulars of his capture by three militia-men, Paulding, Van Wert and Williams. He further ascertained that Lieutenant-Colonel Jameson, (who, in the absence of Colonel Sheldon, then had command of the dragoons,) had sent the prisoner to General Arnold's headquarters, accompanied by a letter of information respecting his capture. At the respectful but earnest solicitations of Major Tallmadge, Anderson was brought back to Northcastle, but Jameson persisted in sending the letter forward to General Arnold. The observation of the Major soon led him to the conclusion that the prisoner had been *bred to arms*, and communicated his suspicions to Lieut.-Colonel Jameson—requesting him to notice his gait, especially as he turned on his heel to retrace his course across the room.—The Major remained with him almost constantly, and became deeply interested in his new acquaintance. After dinner on

The Tallmadge House.
Summer Residence of William Curtis Noyes, Esq. Litchfield, Conn.

the 24th, he requested the use of pen, ink and paper, which were readily granted him. He immediately wrote the celebrated letter to General Washington, in which he acknowledged himself to be "*Major John Andre, Adjutant General to the British Army.*" This letter he handed unopened to Major Tallmadge, who read it with deep emotion. The sad and important sequel of the story is familiar to every reader. A court martial of fourteen general officers (General Greene presiding,) adjudged him to be a spy from the enemy, and that, "agreeable to the law and usage of nations, he ought to suffer death." At 5 o'clock in the afternoon of October 2d, Major John Andre died on a gibbet, in the presence of an immense concourse of sympathizing people. His military suit having arrived from New York, he was executed in full uniform. Major Tallmadge walked with him from his place of confinement to the foot of the scaffold, where he bade him an affectionate farewell. Years subsequently, he wrote—"I became so deeply attached to Major Andre, that I can remember no instance where my affections were so fully absorbed in any man. When I saw him swinging under the gibbet, it seemed for a time as if I could not support it. All the spectators seemed to be overwhelmed by the affecting spectacle, and the eyes of many were suffused in tears."

In the autumn of 1780, Major Tallmadge requested permission of the commander-in-chief to attempt the destruction of the enemy's works at Smith's Manor, Long Island—but the General regarded the expedition as too hazardous to be undertaken. Major T. did not, however, abandon the project, but secretly visited Long Island for the purpose of making observations and gaining information. On his return, he made another application, and obtained the consent of General Washington. On the 21st of November, with one hundred dismounted dragoons, he embarked at Fairfield—crossed the Sound, and march toward Fort George, on south side of Long Island. The garrison was surprized and captured—the works were demolished, and the houses, shipping, and an immense quantity of stores, were burnt. Some valuable articles of dry-goods were made up in bundles and bound upon the shoulders

20

of the prisoners, who were pinioned two and two. The victors then re-crossed the island to their boats, with their prisoners and booty. While the main body was thus on the march, the Major selected eight or ten men, mounted them on horses which he had taken at the Fort, and made a digression for the purpose of destroying the king's magazine at Coram—which he accomplished—and, in the course of an hour and a half, joined his associates at a place where he had ordered them to halt. The whole company arrived in Fairfield—only one person engaged in the expedition having been seriously wounded. Among the prisoners taken were one lieutenant-colonel, one lieutenant, one surgeon, about fifty rank and file, and a host of others in the garrison. For this daring and successful exploit, Major Tallmadge received the public thanks of the commander-in-chief and of the Congress of the United States.

He continued in actual service until the close of the war, and was engaged in several other desperate enterprizes. Our article, however, is already too long, and we must close the narrative of his revolutionary services with the relation of a single additional fact. From 1778 to 1783, an important and confidential correspondence was carried on between General Washington and Major Tallmadge, a large part of which is still in possession of the Tallmadge family.

In November, 1782, he purchased of Mr. Thomas Sheldon, (for the sum of £800,) the premises in North street in this village, still known as *The Tallmadge Place*. In the purchase-deed of this property he is styled "late of Long Island, now of the Continental Army." He continued in the public service about a year longer, when the army was disbanded, and the subject of this sketch retired to private life with the rank of Colonel. Before separating, the officers of the army formed themselves into a national association called *The Society of the Cincinnati*, of which Washington was chosen the first President. At the same time, a similar Society was formed for each State. Colonel Tallmadge was chosen the first Treasurer and subsequent President of the Connecticut Society.

On the 16th of March, 1784, Colonel Tallmadge was united in marriage to Mary Floyd, (daughter of General William

Floyd, of Mastic, L. I., a Signer of the Declaration of Independence,) and at once took up his residence in this village. Here he engaged extensively and successfully in merchandizing until 1801, when he was elected a member of the Congress of the United States. For a period of sixteen years, (by re-election every two years,) he held his seat in that distinguished body. Once more retiring from public life, he devoted himself with even more than his usual zeal, to the advancement of every good cause. For many years he was an officer and liberal benefactor of various charitable institutions and societies; while his contributions to the needy in his own town were much more frequent and extensive than were known to the public.

On the 3d of June, 1805, Mrs. Mary Tallmadge died in Litchfield, leaving five sons and two daughters, viz., William S., Henry F., Maria, Frederick A., Benjamin, Harriet W., and George W. May 3d, 1808, Colonel Tallmadge married Maria, daughter of Joseph Hallett, Esq., of New York. He died at his residence in this village, March 13, 1835, in the 82d year of his age. The Sermon preached at his funeral by the Rev. Dr. Hickok, was published.

Colonel Tallmadge possessed a tall and portly figure, and a courtesy and dignity of manner, which seem to have belonged peculiarly to the era in which he lived. At the same time he was as accessible to the humblest as he was the highest in the land. All loved and reverenced him. The old soldiers of the Revolution were wont to seek his assistance and advice—and they were ever received with cordiality, and their wishes attended to. Officers, also, of every grade, frequently visited him, and never failed to meet with a hospitable welcome. There are persons yet living, who recollect the interesting and affecting interview between him and Lafayette, at New Haven, where they met in 1824, after a separation of more than forty years. They embraced and wept, as they recurred to the trying scenes through which they had passed and the many changes which time had wrought, since, in the ardency of youth, they had parted on a distant battle-field.

The beautiful homestead where Colonel Tallmadge spent more than fifty years of his life, adjoins that where his comrade in arms, Colonel Sheldon, spent his childhood, youth and early manhood.

THE HONORABLE TAPPING REEVE, *LL. D.*, became a resident of Litchfield in 1772, and spent more than *fifty years* of his life in this town. A son of the Rev. Abner Reeve of Southold, Long Island, he was born in that place in October, 1744. He graduated at the College of New Jersey in 1763, and spent four years as a tutor in that institution. On the 24th of June 1773, he married Sally Burr, a daughter of President Burr of New Jersey College, and a grand-daughter of the renowned President Edwards. So long as she lived, she was an invalid, and for many years her husband spent a large portion of his time in ministering to her wants. "Though his domestic afflictions withheld him from the active scenes of the Revolution," says Dr. Beecher, in his Funeral Discourse, "none entered more deeply into his country's cause than he. He shared with his generation all the vicissitudes, hopes, fears, self-denials and losses, of that arduous day. He possessed, though in early life, the confidence, and participated in the counsels, of the wise and great and good men of that era ; and, at the moment of greatest dismay, when Washington fled with his handful of troops through the Jersies, and orders came for New England to turn out *en masse* and make a diversion to save him, the Judge was among the most ardent to excite the universal movement, and actually went in the capacity of an officer to the vicinity of New York, where the news met them of the victories at Trenton and Princeton, and once more Washington and the country were delivered." At one time, he had the honor of entertaining at his house in this village, General LaFayette and some of his brother officers, who were passing through this region on important public business. In 1784, he opened his celebrated Law School, of which he was the Principal for nearly forty years. Though fitted to shine in public life, and though official honors were always within his reach, he seems rather to have shunned than sought promotion. He was once elected a Representative, and once only a member of the Council. He was an enthusiast in his profession, and had indeed but little taste for anything else of a secular nature. In 1798, he was appointed a Judge of the Superior Court and of the Supreme Court of Errors. Here his peculiar talents found ample scope for their full development. Until the adoption of the Constitution of 1818, all our Judges were elected annually by the Legislature. Judge Reeve gave such universal satisfaction, that he continued to be re-appointed from year to year until 1814, when he was promoted to the office of Chief Justice. On reaching the age of seventy years, he retired to private life—still, however, devoting much of his time to his favorite Law School. He died here, December 13, 1823, in the 80th year of his age. He was eminently distinguished for his piety and learning. In seasons of revival, and indeed at all times, no layman in the parish was so efficient as a co-laborer with the pastor, as Judge Reeve.

Mrs. Sally Reeve died soon after the war, leaving an only son, Aaron Burr Reeve. The latter, died in Troy, N. Y., in 1809, leaving an only son, Tapping Burr Reeve, who received his first degree at Yale College in 1829, and died the same year. With him the family of Judge Reeve became extinct. April 30, 1798, the Judge married a second wife—Betsey Thompson—who survived him a few years.

MAJOR MOSES SEYMOUR was born in Hartford, July 23, 1742, and became a resident of Litchfield in early manhood. Early in the war of the revolution, he was commissioned as Captain of the troop of horse attached to the 17th regiment of Connecticut militia. In June, 1776, Elisha Sheldon, Esq., of Salisbury, was appointed Major-Commandant of the Fifth Regiment of Cavalry; and the subject of this sketch received the appointment of Captain of one of the companies of this regiment. Though Major Sheldon was subsequently transferred to the command of the Second Regiment of Dragoons in the continental army, Captain Seymour retained his connection with the Fifth until the close of the war.

In April, 1777, on the occasion of the Danbury Alarm, Captain Seymour mustered his troops and proceeded forthwith to assist in repelling the invason of Governor Tryon. He participated in the skirmishing which followed the retreat of the enemy toward the Sound. At the capture of Burgoyne, in October of the same year, he was once more at the head of his favorite corps, and did good service in that most important and decisive engagement. A day or two after the terms of capitulation were signed, the American officers invited Burgoyne and his associate-officers to dine with them. At this interesting festival Captain Seymour was present. His account of the conversations that took place on the occasion, between the conquerors and the conquered, and particularly his minute recital of the toasts given on both sides, are still remembered with interest by his neighbors. The utmost courtesy and good feeling prevailed on the part of the principal officers, and the responses to the sentiments given were hearty and enthusiastic. At length, General Burgoyne was called upon for a toast. Every voice was for the moment hushed into the deepest attention, as he arose and gave—"*America and Great Britain against the world!*" The response which followed may be imagined.

During the night which succeeded the final battle between Generals Gage and Burgoyne, Captain Seymour watched with a British officer who had been wounded and carried off the field in the midst of the engagement. Soon after he had entered the room, the officer, who had not before learned the fate of the day, enquired eagerly of Captain S. as to the result. On hearing that the British had been defeated, he remarked —"Then the contest is no longer doubtful; *America will be independent.* I have fought earnestly for my king and country, but the contest is ended!" The kindness of Captain Seymour to him, an enemy, deeply affected him. He thanked him again and again; and finally offered him his watch and other rewards, which were of course refused. The gallant American did all in his power to relieve the distresses and soothe the mind of his charge—but his wounds proved fatal.

During the greater part of the war, Captain Seymour was stationed at Litchfield as a Commissary of Supplies for the army. In this department of the public service, his zeal and efficiency were conspicuous, and duly appreciated by Governor

Trumbull, General Wolcott, and others. Few men in this section of the State labored as untiringly or accomplished more. I have elsewhere stated that Litchfield was a depot for military stores and provisions. Captain Seymour was employed not only in the purchase of these articles, but assisted in storing and guarding them while here, and in superintending their transportation wherever they might be ordered by the competent authorities. In September, 1781, we find him with his dragoons, by order of General Wolcott, guarding a train of wagons loaded with supplies for the French Army, from Litchfield to Fishkill.*

With the Peace of 1783, the subject of this sketch retired to private life with the rank of Major. In 1789, he was elected by his fellow-citizens to the office of Town Clerk—a post to which he was annually re-elected during the remainder of his life, a period of *thirty-seven years!* This uninterrupted bestowment of an office upon one individual for so long a time, is unprecedented in the history of the town. He was also a member of the House of Representatives at sixteen regular sessions, commencing with the October session, 1795. In the early part of the present century, Major Seymour was occasionally a candidate of the political party with which he was connected, for the Council of State. In 1805 he received 7,426 votes, and at the election of the succeeding year he received 7,671 votes, for that office.

Major Seymour was a gentleman of the old school, retaining to the last the manners and costume of that now obsolete class.

On the 7th of November, 1771, he married Molly, daughter of Colonel Ebenezer Marsh, and had five sons and one daughter—the latter alone surviving at the present time. Of these

* The French Commissary, Jujardy N. Granville, (who appears to have possessed a very imperfect knowledge of our language,) left the following curious acknowledgment of the service, which is on file in the Comptroller's Office :

"We, Commissary of War, employed in the Army of Rochambeau, Certified that the Detachment composed of 24 Dragons or Light Horses commanded by Mr. Moses Seymour, capitaine, came on with our teams and stores from Litchfield. We certified beside that the said Capitain Moses has taken a great care for the security of our convoy and bagage while he stay with us till this place.

JUJARDY N. GRANVILLE.

Fishkill, Sep 22, 1781."

five sons, one became distinguished as a financier and Bank President; two became High Sheriffs of this County; one was a Representative, Senator, and Canal Commissioner, in the State of New York; and one was for twelve years a United States Senator from Vermont—the most remarkable family of sons ever raised in Litchfield. The daughter, Clarissa Seymour, married the Rev. Truman Marsh, for many years Rector of St. Michael's Church in this town.

Major Seymour died at his residence in this village, Sept. 17, 1826, in the 84th year of his age. His remains rest in our East Burying-Ground.

There is yet another name which I would mention with respect in this connection—that of ELISHA MASON, *the last of the Revolutionary Soldiers in Litchfield.* With a patriotism as unquestioned and a zeal as ardent as can be claimed for the most renowned of our heroes, he performed the humbler duties of his sphere as faithfully as they, though all uncheered by the hope of fame or pecuniary reward. He died in this village, June 1, 1858, in the 100th year of his age. I frequently had occasion to consult him on matters of local interest, and found his mind clear and his memory retentive almost to the last. He seemed like one who had come down to us from a distant generation. In the last interview I had with him, (January 18, 1858,) he assured me that he well remembered the first meeting-house ever built in this town, and which was demolished when he was about three and a half years old. He also recollected the old fort which occupied the site of the present Court House, as well at that which stood on Chestnut Hill—both of which were erected as a defense against the Indians. In the great struggle for Independence, he had periled his life in the cause of his country. And what was his reward? On one occasion, at the expiration of a term of service, he was discharged on the Hudson, and paid off in continental currency. Starting homeward on foot, he reached Danbury, where he spent the night. In the morning, on attempting to settle his bill, his continental money was refused. He offered larger and still larger sums—and finally tendered bills to the amount of forty dollars, for his lodging and meals; but the landlord refused to take the currency on *any* terms. Mr. Mason was finally compelled to pawn his rifle to cansel his indebtness. As his wages were but eight dollars per month, he thus offered the avails of five months' services for his keeping for twelve hours! But though so poorly requited by the country for which he had fought, the soldier lived to enjoy the blessings of a free government, and in bequeathing them as a rich legacy to his posterity, he felt himself abundantly repaid for all his toils and privations.

Ten years ago, many an active participant in the stirring events of that great contest which resulted in the freedom of America, still lingered with us; and many a story of personal adventure was told, at many a fire-side circle, to eager listeners. Now, alas! the lips of those venerable men are forever sealed. Henceforth their chivalric deeds will live only in uncertain Tradition, or in the results which an all-wise Providence shall cause to flow from them. While enjoying the rich blessings which they assisted in achieving and transmitting to us, let us not fail to cherish their memory and emulate their potriotism.

CHAPTER IX.

PROGRESS AND IMPROVEMENT.

THOUGH descendants of the puritans, and perhaps somewhat puritanic themselves, the first settlers of Litchfield and their immediate successors were not of that class who proscribed wholesome amusement and recreation. Their manners and customs were indeed simple. Industry and frugality were regarded as essential requisites. As already intimated, every man was from necessity a soldier and a hunter; and the duties incumbent upon him in these capacities were full of bold adventure and healthful excitement. Where game was so abundant, a hardy and athletic people like our fathers could not have wanted for sport. Our streams and lakes, too, with their teeming abundance, afforded pleasant and profitable employment for such as had no better business.

Husking-Parties, Apple-Bees, Raisings, Quiltings, Weddings, Spinning-Parties, and Balls, were made occasions of hilarity and social good-cheer—though generally conducted with rustic simplicity and the strictest regard to economy. Mr. Morris says—"When young people of both sexes assembled together for amusement, they employed themselves principally in dancing, *while one of the company sang*. The first use of the violin in this town for a dance, was in the year 1748. The whole expense of the amusement, although the young people generally assembled, did not exceed *one dollar*, out of which the fiddler was paid! When this instance of profusion took place, parents and old people exclaimed that they should be ruined by the extravagance of the youth. In 1798," continues the same writer, "a ball, with the customary entertainment and variety of music, cost about $160, and nothing was said about it. It is not to be inferred from this difference, that our youth had become more vicious than formerly; but it

OLIVER WOLCOTT.

Oliv. Wolcott

Hollister's History of Connecticut.

serves to show a material change in the wealth and character of the people."

Tradition yet tells of the festivities and merry-makings that took place on Litchfield Hill, when, a short time before the Revolution, a gallant young officer of the militia led to the hymenial altar the accomplished daughter of one of the magnates of the town; and how, in the midst of their rejoicings, the bride was mysteriously spirited away, and borne on horseback to a quiet inn in Northfield; with what fleetness, on that bright autumnal evening, the bridegroom and his attendants rushed over the eastern hills to the rescue; how, on their arrival, the little inn was suddenly illuminated, the violin struck up a merry tune, the dance commenced, and the festive-board was spread; and how, an hour or two later, the cavalcade, like a triumphal procession, returned to the village. Long years thereafter, when the wars with the mother-country were over and a grateful people were enjoying the liberties which that bridegroom, on the battle-field and in the council-chamber, had assisted in achieving, the venerable couple would sometimes tell, to their children and their children's children, the story of the "stolen bride."

The establishment of the LITCHFIELD LAW SCHOOL by Judge Reeve, in 1784, and the LITCHFIELD MONITOR (a weekly newspaper,) by Mr. Thomas Collier, during the same year, affords indication of the growing importance of the town, and at the same time tended to give it a wider reputation. The intelligence and social position of its inhabitants, no less than the beauty of its location, drew hither the wealthy and distingnished from abroad—some, for the purpose of enjoying the congenial quiet of the place; others, to participate in its superior educational advantages. New and more *fashionable* pastimes were now introduced among our people. In May, 1785, several Theatrical Performances came off in this village, the principal characters being sustained by students of Yale College. The Monitor says—"Distinguished Merit and literary Ability were so evidently conspicuous and amply displayed on the Occasion, as would have done Honour to a British Theatre." In July, 1787, Mr. Pool, an American Circus-Rider, announced that he would give an exhibition "in Mr. Buel's Orchard, Litchfield." In November, 1789, Shakspeare's Plays were performed in "Mr. Buel's Ball-Room," by a company of strolling actors; and about the same time, "the Surprizing Performances of the celebrated John Brannan and wife, from Dublin, in the Curious and Ingenious Art of dancing on the Slack-Wire," was advertized.

Toward the close of the last century, the Hon. Messrs. Tracy and Allen, both of Litchfield, were in Congress at the same time with the Hon. Chauncey Goodrich, whose wife was a Litchfield lady—a daughter of Governor Wolcott. During the same period, also, the Hon. Oliver Wolcott, Jr., of this town, (then a member of the Cabinet,) was residing at the seat of government with his family. Thus, the talent and beauty of Litchfield, (both of which had by this time become famous,) formed quite an element in the society of the national capital. An anecdote of General Tracy has been preserved, commemorative at once of Mrs. Wolcott's attractions and his own peculiar wit. Mr. Liston, the then British Ambassador, who was thoroughly English in his ideas, on some occasion said to him, "Your countrywoman, Mrs. Wolcott, would be admired even at St. James." "*Sir*," retorted the Senator from Connecticut, *she is admired even on Litchfield Hill!*"

Of the object of "Sabbath-Day Houses," I have already spoken. The Rev. Henry Ward Beecher, in an address on the anniversary of the Landing of the Pilgrims, delivered in New York, December 20, 1853, alluded incidentally to the opposition made to the introduction of *stoves* into the old meeting-house in Litchfield during the ministry of his father. This allusion called up divers reminiscences of the fierce war that was waged on the occasion. A New York correspondent of the *Enquirer* thus wrote—"When the heresy was broached, you probably recollect the intense excitement that prevailed on Litchfield Hill. The parties were formed—the Stove Party and the Anti-Stove Party. For a time the storm raged fearfully; but the Stove Party at length triumphed, and on the following Sabbath the stove was in its place." The writer then proceeds to give the *results*. One maiden lady, of the anti-stove party, "commenced fanning herself, and at length apparently swooned away"—declaring, when she recovered, that "the heat of that horrid stove had caused her to faint." The *Cleveland* (Ohio) *Herald* copied Mr. Beecher's remarks, adding—"We have a Litchfielder right by us, who remembers all about that stove, and its advent into the old meeting-house on Litchfield Hill"—and the editor proceeds to give the recollections of the gentleman referred to. The editor of the *Hartford Daily Courant* appended the following remarks:

"Now we have a word to say in the matter. Violent opposition had been made to the introduction of a stove into the old meeting-house, and an attempt made in vain to induce the Society to purchase one. The writer was one of seven young men who finally purchased a stove, and requested permission to put it up in the meeting-house on trial. After much difficulty, the committee consented. It was all arranged on Saturday afternoon, and on Sunday we took our seat in the Bass, rather earlier than usual, to see the fun. It was a warm November Sunday, in which the sun shone cheerfully and warmly on the old south steps and into the naked windows. The stove stood in the middle aisle, rather in front of the Tenor Gallery. People came in and stared. Good old Deacon Trowbridge, one of the most simple-hearted and worthy men of that generation, had, as Mr. Beecher says, been induced to give up his opposition. He shook his head, however, as he felt the heat reflected from it, and gathered up the skirts of his great-coat as he passed up the broad isle to the Deacon's Seat. Old Uncle Noah Stone, a wealthy farmer of the West End, who sat near, scowled and muttered at the effects of the heat, but waited until noon, to utter his maledictions over his nut-cakes and cheese at the intermission. There had in fact been NO FIRE IN THE STOVE—the day being too warm. We were too much upon the broad grin to be very devotional, and smiled rather loudly at the funny things we saw. But when the editor of the village paper, Mr. Bunce, came in, (who was a believer of stoves in churches,) and with a most satisfactory air, warmed his hands by the stove, keeping the skirts of his great-coat carefully between his knees, we could stand it no longer, but dropt invisible behind the breastwork. But the climax of the whole was, (as the Cleveland man says,) when Mrs. Peck went out in the midst of the service! It was, however, the means of reconciling the whole society; for, after that first day, we heard of no more opposition to the warm stove in the meeting-house."

On referring to the Society's Records, I find the subjoined reference to the transaction mentioned in the article from the Courant:

"The following representation in writing, viz.,

"An Association of Young Men, inhabitants of the Town of Litchfield, desire the First Ecclesiastical Society, by their Committee, to accept of a Stove and Pipe for their meeting-house. They request the Committee would consult the Society, and inform the undersigned where they would wish to have it placed.

JOHN P. BRACE,
HIRAM WALLACE, } Committee.
L. GOODWIN,

Litchfield, Oct. 18, 1816."

—having been presented to the Society's Committee, and the Society having been informed by their said Committee that they had accepted the Stove and Pipe referred to in said representation—Whereupon,

VOTED, That the Society's Committee be, and they are, instructed and directed to designate the place in which the said Stove shall be located, and give the necessary directions regarding the mode in which the said stove, and the pipe thereto attached, shall be erected.

Attest, J. W. HUNTINGTON, Clerk."

In nothing, perhaps, has there been a greater change during the last seventy-five years, than in the mode of traveling and carrying freight. Until the close of the Revolution, traveling, especially in the inland towns, was performed almost exclusively on horseback. The saddle and the pillion were regarded by the upper and middle classes as articles of special convenience and gentility—much more so than carriages and coaches now are. Horses were trained to *carry double*; and it was not an uncommon thing to see father, mother, and at least one child, mounted on the some horse at the same time. Long journeys were sometimes taken with this tripple load. For years after the Old Forge, in the western part of this town, was erected, the ore for its use was brought from the iron-mines of Kent in *bags* slung across the backs of horses; and the bar-iron manufactured there, was bent in the form of ox-bows, and carried to market on horseback! Ox-carts and ox-sleds were common, and journeys of hundreds of miles wer not unfrequently made in these tedious vehicles. Many of the ambitious and hardy young men of this town, who emigrated to Vermont, to the Genesee Country, and New Connecticut, went *on foot*—each carrying a pack, in which was enclosed, as an indispensable part of his outfit, a *new axe*. Some who *thus* went, became men of wealth and distinction.

There was no *public* conveyance between Litchfield and the neighboring or more remote towns, for a period of nearly seventy years after the settlement of the place commenced. As early as 1766, it is true, Mr. William Stanton was a post-rider between Litchfield and Hartford; but as it is understood that his journeys were performed on horseback, the inference is that he did not make a business of carrying passengers! Indeed, during the revolution, all regular communication between the interior towns was suspended, even where it had before existed; but *expresses* were sent hither and thither, as the exigences of the hour might demand. Litchfield was on the great inland route from Boston to New York, as well as from Hartford to West Point, so that the amount of travel through the town was very great.

The establishment of a weekly paper in this village, in 1784, seemed to call for *some* method of obtaining and circulating the "news." There was not a Post Office or a Mail Route in the County of Litchfield; and how the subscribers contrived to get their papers, may well be regarded as a mystery by the publishers of our day. In 1789, Jehiel Saxton, a post-rider between New Haven and Lenox, passed through this town on his route, at stated intervals. In 1790, another of this interesting class of primitive letter-carriers and errand-men, commenced his long and lonely ride over the almost interminable succession of hills, between "the Litchfield Court-House" and the city of New York—leaving each place *once a fortnight*. That was a proud day for Litchfield—perhaps for *New York* also!

But at length the enterprize of the printer accomplished what the Government had failed to do. In January, 1791, the *Monitor* contained the following announcement:

"POST-OFFICE ESTABLISHMENT.—The Public, particularly Gentlemen in the Town and Vicinity of Litchfield, have some time lamented the want of a regular and weekly Intercourse with the City of Hartford, by a Post immediately from this Town—are respectfully assured, that a Post in conjunction with Mr. Isaac Trowbridge, the Rider from New York, will start from this Office for Hartford regularly, once a week, commencing on Monday next, the 31st inst. This Establishment has met the Sanction and Encouragement of Mr. Trowbridge; and the Undertakers will be subject to the same Regulation and Responsibility required by the Postmaster General. Consequently, every Duty annexed to the Business will be strictly and pointedly observed.

" And that the Public may be better accommodated, and derive a safe Repository for their Letters, &c., a POST-OFFICE is opened in Collier's Printing Office—at which Place all Despatches, to be transmitted through the Medium of either Post, must be deposited. During the Winter, (and till the 1st of May next,) the Post from New York will ride once a fortnight, and arrive on Tuesday Evening, commencing the 5th of the ensuing month. Those who have Business or Letters are requested to leave their directions at this Office, for New York on *Tuesday*, for Hartford on *Saturday* Evenings, preceding the days of departure; as the Posts will positively start at an early Hour. Letters will be received at this Office for any part of the United States.

Litchfield, Jan. 24, 1791."

A memorial of those days may still be seen about half a mile west of the Court-House, in the highway—a mile-stone bearing the following inscription, viz.:

" 30 Miles to
Hartford.
102 Miles to
New York.

J. Strong,
A. D. 1787."

Forty and fifty years ago, several of these relics, of *red sand stone*, were scattered along the main route through the township, from east to west; but they have nearly all disappeared. The one above referred to, is of white marble, and was doubtless erected by the Hon. Jedediah Strong, who, at the date given, resided on the adjacent premises, and who appears to have been unwilling that an *ordinary* stone should stand so near his dwelling. He was evidently quite satisfied with his achievment, as, in his subsequent advertizements, he designates the locality of his residence as " near the *marble mile-stone*," etc.

On the 20th of February, 1792, the President of the United States approved and signed the Post Office Bill, by which, on and after the 1st day of June following, a Post Road was established from New York to Hartford, via. White Plains,

Northcastle, Salem, Pound Ridge, Ridgefield, Danbury, Newtown, New Milford, *Litchfield*, Harwinton, and Farmington. A Government Post Office was established in this town during the same year; and though for a while the only one in the county, it was not very generally patronized, if we are to form our opinion from the following and other similar advertizements:

"LIST OF LETTERS at the Post Office in Litchfield last quarter: Noble Bostwick, New Milford; Justus Cook, Northbury; David Fancher, Watertown; Reuben and John Miner, Winchester; Jonathan Werden, Salisbury. B. TALLMADGE, *P. M.*
Litchfield, Nov. 1, 1792."

Within the half-dozen years next succeeding the latter date, commenced what may be characterized as *The Era of Turnpikes and Stage-Coaches*—which continued in its glory for something over forty years. During this period, very much was done to improve the routes of travel and to facilitate communication of town with town. Turnpike Companies were organized in all parts of the State, and turnpike stock was regarded by capitalists as a safe, profitable and permanent investment. The Litchfield and New Milford Turnpike Company was incorporated in October, 1797; the Litchfield and Harwinton Company, in October, 1798; and the Litchfield and Canaan Company, in May, 1799. Then followed Straits' Turnpike, from Litchfield to New Haven, the Litchfield and Cornwall, the Litchfield and Torrington, and the Litchfield and Plymouth Turnpikes—so that, in due time, it became almost impossible to get *into* or *out of* our borough without encountering a toll-gate. Four-horse Stage Coaches gradually came into use from the time that Turnpikes became general; and ultimately Congress enacted that the U. S. Mails should be thus conveyed on all the principal routes. Litchfield now became an important centre of travel. Daily lines of Mail Stages were established between this village and Hartford, New Haven, Norwalk, Poughkeepsie, and Albany. One after another, Post Offices were established in all the towns and principal villages in the County; notwithstanding which, the business of the Litchfield Office has been constantly on the increase. Staging continued to be an extensive and profitable business in this town, until the opening of the Housatonic Railroad, in 1837, at which time the Poughkeepsie and Albany lines were discontinued. Two-horse Mail Wagons have since run from this village to meet the railroad trains at West Cornwall and New Milford. In 1848, the Naugatuck Railroad was completed from Bridgeport to Winsted—running through the entire length of this township, near its eastern boundary. Since that time, our *only* four-horse stage is that running from the village to the Litchfield Station on the Naugatuck Road.

There are now six Post Offices in this township, viz., those of Litchfield, South Farms, Milton, Northfield, Bantam Falls, and Campville. In 1851, an office was established at the Litchfield Station, called "East Litchfield"—of which Messrs. William Butler and Charles Carter were successively Postmasters. It has since been discontinued. A Return from the General Post Office, published some half-dozen years since, shows that the yearly receipts at the Litchfield Post Office exceeded those of any other office in the State, except those located in the *cities*.

The following is believed to be a complete list of Postmasters at the Litchfield Office, from its establishment to the present time, viz., Benjamin Tallmadge, Frederick Wolcott, Moses Seymour, Jr., Charles Seymour, George C. Woodruff, Jason Whiting, Reuben M. Woodruff, Leverett W. Wessells, and George H. Baldwin.

The Postmasters for this town, for the year 1858–'9, are—Litchfield, Geo. H. Baldwin; South Farms, W. L. Smedley; Northfield, John Catlin; Milton, H. Kilbourn; Bantam Falls, L. Kenney; Campville, J. M. Camp.

CHAPTER X.

ECCLESIASTICAL MATTERS.

FIRST SOCIETY.

IN a preceding chapter, I have given with some particularity an account of the settlement of the Rev. Timothy Collins, and of the erection of the first meeting-house in this town. The building was clapboarded, but had neither steeple or bell. Mr. Morris informs us that at the " raising," all the adult males residing in the township, sat on the sills at once! Mr. Collins was ordained as the first pastor of the First Church, June 19, 1723. There is no evidence, either recorded or traditionary, which would lead us to suspect that aught but the most perfect harmony existed between pastor and people, during the early part of his ministry. The first inference to the contrary may be drawn from the doings of a town meeting held December 25, 1728, when a memorial from Mr. C. was read, and the consideration thereof " postponed till the next meeting"—which, however, was not called until nearly three months afterward. It appears from the records of the meeting in March, that the memorial had reference to " the discount of money since the agreement was made" between the parties. It was finally resolved to pay him ten pounds per year in addition to the eighty pounds originally agreed upon as his salary—" until the town shall see cause to order otherwise."

On the 14th of April 1731, the first vote was passed for "seating the meeting-house." In the doings of the same meeting occurs the following entry : " Voted, *after dark*, that Mr. Collins have the choice of the pews for himself and family." The peculiar significance of the wording of this vote, will be understood when taken in connection with a previous vote, which provided that " no act of the town should stand in force that was passed *after day-light failed to record it*."

The controversy which began in a dispute concerning the salary of Mr. Collins, was continued through a long series of years, and increased in importance and acrimony. Though a decided majority of the church and society took sides against their pastor, there was still a respectable minority who sustained him. In 1744, the town voted " not to make any rate for Mr. Collins under present difficulties." At the same time a committee was appointed to treat with the pastor respecting his salary " and *absence from the work of the ministry*." In December, 1745, a committee was appointed " to eject Mr. Collins from the Parsonage Right." In December, 1750, Mr. C. was desired " to resign his ministerial office." During the succeeding month, a committee was appointed to carry a charge against Mr. C. to the Consociation, " for unfaithfulness in the ministerial office." To this last vote, Serg't. Joseph Mason, Lieut. Moses Stoddard, and Messrs. George Marsh, Archibald McNeile, John Marsh, William Peck, Sylvanus Stone, Asa Hopkins, and Alexander McNeile, " did protest." Two years later, a similar vote to the last was offered in town meeting, and negatived by a decided majority—yeas 13; nays 41.

After a ministry in this town of about thirty years, Mr. Collins vacated the pulpit in 1752. Though his pecuniary contest with the town continued for a few years later, he seems to have been not unpopular either as a citizen or civilian. Like many of the clergy of that day, he had received a medical education, and he continued here as a practicing physician during the remainder of his life. He was elected by the voters of this town to the offices of Lister and Selectman, and was appointed by the Legislature a Justice of the Peace for Litchfield County. In 1755, he was appointed a Surgeon of one of the Connecticut Regiments in the Expedition against Crown Point. He is represented to have been a gentleman of good talents and stately demeanor, but with manners by no means conciliatory or popular. It is worthy of mention, as indicating that he may have been " sinned against" in his controversy with the town, that he was *successful* in the only lawsuit growing out of it. He died in Litchfield in 1776.

In February, 1753, the town voted a call to the Rev. Judah Champion, of East Haddam, who had graduated at Yale College in 1751. Two thousand pounds, old tenor currency, was voted as his settlement, and eight hundred pounds, old tenor, was voted as his yearly salary. Mr. Benjamin Webster was appointed to visit Mr. Champion, and deliver to him these votes of the town. Mr. Champion accepted the call, and was ordained as pastor of the First Church, July 4, 1753.

On the 30th of December, 1760, the town voted to build a new meeting-house on the Green; and Mr. Joseph Vaill, Mr. Alexander McNeile, Deacon Peter Buel, Jacob Woodruff, Esq., and Captain Solomon Buel, were appointed a Building Committee. At the same time, Reynold Marvin, Esq., was designated as the Town's Agent to apply to the County Court for a committee to fix the place for said meeting-house; and Col. Ebenezer Marsh, Timothy Collins, Esq., and Capt. Elisha Sheldon, were appointed to wait on the Committee of the Court. The edifice was erected near the site of the old one, and was 63 feet long by 42 feet wide, with a steeple and bell. It was completed during the autumn of 1762. The old meeting-house was sold at auction in November of that year—Mr. Asa Hopkins, Vendue Master.

Mr. Champion proved to be an able and popular minister, and continued here in the pastoral office until 1798. He died in this town, October 5, 1810, in his 82d year.

From the organization of the town to the year 1768, all business relating to schools and ecclesiastical affairs was transacted in town meeting. The Society of South Farms (or the Second Society of Litchfield) having been incorporated, the First Society met for the first time, May 9th, 1768. Elisha Sheldon, Esq., was chosen Moderator; Isaac Baldwin, Esq., Clerk; Mr. Joshua Garrett, Treasurer; and Mr. Edward Phelps, Jr., Capt. Oliver Wolcott and Capt. William Marsh, Society's Committee. There was little done at these Society's Meetings, from year to year, except to appoint officers, Committees, and Choristers. Now and then we find an entry in the records of a different character. Thus—December, 1772—measures were taken for "*coloring* the meeting-house, and putting up *Electrical Rods*." At the same meeting, the Society's Committee were directed "not to let the Town's Stock of *Powder and Ball* to be stored in said house." Two years later it was voted that "*the new method of Singing* at present taught by Mr. Lyman," should be introduced into the public worship of the congregation; and the singers taught by Mr. Lyman were granted "the use and privilege of the Front Seats in the Gallery." The subject of the minister's salary still gave the Society much trouble. Mr. Champion complained of the depreciated and fluctuating currency, as Mr. Collins had done before him. To obviate this difficulty, the Society, in 1779, voted to give him as his salary for the then current year, the sum of seventy-five pounds sixteen shillings, money, "to be paid in the following articles at the usual prices affixed, viz., Wheat at four shillings per bushel; Rye at three shillings do.; Indian Corn at three shillings do.; Flax at six pence per lb.; Pork at twenty-five shillings per cwt.; Beef at twenty shillings do.; Tried Tallow at six pence per lb.; Lard at five pence do; Oats at one shilling per bushel."

Mr. Champion's successor was the Rev. Dan Huntington, who, at the time he received the call to settle here, was a tutor in Yale College. He was ordained in October, 1798. As he was a gentleman of learning and eloquence, the church and society were delighted with their new pastor; and he appears to have been no less pleased at being settled in such a place and over such a people. He thus wrote concerning them —"A delightful village, on a fruitful hill, richly endowed with its schools, both professional and scientific, and their accomplished teachers; with its venerable Governors and Judges; with its learned lawyers, and Senators, and Representatives, both in the National and State Departments; and with a population enlightened and respectable—Litchfield was now in its glory." During Mr. Huntington's ministry in this place, a remarkable religious awakening overspread this and and the adjacent parishes, resulting in the hopeful conversion of about three hundred persons among the different denominations of Litchfield. "This town," says Mr. Huntington, "was originally among the number of those decidedly opposed to the movements of former revivalists; and went so far, in a regular church meeting called expressly for the purpose under the ministry of the venerable Mr. Collins, as to let them know, by a unanimous vote, that they did not wish to see them. The effect was, they did not come. The report circulated, that Litchfield had "voted Christ out of their borders." It was noticed by some of the older people, that the death of the last person then a member of the church, was a short time before the commencement of our revival."

Previous to the settlement of Mr. Huntington, the society voted him a "settlement" of one thousand dollars, and an annual salary of four hundred dollars; also, agreeing to continue to Mr. Champion, during life, a salary of one hundred pounds. In December, 1805, a subscription was made of funds to be placed at interest, for the purpose of *adding* two hundred dollars to the salary of the pastor. It would seem, however, that notwithstanding these efforts to increase his income, Mr. Huntington had resolved upon leaving. The Church and Society, in February, 1807, voted *not to concur* in his request that a separation should take place between them. A Council, however, was called, and the connection amicably dissolved. In March, 1810, the Society voted a unanimous call to the Rev. Lyman Beecher, which was accepted, and he was installed on the 30th of the succeeding May—President Dwight, of Yale College, preaching the installation sermon. After a successful ministry in this town of about sixteen years, he accepted a call from the Hanover-street Church, Boston, and was dismissed, February 21, 1826. His successor in the ministry here, was the Rev. Daniel Lynn Carroll, who was ordained October 3, 1827; and was dismissed, at his own request, March 4, 1829.

In 1827, the Society voted to erect a new church-edifice; and Messrs. Frederick Wolcott, Stephen Deming, Salmon Buel, William Buel and Leonard Goodwin, were appointed a Building Committee. The House was dedicated on the same day that the installation of Mr. Hickok took place.

The Rev. Laurens P. Hickok, of Kent, was the next pastor, having been installed July 15, 1829. During his ministry here, of about seven years, 214 persons united with the church. Ninety-five of these were added at two communion seasons in the autumn of 1831—being a part of the fruits of the great revival of that year. In September, 1836, Dr. Hickok having been elected Professor of Theology in the Western Reserve College, Ohio, requested a dismission from his pastoral charge, which was reluctantly granted—and he was dismissed, November 15, 1836.

June 12, 1838, the Rev. Jonathan Brace, of Hartford, was ordained as pastor of the church; and was dismissed, at his own request, February 28, 1844. During his pastorate of about six years, not far from one hundred and fifty persons united with the church.

The Rev. Benjamin L. Swan was installed as the eighth pastor, October 22, 1846, and closed his labors here, on the 10th of May, 1856—having supplied the pulpit with much ability and acceptance for nearly ten years.

The present pastor, the Rev. Leonard Woolsey Bacon, was ordained, November 16, 1856, on which occasion the ordination sermon was preached by his father, the Rev. Leonard Bacon, D. D., of New Haven.

Deacons of the First Church, (from 1723 to 1859.)—John Buel, Nathaniel Baldwin, Benjamin Hosford, Benjamin Kellogg, Benjamin Webster, Thomas Harrison, Peter Buel, Moses Stoddard, Andrew Adams, William Collins, Ozias Lewis, Thomas Trowbridge, Andrew Benedict, Frederick Buel, Truman Kilbourn, Charles Adams, Cyrus Catlin, Henry W. Buel, and Henry B. Bissell.

Clerks of the Society.—Isaac Baldwin, Roger Skinner, Abel Catlin, Luke Lewis, Samuel Buel, Jabez W. Huntington, Joseph Adams, Frederick Deming, Samuel P. Bolles, George C. Woodruff, Sylvester Galpin, Francis Bacon, James G. Batterson, Reuben M. Woodruff, Frederick D. McNiel.

Treasurers of the Society.—Joshua Garrett, Abraham Bradley, Isaac Baldwin, William Stanton, Moses Seymour, Samuel Buel, Joseph Adams, Luke Lewis, Frederick Deming, Sylvester Galpin, George C. Woodruff, Charles Adams, Sam'l P. Bolles, Chauncey M. Hooker, Henry W. Buel.

In 1735, Mr. John Davies, of Kinton, Hertfordshire, England, purchased a tract of land in the south-west corner of this town, and not long after took up his abode in that wild and unfrequented region. He was warmly attached to the doctrines and forms of the Church of England, and was for some years the only Episcopalian in Litchfield. The unpopularity of Mr. Collins, of the congregational society, at length induced several of the leading members of his congregation to withdraw themselves from his ministry, and to look elsewhere for religious instruction. On the 5th of November, 1745, a meeting was called at the house of Captain Jacob Griswold, by Messrs. Jacob Griswold, Joseph Kilbourn, John Davies, James Kilbourn, Thomas Lee, Samuel Kilbourn, Abiel Smith, Joseph Smith, Abraham Kilbourn, Elijah Griswold, Isaac Bissell, William Emmons and Daniel Landon—at which the *First Episcopal Society* of Litchfield was organized. The first service after the English ritual, was performed in this town by the Rev. Dr. Samuel Johnson, President of King's (now Columbia) College in the city of New York. At an adjourned Town Meeting, held on the 16th of February, 1747, it was voted, that "those who declared themselves members of the Church of England the last year, shall be discharged from paying their Minister's Rate for the last year—they paying two-thirds of the Rate that was made for them to pay the last year." This was one short step toward *toleration.* In that year Mr. John Davies deeded to the Episcopal Society in Litchfield, a tract of land situated about one mile west of the present Court House, containing fifty-two acres. This deed was in the form of a lease, for the term of nine hundred and ninety-eight years, for the use of the "Society for Propagating the Gospel in Foreign Parts"—for which there was to be paid "one pepper-corn annually, at or upon the Feast of St. Michael the Archangel, if lawfully demanded." About the same time, Mr. Daniel Landon deeded to Capt. Jacob Griswold and Captain Joseph Kilbourn, a tract of fifty acres, "lying westward of the Great Pond, near a mountain called Little Mount Tom," to hold for the use of said Society for Propagating the Gospel, "to be by said Society applied and appropriated for the benefit of the

23

Minister of the Episcopal Church in Litchfield." The first church edifice of the parish was raised upon the first named of these tracts, April 23, 1749. It was covered—seats, pulpit, reading desk and chancel were made—and it was used in this condition for about twenty years before it was *finished.* It was named *St. Michael's*, by request of Mr. Davies. It stood (as did also the house of Captain Griswold, in which the society was organized,) nearly opposite the present residence of John E. Sedgwick, Esq., and continued to be occupied as a place of public worship for over sixty years.

In 1749, John Davies, Jr., (the only surviving son of the first benefactor of the parish,) came over from Hertfordshire, with a wife and several young children,* and settled near his father, south-west of Mount Tom, at a place still known as *Davies Hollow.* As he was a gentleman of good estate, and an ardent Churchman, his arrival was regarded as an important accession to the Episcopal Society. He had previously crossed the ocean two or three times on tours of observation. His wife—whose maiden name was Mary Powell—was very reluctant to leave her native land; and had it not been for the fact that one or more of her children were already in the family of their grand-parents in Litchfield, it is doubtful if she would have been induced to come. That she should have regarded her new home in the wilderness as cheerless and lonely, compared with the scenes she had left, is not to be wondered at. In writing home to her English friends, she is said to have described herself as "entirely alone, having no society, and *nothing to associate with but Presbyterians and Wolves.*" The reader may be interested in the fact, that though the wolves long since disappeared from Davies Hollow, some of the descendants of the excellent lady who thus wrote, are now numbered among the sect of christians which she seems to have regarded with such abhorrence.

* William, Mary, Walter and James, were born in Hertford; the other children, viz., Catharine, Elizabeth, Ann, James J., David, Rachel, George and Thomas, were born in Litchfield. These were all children of Mr. Davies' second wife, Mary Powell. His first wife, Elizabeth Brown, was the mother of John, Thomas (the Rector of St. Michael's,) and William who died young. The youngest son, Thomas, was born about the time of the death of his elder brother of the same name.

From the organization of the society in 1745, to 1754, they were without a settled minister. The Rev. Drs. Mansfield, Johnson, Cutler and Beach, occasionally officiated here; and in the absence of a clergyman, prayers were sometimes read by Messrs. Davies, Landon and Cole. The first Rector of St. Michael was the Rev. Solomon Palmer, *M. A.*, who had been pastor of the Congregational Church in Cornwall from 1741 to 1754. In March of the preceding year, to the great surprize and grief of his people, he on the Sabbath publicly announced himself an Episcopalian in sentiment. He soon after sailed for England, where he was ordained Deacon and Priest by the Rt. Rev. Zachary Pierce, Bishop of Bangor; and returned to this country during the same year (1754,) bearing a commission from the Venerable Society as missionary for Litchfield, Cornwall and Great Barrington. His salary from the Society was £60 per annum. With the exception of about three years, (during which time he was Rector of Trinity Church in New Haven,) Mr. Palmer continued to reside in Litchfield, in the exercise of his pastoral duties, until his death, which took place November 1, 1771, at the age of 62 years. He was buried near the old parish church, one mile west of the present edifice—where, Mr. Jones informs us, his tomb-stone was standing in 1812. His epitaph has recently been carved on a handsome modern monument in the West Burying Ground.

His successor in the ministry of St. Michael's, was the Rev. Thomas Davies, *M. A.*, (son of Mr. John Davies, Jr.,) who was born in Hereford, England, January 2, 1737, and was brought to Litchfield by his father in 1745, when but little more than eight years old, and was left here with his grand-parents. This was some four years before his parents became *residents* of this town. Having graduated at Yale College in 1758, and pursued the usual course of theological studies, Mr. Davies sailed for England, and was there ordained Deacon by the Archbishop of Canterbury, at Lambeth, on Sunday, August 23, 1761, and was ordained Priest by the same prelate on the following day. Like Mr. Palmer, he returned hither as a missionary of the English Society "for Litchfield county and the parts adjacent." By a subsequent and more definite appointment, the parishes of New Milford, Roxbury, New Fairfield, New Preston and Sharon, were designated as his field of labor. On the removal of Mr. Palmer to New Haven in 1763, he became the minister of St. Michael's, and remained here in charge of the parish until his decease, May 12, 1766. His Memoirs and Diary, (with a likeness,) were published in New Haven in 1843—edited by the Rev. Mr. Hitchcock. The volume contains the record of a large number of Baptisms and Marriages in Litchfield. As heretofore intimated, Mr. Palmer returned to Litchfield and continued his pastoral duties in this place during the remainder of his life. Mr. Benjamin Farnham, a candidate for Holy Orders, officiated in the parish for a few months, until the arrival of the Rev. Richard Moseley, who was sent hither as a missionary of the Society in England. Mr. M. was not welcomed with any degree of cordiality, and was never recognized by the congregation as their pastor. He consequently returned to England, and carried with him such an "ill report" of the parish as to cause a suspension of the annual allowance from the English Society for the year 1773. On a due representation of the facts in the case, the salary was restored in 1774.

The Rev. James Nichols, a native of Waterbury and a graduate of Yale College, became Rector of the parish, April 20th, 1775. Though he is represented to have been a talented and popular preacher, the excitement consequent upon the Revolution drove him from the pulpit, and the church was closed until 1780. Mr. Nichols then resumed his ministerial duties, and the society from that time gradually increased in numbers

* The Episcopalians of Litchfield have good cause to remember the Davies family with gratitude. John Davies, Sen., (in addition to the gift of the lands referred to,) was perhaps the most liberal contributor towards erecting the first Episcopal church in this town. He died November 22, 1758, and his remains were brought seven miles from his residence and interred in our West Burying Ground, where they rest without a stone to mark the spot. He ordered gifts of mourning apparel to be made to his colleagues in erecting the church. John Davies, Jr., in January, 1794, gave a piece of land near his residence in Davies Hollow, for a church and burying-ground, on which, mainly at his own expense, a place of worship was erected. Aged and infirm, he sat in the door of his house and witnessed the raising of the building. He departed this life, May 19, 1797, in his 84th year. His widow, Mary, died December 15, 1801, in her 76th year.

On the organization of the town of Washington in 1779, Davies Hollow was annexed to that township.

and in public favor. On the 26th of October, 1784, it was incorporated by an Act of the General Assembly of the State, and thereupon it was duly organized according to law.

Episcopacy in Litchfield had thus far been tolerated, and the the members of the society had for the most part been treated by their fellow-townsmen with the ordinary courtesies of life; but a large majority of the people of the town as well as of the members of the colonial and State governments, seem to have been particularly loth to do anything that might look like *encouraging* dissent from what had so long been the established religion of Connecticut. In 1785, an "Address of Thanks" to the Legislature was drawn up by the Rev. Mr. Nichols and signed by Daniel Landon, Jr., in behalf of the society, for the act of incorporation. "Wishing the favor of a *Justice of the Peace to adorn our Society*," (wrote Mr. Landon,) "they nominated Mr. Seth Landon, with some others, as a fit person to fill that office." *Seventeen years* after this request was made, Mr. Seth Landon was for the first time appointed to the office for which he was thus nominated; nor do I find that, in the intermediate time, more than one Episcopalian was appointed to the magistracy for this town! It was not until the Jeffersonian Campaign, when Messrs. Champion and Huntington began to introduce *politics* into their sermons and prayers, that Episcopacy became sufficiently formidable in the town to *demand* its full share of civil and political rights.

Mr. Nichols resigned his charge of the parish in May, 1784; and on the 9th of September, 1785, the Rev. Ashbel Baldwin, (a native of Litchfield and a graduate of Yale College,) became the Rector of St. Michael's, and continued to occupy the position for about eight years—when he was succeeded by the Rev. David Butler, (afterwards *D. D.*) *His* successors have been the Rev. Messrs. Truman Marsh, Isaac Jones, John S. Stone, *D. D.*, William Lucas, Samuel Fuller, *D. D.*, William Payne, John J. Brandagee, Benjamin W. Stone, J. M. Willey, and the present Rector, Rev. H. N. Hudson.

In 1796, during the ministry of Mr. Butler, a large number of Episcopalians residing in the west part of the town seceded from the first Episcopal Society, and erected a new church.

The edifice, which stood upon the hill nearly opposite the Burying-Ground at Bantam Falls, was fifty feet long by thirty-six broad, and was surmounted by a tower, bell, and steeple. It was planned and built by Mr. Giles Kilbourn, who died on the 13th of September, 1797, and his funeral was the first attended within its walls.* In October, 1797, the seceders petitioned to be released from paying taxes to the First Episcopal Society, and for permission to organize themselves into a distinct Society. On the 6th of November following, this petition was granted; and on the 14th, the "Second Episcopal Society of Litchfield" was duly organized, with the following officers, viz., Messrs. David Kilbourn, John Landon and Sylvanus Bishop, Society's Committee; James Kilbourn, Clerk; and Heber Stone, Treasurer. In 1803, the two Societies were amicably united, and so continue at the present time—though they manage a portion of their affairs independently of each other, and have different Rectors. The Old West Church (as it was called,) was occupied as a place of public worship about forty-six years, and was taken down in the summer of 1843—a smaller edifice having about that time been erected a few rods farther west. Services were held for the first time in the new church—which bears the name of *St. Paul's*—on Sunday, December 24th, 1843, by the Rev. G. C. V. Eastman, the newly appointed Rector.

At the commencement of Mr. Marsh's ministry in this town, in 1799, he agreed to preach one-fifth of the time in Milton, where there were a few families of Episcopalians; and in 1802 a neat and convenient church was erected in that section of the town. It was raised on the 25th of June, 1802; finished in 1827; consecrated by Bishop Brownell in 1837, and is still in use.

There is also a flourishing Episcopal church and society in Northfield, in the south-east part of this town, under the care of the Rev. Frederick Holcomb, *D. D.*, of Watertown.

* Mr. K. was enthusiastically devoted to his business as a Builder, and did much in his generation to improve the architecture of this vicinity. The Tallmadge House, and the present residences of William Deming and Henry R. Coit, Esq's., (all in this village,) were built by him. An obituary notice of him in the Monitor, (which is understood to have been written by the Rev. Dr. Butler,) says—"He was a man of uncommon industry, and a very valuable member of society." His funeral sermon was preached by Dr. Butler.

In June, 1790, the Rev. *Freeborn Garretson*, one of the ablest and most earnest Apostles of Methodism in America, visited Litchfield on his way from the Hudson river to Boston. He was at that time Superintendent of the Northern District, and, in his itinerant journeyings, was almost invariably attended by his colored servant, *Harry*, who was himself a licensed preacher of no mean distinction. They traveled together on horseback, apparently vieing with each other in their zeal for the promotion of the cause of their common Master. On Wednesday, June 23d, (as we learn from Dr. Stevens' *Memorials of Methodism*,) Mr. Garretson "rode seven miles to Litchfield, and was surprized to find the doors of the Episcopal church open, and a large congregation waiting for him. He discoursed from the words—'Enoch walked with God,'—and believed good was done. *He left Harry to preach another sermon*, and went on to the centre of the town; the bell rang, and he preached to a few in the Presbyterian meeting-house, and lodged with a kind churchman." On the same day, Mr. Garretson wrote in his Diary—"I preached in the skirts of the town, where I was opposed by ——, who made a great disturbance. I told him the enemy had sent him to pick up the good seed; turned my back on him, and went my way, accompanied by brothers W. and H. I found another waiting company, in another part of the town, to whom I declared, 'Except ye repent ye shall all likewise perish.' In this town we have given the devil and the wicked much trouble; we have a few good friends." On his return from Boston, Mr. Garretson again preached in Litchfield—Friday, July 13, 1790. So far as I have learned, these were the *first* Methodist sermons ever preached in this town.

The *Litchfield Circuit* was organized during the spring of 1790, and embraced, according to Mr. Stevens, "the north-western section of Connecticut." In May, 1791, the Rev. Messrs. Matthias Swain and James Covel were appointed by the conference to labor in this Circuit. Their immediate successors, previous to the commencement of the present century, were, Rev. Messrs. Lemuel Smith, Samuel Ostrander, Philip Wagner, James Coleman, Enoch Mudge, F. Aldridge, Jesse

Stoneman, Joseph Mitchell, Daniel Dennis, Wesley Budd, Ezekiel Canfield, William Thatcher, Ebenezer Stevens, Freeman Bishop and Augustus Jocelyn.

On the 21st of July, 1791, the famous Bishop Asbury preached in the Episcopal church in this town. In reference to his visit here, he wrote—" I think Morse's account of his countrymen is near the truth ; never have I seen any people who could talk so long, so correctly, and so seriously, about trifles." A hard hit, certainly !—is it not too well deserved ?

I have found no *records* whatever, indicating the progress of this denomination in Litchfield, for many years subsequent to the last of the dates here given. The names of the following persons in our Grand List for 1805, are put down as " members of the Methodist Society," viz., Noah Agard, Isaac Baldwin, Ebenezer Clark, Thomas F. Gross, Elisha Horton, Samuel Green, Jonathan Hitchcock, Roswell McNeil, Jonathan Rogers, Daniel Noyes, John Stone and Arthur Swan.

In 1837, a handsome church edifice was erected by the Methodists, in Meadow street, in this village, which was dedicated on the 27th of July of that year. The dedication sermon was preached by Professor Holdich, of the Wesleyan University ; and an appropriate discourse was delivered by the Rev. Mr. Washburn. The following clergymen have since been stationed here, generally for two years each—Rev. Messrs. Charles Chittenden, Keyes, Gad Smith, Jason Wells, D. L. Marks, William Dixon, Joseph Henson, William B. Hoyt, N. C. Lewis, H. N. Weed, Lounsbury, and William Howard.

The number of members of this church, as reported to the Conference about a year since, is 113.

In addition to the church in this village, there is a Methodist church in Milton and another on Mount Tom.

The late Rev. Horace Agard, and the Rev. Joseph L. Morse, are, so far as I can learn, the only *natives* of the town who have become Methodist ministers.

There is a flourishing Baptist Church and Society at Bantam Falls, under the charge of the Rev. Mr. Ganun. Formerly there was a Baptist Church in Northfield, which flourished for several years under the pastoral care of the Rev. Messrs. Seth Higley and Levi Peck.

BIOGRAPHICAL NOTES

of Natives and Residents of the Town of Litchfield.

ADAMS, Samuel, a native of Milford and long a resident of Stratford, came to this village to reside a few years previous to his death—which took place here, November 12, 1788, in the 85th year of his age. He had been a prominent lawyer and Judge of the Fairfield County Court. His widow, Mrs. Mary Adams, died in this town, August 29, 1803, *in the one hundred and sixth year of her age.* "She retained," says the *Monitor*, "her memory, reason and activity remarkably, until about two years before her death. After she was an hundred years old, she rode on horseback thirty miles in one day." She was a daughter of Mr. Zachariah Fairchild, and was born in Stratford, May 7, 1698; thus having lived in three centuries!

ADAMS, Andrew, *LL. D.*, (son of the preceding.) resided in this town about thirty years, and became Chief Justice of the State. He died in this village, while holding that office, Nov. 27, 1797, aged 62. [See pp. 144 and 145. of this volume.]

ALLEN, John, a native of Great Barrington, Mass., was admitted to the Litchfield Bar in 1786, and continued to reside here as a practicing lawyer until his death, in the year 1812. He was a Representative at seven sessions; Clerk of the House in 1796; member of Congress from 1797 to 1799; and member of the State Council from 1800 to 1806. He not only possessed great powers of mind, but was remarkable for his imposing presence—having been nearly seven feet in height, and with a proportionably heavy frame. He was buried in our East Graveyard.

ALLEN, John W., (son of the preceding,) was born in Litchfield, but left his native town soon after the death of his father. Having studied law, he settled in Cleveland, Ohio, where he became eminent in his profession. In 1837, he was elected a member of Congress from Ohio, and was re-elected in 1839. He has also been Mayor of Cleveland, Presidential Elector, etc.

ALLEN, General Ethan, the Hero of Ticonderoga, was born in Litchfield, January 10, 1737-'8; and died in Burlington, Vermont, February 13, 1789, aged 51 years. [See pp. 135, etc. of this volume.]

AGARD, Rev. Horace, (son of Mr. Noah Agard,) was born in Litchfield, received a license to preach from the Methodist Conference, and for some time labored successfully in his native town. Removing to the State of New York, he was ordained Deacon in Paris, by Bishop George, in 1821, and two years later he was ordained Elder at Westmoreland, N. Y., by the same Bishop. For eleven years out of nineteen of effective service in the ministry, he was Presiding Elder of the Susquehanna and Berkshire Districts. He died in the faith, January 8, 1850.

BACON, Asa, a resident of Litchfield from 1803 to 1852, was born in Canterbury, graduated at Yale College in 1793, and died in New Haven in February, 1857, aged 86. He was one of the most eminent lawyers at the Litchfield bar. His widow, (a daughter of the late Hon. Epaphroditus Champion, of East Haddam,) is still living in New Haven.

BACON, Epaphroditus Champion, (eldest son of the preceding,) was born in Litchfield in 1811 ; graduated at Yale College in 1833 ; and settled in his native town as a lawyer. In 1839, he was a Delegate to, and Secretary of, the National Convention which met at Harrisburg and nominated General Harrison for the Presidency of the United States. Mr. Bacon was elected a Representative from this town in 1840, and again in 1841. He was a diligent antiquarian and genealogist. While traveling in Europe, he died at Seville, Spain, January 11, 1845, aged 34 years.

BACON, Lieutenant Frederick A., (son of Asa Bacon, Esq.,) was born in Litchfield in 1813 ; entered the Navy in his youth, and was attached to the U. S. Schooner *Sea Gull* of the Exploring Expedition, which foundered off Cape Horn, May 1st, 1839, and all on board perished. He was 26 years of age. Lieut. Bacon was married, and left one son.

BACON, General Francis, (youngest son of Asa Bacon, Esq.,) was born in Litchfield in January, 1820 ; graduated at Yale College in 1838 : studied law with the Hon. O. S. Seymour, and settled as a lawyer in his native town. With the exception of two or three years, he continued to reside here until his death. In 1847 and 1848, he was First Clerk of the House ; and in 1849, he was elected to the Senate of this State. He was also Major General of all the Militia of Connecticut. He died in this town, September 16, 1849, aged 29 years and 8 months. General Bacon married Elizabeth Dutcher, of Canaan, and left one daughter, Kate.

BALDWIN, Isaac, graduated at Yale College in 1735, settled in Litchfield in 1742, and died here, January 15, 1805, aged 95 years. He was a Representative at ten sessions, Clerk of the Probate Court twenty-nine years, Town Clerk thirty-one years, and Clerk of the Court of Common Pleas forty-two years !

BALDWIN, Rev. Ashbel, (son of Isaac Baldwin, Esq.,) was born in Litchfield, March 7, 1757, and graduated at Yale College in 1776.

He was ordained Deacon at Middletown, by Bishop Seabury, Aug. 3, 1785—*being the first Episcopal ordination in the United States.* In September following, he was ordained Priest by the same Bishop. From 1785 to 1793, he was Rector of St. Michael's church in this town, and was afterwards for about thirty years Rector of Christ Church, Stratford. He was Secretary of the Diocese of Connecticut, and member of the General Convention. Mr. Baldwin died in Rochester, N. Y., February 8, 1846, in his 89th year. From his register it appears that he had preached and performed service about 10,000 times; baptized 3,010 persons; married 600 couple; and buried about 3,000 persons!

BALDWIN, William B., (son of Captain Horace and grandson of Isaac Baldwin, Esq.,) was born in Litchfield, January 7, 1803, and has been for more than twenty years past one of the editors and proprietors of the New Haven Daily and Weekly *Register.* He has also been State Printer, member of the Common Council of the City of New Haven, &c.

BARNES, Amos, (son of Mr. Enos Barnes,) was born in Litchfield, and settled in Pittsfield, Mass., where he still resides. He was an officer in actual service in the last war with Great Britain; has since been a Selectman, Magistrate, and Trial Justice of the Police Court; and in 1837 and again in 1838, he was elected a member of the Massachusetts House of Representatives.

BEEBE, Bezaleel, a Colonel in the continental army, was born in Litchfield, April 28, 1741; died May 28, 1824. [See p. 145.]

BEECHER, Lyman, *D. D.*, was born in New Haven, October 12, 1775; graduated at Yale College in 1797; and was ordained pastor of a church in East Hampton, L. I., in December 1798, with a salary of $300 per year. In 1810, at the age of thirty-five years, he was installed pastor of the First Church in Litchfield, and remained here in that capacity for a period of sixteen years. This was, as he himself states, by far the most active and laborious part of his life. In addition to his ordinary pastoral services, he was probably more conspicuously identified with the establishment of the great benevolent associations of the day, than any other country pastor in New England. Returning, full of zeal, from the first meeting of the American Board of Commissioners for Foreign Missions, in 1812, he called together, in this village, several clergymen and laymen from various parts of the county, who organized the *Litchfield County Foreign Mission Society*—THE FIRST AUXILIARY OF THE AMERICAN BOARD. He was active in all the reforms of that period. His *Six Sermons on Intemperance*, which were preached in our old meeting-house in 1826, were widely circulated on both sides of the Atlantic, and were among the earliest and most effective means in arousing the Christian world to the evils of intemperance. In 1826, Dr. Beecher became pastor of the Hanover street Church in Boston; and in 1832, he accepted the Presidency of Lane Theological Seminary in Ohio, in which latter office he continued for some ten years. Subsequently, for a few years, he was engaged in preparing his Works for the press. He now resides in Brooklyn, New York. Dr. Beecher has been three times married, and has had thirteen children, viz., 1 Catharine E., distinguished as an author; 2 Rev. William H.; 3 Rev. Edward, *D. D.*, ex-President of Illinois College; 4 Mary Foote, m. the Hon. Thomas C. Perkins, of Hartford; 5 Harriet, died young, on Long Island; 6 Rev. George, died in Chilicothie, Ohio; 7 Harriet, m. Rev. Dr. Calvin E. Stowe, now of Andover, Mass.; 8 Rev. Henry Ward; 9 Rev. Charles, of Georgetown, Mass.; 10 Frederick, died young, in Litchfield; 11 Isabella Holmes, m. John Hooker, Esq., of Hartford; 12 Rev. Thomas K., of Elmira, N. Y.; 13 Rev. James C., Seamen's Chaplain in China. Of these, Mrs. Stowe, Henry Ward, Charles, Frederick, Mrs. Hooker, and Thomas K., were born in Litchfield.

BEECHER, Rev. Henry Ward, was born in Litchfield, June 24, 1813; graduated at Amherst College in 1834; was licensed to preach in April, 1838; and was settled as pastor of a church in Lawrenceburgh, Indiana, in the fall of the same year. From August 1839 to October, 1847, he was pastor of a church in Indianapolis, Indiana; and since the last named date he has been pastor of the Plymouth Church, Brooklyn, N. Y. He is a powerful and popular preacher and lecturer, and is said by the New American Cyclopedia to have "the largest uniform congregation in the United States." He is the author of a volume of *Lectures to Young Men; The Star Papers*; *Views and Experiences; Talks about Fruits, Flowers, and Farming*, &c.; and two volumes of extracts from his extemporaneous discources, noted down, edited, and published, by members of his congregation, have had an extensive circulation. Mr. Beecher was married, Aug. 3, 1837, to Eunice, daughter of Dr. Artemas Ballard, of W. Sutton, Ms.

BEERS, Seth P., was born in Woodbury, July 1, 1781, studied law with the Hon. Ephraim Kirby, and at the Litchfield Law School, and was admitted to the bar on the 20th of March, 1805. He has ever since resided in this village. In November, 1813, he was appointed by President Madison, Collector of the Direct Taxes and Internal Revenue of the United States, for Litchfield county, and held the office until it was abolished in 1820. He was also State's Attorney for five years, and a Representative in 1820, 1821, 1822 and 1823. In 1821, he was Clerk of the House, and during the sessions of the two succeeding years he was Speaker. In 1824, he was elected a State Senator, and, while holding that office, the Legislature appointed him Assistant Commissioner of the School Fund. On the resignation of the Hon. James Hillhouse, he was appointed sole Commissioner, June 1, 1825, and resigned said office to take effect December 1, 1849. The Legislature passed a unanimous vote of thanks to Mr. Beers "for his long, laborious and faithful labors as Commissioner of the School Fund." Mr. B. has also been a candidate for Congress; and in 1839, he was the regular democratic nominee for Governor. He was a Presidential Elector in 1836, and State Superintendent of Common Schools from 1845 to 1849.

BIRD, John, (son of Dr. Seth Bird,) was born in Litchfield, Nov. 22, 1768; graduated at Yale College in 1786; practiced law for a few years in his native town; removed to Troy, N. Y., in 1794, and died there in the year 1806, aged 38 years. He had been a member of the Legislature of New York, and a member of Congress from that State. Ex-President Van Buren thus writes to the author of this volume concerning him: "John Bird I did not know personally, but have always taken much interest in his character and career. He must, according to all accounts, have been one of the very ablest men in the State, though a very eccentric one. There have been but few men among us, who have left behind them so many racy anecdotes illustrative of their peculiarities." His first wife was a daughter of Col. Joshua Porter, of Salisbury; his second wife was Sally Buel, daughter of Mr. David Buel, of Troy, formerly of this town. He left several children.

BIRGE, Gen. John Ward, was born in Litchfield, January 7, 1803, and in his youth went to reside with an uncle in Cazenovia, N. Y. He received his medical degree at Geneva College, and is a successful practitioner in Utica, where, as a surgeon and occulist, he has a high reputation. He is, however, principally famous for his connection with the Patriot War in Canada in 1837-'8. He had previously been Colonel of the Eighth Regiment of New York State Cavalry; and, while holding the office of Brigadier General, (an extensive organization being perfected along the lines, having for its object the freedom of the Canadas from British rule,) he was waited upon by a deputation from the executive committee having the matter in charge, who urged upon him the acceptance of a Major General's commission, with the command of the second of the three Divisions. After some hesitation, he accepted the position, and fixed his headquarters at Watertown, N. Y. The confidence and enthusiasm of the people on the subject, for fifty miles on each side of the lines, was so unbounded, that such a thing as failure seems not to have been thought of. The whole plan of operations, however, was frustrated by a rash attempt of Colonel Von Shoultz, a gallant Polander, to land at Prescott with his regiment. *Success* would have made Heroes and Patriots of the chief actors in the enterprize; *failure* made them Rebels and Traitors. Von Shoultz and others were hanged, some were banished, and some (among whom was the subject of this sketch) were tried for a breach of the neutrality laws. General Birge is a son of the late Joseph Birge, Esq., who died in this town in 1854.

BISSELL, George Beckwith, (son of Mr. John Bissell,) was born in Litchfield, Sept. 12, 1823, entered the United States Navy in his youth. In August, 1846, he was attached to the U. S. Brig *Truxton* when she was wrecked on the coast of Mexico, and with others was seized and held as a prisoner of war. On his release, he made a visit to his native town; but soon re-joined the Navy, and for eighteen months was attached to the scientific department at Washington. He joined the Frigate Cumberland in New York, as Sailing Master, on the 31st of August, and died at the Naval Hospital in Brooklyn, September 10, 1848, aged 25 years. His remains were brought here for interment. His elder brothers, John Bissell, Jr., and Edward Bissell, Esq'rs., (both lawyers in New York city,) were born in the State of New York, but resided many years in Litchfield. The latter has been a Purser in the Navy.

BISSELL, Lyman, (son of Mr. Hiram Bissell,) was born in Litchfield, October 19, 1812; was Captain in the United States Army, and Paymaster of the New England Regiment, in the War with Mexico; and is still an officer in the Army.

BRACE, John P., was born in Litchfield, February 10th, 1793; graduated at Williams College in 1812; and was for some years Principal of the Litchfield Female Academy, and subsequently of the Hartford Female Seminary. For eight or ten years past, he has been one of the editors of the Hartford Daily and Weekly *Courant.* Mr. Brace is the author of *Lectures to Young Converts*, *Tales of the Devils*, and *The Fawn of the Pale Faces.*

BRACE, Charles Loring, the celebrated traveler, is a son of John P. Brace, Esq., and was born in Litchfield, June 19, 1826. Having graduated at Yale College in 1846, and pursued a course of theological studies, he spent several years traveling in Europe; as a part of the fruits of which, he has given to the public three or four very interesting volumes, viz., *Hungary in* 1851, *Home Life in Germany*, *The Norse Folk*, &c. In May, 1851, during the Hungarian struggle for independence, Mr. Brace was seized as a spy by the Austrian authorities, and imprisoned at Gross Wardein; but after a lapse of thirty days, he was released through the intervention of Mr. McCurdy, then American Minister to Austria. He is now Secretary of the Children's Aid Society in the city of New York.

BRADLEY, Abraham, (son of Abraham Bradley, Esq.,) was born in Litchfield, February 21, 1767, studied law, and became a Judge in Luzerne county, Penn. From 1799 to 1829, he was First Assistant Postmaster General of the United States. He drew and published a Map of all the Post Roads in the Union, with the Post Offices and distances clearly defined. He died at his residence in the city of Washington a few years since.

BRADLEY, Dr. Phineas, (brother of the preceding,) was born in Litchfield, July 17, 1769; married Hannah Jones, of this town, and settled here as a physician and druggist. When the office of Second Assistant Postmaster General was created by Congress, Dr. Bradley was appointed, and retained the position for about twenty-five years. He was a gentleman of wealth, and distinguished for his hospitality and benevolence. He died at his beautiful seat, *Clover Hill*, two miles north of the national capitol, in the spring of 1845, aged 76.

BRADLEY, William A., (son of the preceding,) was born in Litchfield, July 25, 1794, and settled in the City of Washington, where he still resides. He has been President of the Patriotic Bank, Postmaster, and Mayor of the city.

Julius Catlin

BUEL, David, Jr., born in Litchfield, October 22, 1784; graduated at Williams College in 1805; settled as a lawyer in Troy, where he still resides. In 1821, he was a Delegate to the Constitutional Convention of his adopted State; for some years held the office of First Judge of the Court of Common Pleas for Renselaer county; and in 1842, he was elected a Regent of the State University—a position which he still holds. From 1829 to 1847, Judge Buel was a Trustee of Williams College. May 24th, 1814, he married Harriet, daughter of John G. Hillhouse, Esq., of Montville, Conn., and has several sons and daughters,

BUSHNELL, Rev. Horace, *D. D.*, (son of Ensign Bushnell, Esq.) was born in Litchfield in 1802; graduated at Yale College in 1827, and was a Tutor in that institution from 1829 to 1831. For the last twenty-seven years, he has been pastor of the North Congregational Church in Hartford. He received the degree of Doctor of Divinity from the Wesleyan University in 1842, and from Harvard College in 1852. Besides a large number of published Addresses and Sermons, he is the author of several theological works that have elicited much attention on both sides of the ocean—among which are *God in Christ*, *Nature and the Supernatural*, and *Sermons for the New Life.*

CATLIN, Julius, (son of Mr. Grove Catlin,) was born in Harwinton in 1799. When he was about one year old, his parents removed to this village, and this continued to be his *home* for the succeeding twenty years, though at the age of fifteen he commenced his clerkship in Hartford. He became a successful merchant in that city, where he still resides. Many years ago he was a Director of the Connecticut Branch of the United States Bank, and was one of the Committee appointed to wind up the affairs of that institution, when the parent Bank had been crushed by the veto of General Jackson. In 1846, he was appointed Commissary General of the State, and subsequently he held the office of Auditor of Public Accounts. The President of the United States, in 1847, commissioned Colonel Catlin as a member of the Board of Visitors to the National Military Academy at West Point. In the autumn of 1856, Colonel Catlin and ex-Governor Dutton were chosen Presidential Electors for the State at large. At the annual election in April, 1858, the subject of this sketch was chosen Lieutenant-Governor of Connecticant—an office which, by re-election in April last, he still holds. It is pleasant to his Litchfield friends to know that long absence has not obliterated his recollections of these cherished scenes. In a recent letter to the author of this volume, he says—"I look back with delight on the many days and years of my childhood and youth spent at my happy home. My recollections of Litchfield are indeed pleasant. *I love its very name*, and shall ever take a deep interest in the welfare of the place." Would that *all* the emigrant Sons of Litchfield might carry with them, and retain through life, the same genial love for their early homes! In 1829, Mr. Catlin married Mary Fisher, of Wrentham, Mass., (a sister of the wife of the Rev. Joel Hawes, D. D.,) and has had five children, three of whom are living. For the last fifteen years, he has resided in Asylum street, on the height of ground adjacent to the Railroad—formerly known as the *Sigourney Place*—one of the most beautiful situations in Hartford.

CATLIN, Putnam, (son of Mr. Eli Catlin,) was born in Litchfield, studied law with General Tracy, and was admitted to the bar in this town in 1786. He settled in Montrose, Penn., and there held the office of Judge of the Court of Common Pleas. He was the father of George Catlin, the celebrated artist and historian of the American Indians, who was himself educated in Litchfield.

CHURCH, Samuel, *LL. D.*, a native and former resident of Salisbury, came to Litchfield to reside in 1845, and remained here until his death in the autumn of 1854. He had long been in public life; and, while residing in this town, was chosen Chief Justice of the State and received the degree of Doctor of Laws from Trinity College.

COLLIER, John Allen, (son of Capt. Thomas Collier, editor of the *Monitor*,) was born in Litchfield, November 13, 1787; settled as a lawyer in Binghamton, Broome county, N, Y., and still resides there. He has been a member of Congress, Comptroller of the State, Commissioner to revize and codify the laws, Senatorial Elector for President and Vice President of the United States, and Delegate to and Chairman of the Whig National Convention of 1848. Mr. Collier has long been one of the most eminent lawyers of the State of New York. He was offered a foreign embassy by President Fillmore.

COLLIER, General James, (brother of the preceding,) was born in Litchfield, May 30, 1789; settled in the State of New York, and was Quartermaster and acting Adjutant at the Battle of Queenstown, and participated in that fight. In 1819, he removed to Steubenville, Ohio, his present residence, where he has held the offices of Colonel, Mayor of the city, State's Attorney of the county, and Paymaster General of Ohio. A few years since, he was a Commissioner, with Thomas Ewing and John Brough, to settle the boundary between Ohio and Virginia in conjunction with commissioners from the latter State. In April, 1849, General Collier was appointed by President Fillmore Collector of the Customs for Upper California, with orders to take the overland route to the Pacific. He accepted the post, and, under the escort of a company of dragoons, started for his field of labor. He was five months on his journey, sometimes fighting his way through hostile tribes of Indians, who succeeded in killing three of his men, wounding another, and stealing twenty-seven mules and all his horses. On his arrival at San Francisco, he found the Territory of California governed exclusively by military authority. Being the only civil officer of the federal government on the ground, he was not only Collector, Appraiser, Naval Officer and Surveyor, but was obliged also to perform the duties of District Judge, District Attorney, and Marshal. On being recalled by a new national administration, he was met with the charge of being a defaulter to the government; but after a vexatious suit, he was fully exonerated by the U. S. Court.

Julius Deming

DEMING, Julius, an eminent merchant of Litchfield, was born in Lyme, April 15th, 1755, and, about the year 1781, commenced business in this village. A gentleman of remarkable energy and enterprize, he soon visited London, and made arrangements to import his goods direct from that city—which, probably, was not true of any other country merchant in Connecticut. He is universally recognized by our citizens as the most thorough and successful business man who has ever spent his life among us. Prompt in his engagements, scrupulously upright in his dealings, and discreet and liberal in his benefactions, few men in any community ever enjoyed more implicitly the confidence of all. Mr. Deming had little taste for public life. He was three times elected a member of the House of Representatives, and for several years was one of the Magistrates of this county. From 1801 to 1814, he served in the office of County Treasurer. His position and influence were such, that, had he been an aspirant for political honors, there were few offices within the gift of the people of this State which he might not have filled. He died in this town, January 23, 1838, aged 83 years.

DEMING, Miner R., (son of Stephen Deming, Esq.,) was born in Sharon, February 24, 1810; came to Litchfield with his parents in 1820, and continued to reside here for the next sixteen years. In 1836, he removed to Cincinnati; and in 1839, he became a resident of St. Mary's, Illinois. As Brigadier General, he was chief in command of the Illinois State Troops during the famous Mormon War. General Deming died suddenly, of brain fever, September 10, 1845, while holding the office of High Sheriff of Hancock county. For some time before leaving Litchfield, he was a member of the First Church in this village, and one of the Church Committee. He married Abigail Barnum, of Danbury, and left a family.

DUTTON, Henry, *LL. D.*, (of New Haven,) formerly Governor of Connecticut, and now Professor of Law in Yale College, was born in Plymouth, February 12, 1796. During the following summer, his father, Mr. Thomas Dutton, purchased a place in Litchfield (Northfield Society,) and spent the seven succeeding years in this town, The *earliest* recollections of the Governor are of his Litchfield home. In subsequent years, he returned to Northfield, and taught school two or threeseasons, before his admission to the bar.

GAY, Colonel Fisher, (son of John Gay, Esq.,) was born in Litchfield, October 9, 1733; graduated at Yale College, and settled in Farmington, where he was long a Justice of the Peace and Representative. In the early part of the Revolution he commanded a regiment of Connecticut troops sent for the defense of New York, in which city he died in 1776.

GOULD, James, *LL. D.*, a native of Branford, graduated at Yale College in 1791; settled in Litchfield, and was associated with Judge Gould in conducting the Law School in this town from 1798 to 1820, and subsequently, for about thirteen years, he was the sole Principal of that institution. From 1816 to 1819, he was a Judge of the Supreme Court of this State. Gould's Pleading is a standard work in all our Courts. He was regarded as one of the profoundest lawyers and jurists in the country. The degree of Doctor of Laws was conferred upon him by his alma mater in 1819. He died May 11, 1838, aged 68. Judge Gould married Sally McCurdy, daughter of Gen. Uriah Tracy, and had nine children, viz., 1 William Tracy, now a Judge in Augusta, Georgia. 2 Henry G. 3 James R. 4 Edward S. 5 George, of Troy; now a Judge of the Supreme Court of New York. 6 Julia. 7 Charles, of New York city; late President of the Chicago, Alton and St. Louis Railroad Company, President of the Cumberland Coal and Iron Company, President of the Burns Club, &c. 8 John. 9 Robert Howe, of London.

HOLMES, Uriel, Jr., a native of Hartland, graduated at Yale College in 1784, and settled in Litchfield as a lawyer a few years subsequently. He was elected a Representative nine times, was a Judge of the Litchfield County Court from 1814 to 1817, and during the latter year he was chosen a member of Congress. While residing in Litchfield, he was thrown from his carriage in Canton, from the effects of which he died, May 18, 1827, aged 62. Judge Holmes married a daughter of the Hon. Aaron Austin, and had three children, viz, 1 Henry, *M. D.*, a distinguished physician in Hartford. 2 Uriel, who died July 4, 1818, while a member of the Theological Seminary at Andover. 3 Caroline, died young.

HUNTINGTON, Charles P., (son of the Rev. Dan Huntington,) was born in Litchfield, March 24th, 1802; graduated at Harvard College in 1822; settled as a lawyer in Northampton, Mass., and represented that town in the Legislature in 1834, 1837, 1843, 1852 and 1855—and at the last session named, was chairman of the Judiciary Committee. In 1855, he was appointed Judge of the Superior Court for the Suffolk District, which embraces the city of Boston. Judge Huntington now lives in the vicinity of Boston.

HUNTINGTON, Jabez W., a native of Norwich, graduated at Yale College in 1806; came to Litchfield as a teacher, and student at law, in 1807, and continued to reside here until October 1834, when he returned to Norwich—and died there in 1847, in his 60th year. While a resident of Litchfield, he was elected a Representative, member of Congress, and Judge of the Superior Court. From 1840 until his death he was a member of the U. S. Senate.

KILBOURN, Colonel Charles, (son of Mr. David Kilbourn,) was born in Litchfield, March 3, 1758; fled to Canada in the revolution, and finally settled near Lake Memphremagog, in Stanstead, L. C., where he erected mills of various kinds. The locality still bears the name of *Kilbourn's Mills* on many English and American maps. In the war of 1812, he commanded a corps of provincial troops known as the Frontier Light Infantry. He was also for many years a magistrate, and Justice of the Commissionrrs Court. Colonel Kilbourn died in Stanstead, June 19, 1834, aged 76.

KIRBY, Ephraim, (son of Mr. Abraham Kirby,) was born in Litchfield, February 22, 1757; studied law and settled in his native town. He was often chosen a Representative; appointed Supervisor of the National Revenue for the State of Connecticut in 1801, and U. S. Judge for the Territory of Louisiana in 1804. While on his way to New Orleans, whither the duties of his office called him, he died at Fort Stoddard, Mississippi Territory, October 2d, 1804, aged 47. Col. Kirby married Ruth, daughter of Reynold Marvin, Esq., and left eight children.

KIRBY, Reynold M., Major U. S. A., (son of the preceding,) was born in Litchfield, March 13, 1790. For many years before his death, he was Assistant Adjutant General of the Army.

KIRBY, Edmund, Colonel U. S. A., (brother of the preceding,) was born in Litchfield, April 8, 1794; entered the army as a Lieutenant in 1812; appointed aid-de-camp to his father-in-law, Major General Brown; served in the Blackhawk, Creek and Seminole wars; was chief of the Pay Department, and aid-de-camp to the commander-in-chief, during the late war with Mexico. He died at Avon Springs, N. Y., August 20, 1849, aged 55. On the election of President Taylor, Colonel Kirby was frequently referred to in the public prints as a probable member of the new Cabinet.

MORRIS, James, Jr., was born in Litchfield, January 19, 1752, and graduated at Yale College; was a Captain in the Revolution, and with his company headed one of the columns that led the forlorn hope at the Siege of Yorktown. After the war, he settled in his native parish, South Farms, and was for many years a Justice of the Peace and Representative; and was also the Founder and Principal of *Morris Academy*—an institution which became famous throughout the country. Captain Morris died in this town, September 9, 1814.

OSBORN, Rev. Ethan, (son of Captain John Osborn,) was born in Litchfield, August 21, 1758; graduated at Dartmouth College in 1784; and was settled as pastor of the congregational church in Fairfield, N. J., in 1789. In this small rural parish, Mr. Osborn married 706 couple, attended the funerals of 1500 persons, admitted to his church about 600 members, baptized 1146 persons, and preached 10,164 sermons. His *last* sermon was preached in 1855, when in his 97th year. On Sunday, January 24, 1858, he attended service, addressed the audience in an appropriate manner, and made the concluding prayer—he then being 99 years and 5 months old. He died in Fairfield, May 1, 1858, in his 100th year. He was pastor of the church in that place 54 years.

PECK, John M., *D. D.*, (son of Mr. Asa Peck,) was born in Litchfield, October 31, 1789, and became a celebrated Baptist preacher in Illinois. He was a diligent student, and wrote and published much—especially in relation to the history of the Valley of the Mississippi. The degree of Doctor of Divinity was conferred upon him by Harvard College in 1853. Dr. Peck was an eloquent pulpit orator, and one of the most popular men in Illinois—so much so that the whig party of that State once nominated him as their candidate for Governor. He died at his residence in Rock Spring, Ill., in 1858.

PECK, William V., of Portsmouth, Ohio, one of the present Judges of the Supreme Court of that State, was born of Litchfield parents in Cayuga county, New York, where his father, (Mr. Virgil Peck,) died during his infancy. When the subject of this paragraph was three years old, his mother returned with him to this town, and subsequently married Dr. Abel Catlin, in whose family he was brought up. After spending about twenty years in this village, he settled as a lawyer in Ohio.

PECK, Professor William G., (son of Mr. Alfred Peck,) was born in Litchfield, October 16, 1820; graduated at West Point, where he was for a few years Assistant Professor of Mathematics. As Lieutenant of Topographical Engineers in the U. S. Army, he was associated with Colonel Fremont in his celebrated Exploring Expeditions. He has since been a Professor in the University of Michigan; and is now Professor of Mathematics in Columbia College, New York. He married Elizabeth M., daughter of Professor Charles Davies, *LL. D.*

PHELPS, Samuel Shether, (son of Captain John Phelps,) was born on Chestnut Hill, in the house now owned and occupied by Mr. Willis Law, May 13, 1793; graduated at Yale College and the Litchfield Law School, and settled in Middlebury, Vermont. Having been successively a Paymaster in the war of 1812, aid-de-camp to Governor Galusha, Colonel, member of the Council of Sensors, member of the Legislative Council, and Judge of the Supreme Court, he was elected a Senator in Congress in 1838—an office which held for 12 years. As a lawyer and statesman, he ranked with Clay, Webster, Crittenden and Clayton. Judge Phelps died in 1857.

PIERCE, Colonel John, (son of Mr. John Pierce, of Litchfield,) early entered the public service, and rose to the rank of Paymaster General in the Army, and was a Commissioner for settling the accounts of the army. Though his parents never resided out of Litchfield after their marriage, Colonel Pierce is said to have been born at the house of his maternal grandfather, Major John Patterson, in Farmington. Colonel P. died in New York, August 6, 1788. He was a brother of the late Miss Sarah Pierce, Founder and Principal of the Litchfield Female Academy.

PIERPONT, John, (son of Mr: James Pierpont,) was born in Litchfield, April 6, 1785; graduated at Yale College and at the Litchfield Law School, and settled in Newburyport, Massachusetts, as a lawyer. Abandoning the legal profession, he entered the ministry of the Unitarian denomination, and was for many years pastor of the Hollis-street church, Boston. He is alike distinguished as a poet, preacher and lecturer. Several editions of his *Airs of Palestine*, as well as of his other poems, have been published. Mr. Pierpont now resides in Medford, Mass.

PIERPONT, Robert, (son of Mr. David Pierpont,) was born in Litchfield, May 4, 1791; studied law, and settled in Rutland, Vermont, his present residence. He has been Lieutenant Governor of that State, and Judge of the Supreme Court.

PIERPONT, John, (brother of the preceding,) was born in Litchfield, September 10, 1805; graduated at the Law School in this town, and settled in Vergennes, Vermont. He is now a Judge of the Supreme Court of that State, and has held various other offices.

SEDGWICK, Albert, was born in Cornwall Hollow in the year 1802; removed to Litchfield in 1830, and continued to reside here for the succeeding 25 years. In 1834, he was appointed High Sheriff of this county, an office which he continued to hold (with the exception of one term of three years,) until 1854—when he was appointed by the Legislature Commissioner of the School Fund of Connecticut: In 1855, he removed to Hartford, his present residence.

SEYMOUR, Horatio, *LL. D.*, (son of Major Moses Seymour,) was born in Litchfield, May 31st, 1778; graduated at Yale College and at the Litchfield Law School; and settled in Middlebury, Vt., where he died a year or two since. He was a member of the State Council from 1809 to 1816; and of the United States Senate from 1821 to 1833. In 1834, he was the Whig candidate for Governor of Vermont, but the anti-masonic candidate was elected. He was also for a few years Judge of Probate. Judge Seymour received the degree of Doctor of Laws from his alma mater in 1847.

SEYMOUR, Henry, (brother of the preceding,) was born in Litchfield, May 30, 1780; settled as a merchant at Pompey, Onondaga county, N. Y., where he became wealthy. Removing to Utica, he died there, August 26, 1837. He was a Representative, Senator, Canal Commissioner, Mayor of Utica, and President of the Farmers' Loan and Trust Company. The Hon. Horatio Seymour, *LL. D.*, late Governor of New York, is his son.

SEYMOUR, Origen Storrs, (son of Ozias Seymour, Esq., and grandson of Major Seymour,) was born in Litchfield, Feb. 9, 1804; graduated at Yale College in 1824; settled as a lawyer in his native town. He has been a Representative, Speaker of the House, and member of Congress, and is now a Judge of the Superior Court.

SHELDON, Daniel, Jr., (son of Dr. Daniel Sheldon,) was born in the adjoining town of Washington in 1780, and during the following year his parents removed to Litchfield; and here the subject of this sketch continued to reside until he entered public life. Graduating at the Litchfield Law School in 1799, he accepted a clerkship in the Treasury Department, and retained it until the appointment of Mr. Gallatin as Ambassador to France, when he was nominated and confirmed as Secretary of Legation to that country. When the Ambassador was re-called, Mr. Sheldon remained in France as *Charge d' Affaires* until the arrival of Mr. Gallatin's successor. He died in Marseilles, April 14, 1828, aged 48. His funeral was attended by all the foreign ministers and consuls present in the city, and the flags of all the American ships in port were placed at half-mast.

SKINNER, Roger, (son of Gen. Timothy Skinner,) was born in Litchfield, June 10, 1773; became a lawyer, and removed from this town to Sandy Hill, N. Y., in 1806, where he was elected a Repesentative in 1810, 1811 and 1812, and a Senator from 1818 to 1821. In 1820, he was a member of the Council of Appointment; from 1815 to 1819, U. S. Attorney for the Northern District of New York; and from 1819 until his death, Judge of the U. S. District Court. On being appointed Judge, he became a resident of Albany, at which place he died August 19, 1825. He was an intimate friend of the Hon. Martin Van Buren, who, in a recent letter to the author, says—"Being a widower myself, and he a bachelor, we twice kept house together, and did so at the period of his lamented death. I was with him through his last illness, held his hand when he died, and mourned for him as for a sincere and affectionate friend." The visit of Mr. Van Buren to this town, with Mr. S., about 1820, is well remembered.

SKINNER, Richard, *LL. D.*, (brother of the preceding,) was born in Litchfield, May 30, 1778; graduated at the Law School in his native town, and settled in Manchester, Vermont in 1800. He became State's Attorney, Speaker of the House, Judge of Probate, member of Congress, Chief Justice of the State, and Governor. He received the degree of LL. D. from Middlebury college. Governor Skinner died in Middlebury, May 23, 1833, aged 55.

TALLMADGE, Frederick A., (son of Colonel Benjamin Tallmadge,) was born in Litchfield, August 29, 1792; graduated at Yale College in 1811; and settled as a lawyer in New York city—his present residence. From 1834 to 1836 he was an Alderman; from 1836 to 1840, a member of the State Senate, of which body he was elected President; from 1840 to 1845, and from 1848 to 1853, he was Recorder of the City, and Chief Justice of the Police Court; and from 1846 to 1848, he was a member of Congress. For two or three years past, Mr. Tallmadge has held the office of Superintendent of Police in New York—a very important and responsible post.

TRACY, General Uriah, a native of Norwich and a graduate of Yale College, settled as a lawyer in Litchfield in 1780, and here spent his entire professional life. He was a Representative at nine sessions, member of Congress three years, and U. S. Senator eleven years; and rose to the rank of Major General of militia. He was one of the most brilliant men of his day. General Tracy died in Washington city in 1807, and was the first person buried in the congressional cemetery.

WELCH, John, (son of Major David Welch,) was born in Litchfield, September 23, 1759; graduated at Yale College in 1778; settled as a merchant in his native town, and continued to reside here until his death, which took place December 26, 1845. He was successively a Justice of the Peace, Representative, Senator, member of the Constitutional Convention, Associate Judge of the County Court, and a candidate for Congress. He was successful in business, and left a large estate.

Morris Woodruff

WOLCOTT, Oliver, Jr., *LL. D.*, was born in Litchfield, January 11, 1760; and died in New York, June 2, 1833. He graduated at Yale College, and was successively Comptroller of this State, Auditor and Secretary of the United States Treasury, Judge of the United States Circuit Court, President of the Bank of America, President of the Constitutional Convention of Connecticut, and Governor of his native State from 1817 to 1827. He was one of the most illustrious statesmen of the early days of the republic — the intimate friend and adviser of Washington, Adams and Hamilton; and, for some time previous to his decease, he was the last surviving member of Washington's Cabinet.

WOLCOTT, Frederick, (brother of the preceding,) was born in Litchfield, Novemher 2, 1767; graduated at Yale College in 1787, and died in his native town May 28, 1837. For more than forty years he was constantly in public life—as Clerk of the Courts, Judge of Probate, Representative, member of the State Council, Senator, &c. No man ever lived in the town who enjoyed more implicitly the confidence of the public. There was a dignity and nobleness in his person and manner which left their impress on all who came within the sphere of his influence.

WOODRUFF, General Morris, (son of Mr. James Woodruff,) was born in Litchfield, September 3, 1777; educated at Morris Academy, and was bred a merchant. He commenced his mercantile life with Messrs. David Leavitt and Simeon Harrison; and after his connection with them was dissolved, he prosecuted the business chiefly on his own account for many years. He was through life much employed as Executor, Administrator, and Commissioner, in settling estates, and as Arbitrator, Auditor and Committee appointed by the Courts. He was an active and influential member of the church and ecclesiastical society, and of the community generally to which he belonged; repeatedly discharged the duties of various public offices; represented the town of Litchfield in the Legislature fourteen sessions, and was a magistrate of the county twenty-six years. In 1818, he was appointed Brigadier General of the Sixth Brigade; and in 1824, the Legislature appointed him Major General of the Third Division. From 1829, until his death—a period of eleven years—he held the office of a Judge of the Couny Court, and that of Commissioner which succeeded it; and in November, 1832, he was chosen by the voters of the State at large, an Elector of President and Vice President of the United States. In all the affairs of life, General Woodruff was distinguished by great activity, energy, perseverance, accuracy and fidelity to whatever trust he assumed. Of high integrity himself, he was stern in requiring from others observance of its dictates. Ready to do justice to others; keenly alive to every sense of wrong; penetrating in his scrutiny into the conduct and motives of others; convincing rather than persuasive in his intercourse with men, he impelled their concurrence in his views by producing confidence in the soundness of his judgment and the correctness of his purposes. He was steadfast in his friendships, and few men retain with equal warmth the intimacies begun in early years. The associates of his boyhood were through life his most confiding and devoted friends. The dependance of his neighbors and friends on him for advice and assistance was very great, their confidence was never abused, their reliance never failed; and so his means of usefulness among them were large, and his influence extensive. In his domestic relations he was affectionate and kind—inflexible in retaining a high standard of both filial and parental duty—and never failed to show that the highest good of those who were dependent upon him, was his invariable motive in all his intercourse with them. General Woodruff was nearly six feet in height, stout, erect, active, and of more than ordinary physical strength. Of robust aud vigorous frame and sound constitution, his health was rarely interrupted, and promise of a green old age seemed singularly certain. But in the spring of 1839, his system received a shock followed by an affection of the liver, under which he declined, and on the 17th of May, 1840, he died—illustrating in his dying hour the peace and consolation of the Christian's hope and confidence in the Saviour in whose church on earth he had been numbered for many years. His remains are interred in our East Burying-Ground, where a handsome monument has been erected to his memory. General Woodruff married Candace, eldest daughter of Lewis Catlin, Esq., of Harwinton. Their children were—1 George C., who still resides in Litchfield, and is well known to our readers as a prominent member of the Bar of Litchfield county. 2. Lucy M., m. Hon. O. S. Seymour, of Litchfield. 3 Lewis B., Judge of the Superior Court for the city of New York. 4. Reuben M., *M. D.*, a physician of high attainments, died young in 1849. 5 James, died in infancy.

WOODRUFF, Clark, (brother of the preceding,) was born in Litchfield, August 23, 1791, and was educated at Morris Academy. In 1810, he left his native town, and, passing down the Ohio and Mississippi rivers, he soon established himself as a lawyer in St. Francisville, in the present State of Louisiana. For many years he was reputed one of the ablest, most eloquent and successful advocates at the bar; and in the spring of 1828, he was appointed Judge of the Eighth Judicial District of the State of Louisiana. He also held the office of State Auditor, and Commissioner charged with the subject of Public Improvements in that State, in which he took an active interest. He was also a Trustee af Louisiana College. On resigning his judgeship, he removed to New Orleans, where he resided until a short time previous to his death. He departed this life at his country seat at Carrollton, on the Mississippi, about six miles above that city, on the 25th of November, 1851. Judge Woodruff was a polished, courtly gentleman, of fine address, pleasing manners, and cultivated mind. He married Matilda Bradford, of St. Francisville, a highly accomplished lady, by whom he had three children. The only survivor, Mrs. Octavia Besançon, now lives at Carrollton at the late residence of her father.

The Deming House.
Erected 1793.

APPENDIX.

Colonial and State Officers of Connecticut.

[Complete, from 1635 to 1859.]

	First chosen.	No. years.
Allyn, John, Secretary of State	1664	31
Andros, Sir Edmund, Governor	1687	2
Backus, Thomas, Lieut. Governor	1849	1
Baldwin, Roger S., Governor	1844	2
Baldwin, Edward Law, Executive Secretary,	1844	2
Barnard, Henry, Supt. Common Schools,	1849	5
Beardslee, Cyrus H., Executive Secretary	1827	4
Beers, Seth P.,* School Fund Commissioner	1825	24
Beers, Seth P.,* Supt. Common Schools	1845	4
Betts, Thaddeus, Lieutenant Governor	1834	1
Birge, Alonzo W., Treasurer	1846	1
Bissell, Clark, Governor	1847	2
Bissell, George A., Executive Secretary	1847	2
Billings, Noyes, Lieut. Governor	1846	1
Bishop, James, Deputy Governor	1683	7
Booth, Reuben,† Lieut. Governor	1844	2
Boyd, John,* Secretary of State	1858	2
Brown, Jeremiah, Treasurer	1835	3
Bradley, Charles W., Secretary of State	1846	1
Buckingham, William A., Governor	1858	2
Buell, William H., Comptroller	1858	2
Burnham, Alfred A., Lieut. Governor	1857	1
Burr, Peter, Deputy Governor	1723	2
Calef, Arthur, Treasurer	1855	1
Camp, Daniel W., Treasurer	1854	1
Camp, David N., Supt. Common Schools	1857	2
Carrington, Abijah, Comptroller	1844	2
Catlin, Abijah,* Comptroller	1847	3
Catlin, Abijah,* School Fund Commissioner	1851	1
Catlin, George S.,† Executive Secretary	1831	2
Catlin, Julius,† Lieutenant Governor	1858	2
Clarke, Daniel, Secretary of State	1658	8
Clarke, Thomas, Treasurer	1851	1

Cleveland, Chauncey F., Governor	1842	2
Cleveland, Mason, Comptroller	1846	1
Cleveland, Mason, Sch. Fund Commissioner	1854	1
Coe, Frederick P., Treasurer	1856	1
Colt, Elisha, Comptroller	1806	13
Colt, Peter, Treasurer	1789	5
Cullick, John, Secretary of State	1648	10
Day, Albert, Lieutenant Governor	1856	1
Day, Thomas,* Secretary of State,	1810	25
Dunham, John, Comptroller	1854	1
Dutton, Henry,† Governor	1854	1
Edwards, Henry W., Governor	1833	4
Ellsworth, William Wolcott, Governor	1838	4
Ellsworth, Pinckney W., Executive Secretary	1838	4
Erving, R. Augustus, Executive Secretary	1850	3
Field, William, Comptroller	1836	2
Field, William, Lieut. Governor	1855	1
Fitch, Thomas, Deputy Govornor	1750	4
Fitch, Thomas, Governor	1754	12
Foote, Samuel A., Governor	1834	1
Foote, Joseph F., Executive Secretary	1854	2
Gilbert, Joseph B., Treasurer	1844	4
Gold, Nathan, Deputy Governor	1708	16
Goodrich, Chauncey, Lieut. Governor	1813	2
Graves, Henry B.,* Executive Secretary	1854	1
Griswold, Matthew, Lieut. Governor	1769	15
Griswold, Matthew, Governor	1784	2
Griswold, Roger, Lieut. Governor	1809	2
Griswold, Roger, Governor	1811	1
Hawley, Charles, Lieut. Governor	1838	4
Haynes, John, Deputy Governor	1640	5
Haynes, John, Governor	1639	8
Hillhouse, James, School Fund Commissioner	1810	15
Hitchcock, William R., Executive Secretary	1834	1
Hinman, Royal R.,* Secretary of State	1835	7
Hoadly, Charles J., State Librarian	1856	3
Holabird, William S.,* Lieut. Governor	1842	2
Holley, Alexander H.,* Lieut. Governor	1854	1
Holley, Alexander H.,* Governor	1857	1
Hopkins, Edward, Secretary of State	1639	1
Hopkins, Edward, Deputy Governor	1643	6
Hopkins, Edward, Governor	1640	7
Hovey, James A., Executive Secretary	1842	2
Huntington, Jabez W.,* Executive Secretary	1820	7
Huntington, Jedediah, Treasurer	1789	1
Huntington, Samuel, Lieut. Governor	1784	2
Huntington, Samuel, Governor	1786	10
Huntington, Roger, Comptroller	1834	1
Ingersoll, Jonathan, Lieut. Governor	1816	7

Jones, William, Deputy Governor	1692	5
Kendrick, Green, Lieut. Governor	1851	1
Kilbourn, Henry, Comptroller	1838	4
Kilbourn, P. K.,* Executive Secretary	1857	1
Kimberly. Eleazer, Secretary of State	1696	13
Kingsbury, Andrew, Comptroller	1791	3
Kingsbury, Andrew, Treasurer	1794	24
Lamb, Joseph G., Comptroller	1857	1
Law, Jonathan, Deputy Governor	1724	17
Law, Jonathan, Governor	1741	9
Lawrence, John, Treasurer	1769	19
Leet, William, Deputy Governor	1669	7
Leet, William, Governor	1676	7
Ludlow, Roger, Deputy Governor	1639	3
McCurdy, Charles J., Lieut. Governor	1847	2
Mason, John, Deputy Governor	1660	9
Mather, John P. C., Secretary of State	1850	3
Merrill, Alexander, Comptroller	1855	1
Mills, Roger H., Secretary of State	1849	1
Minor, William T., Governor	1855	2
Mix, Silas, Executive Secretary	1833	4
Palmer, John C., School Fund Commissioner	1850	2
Pardee, Dwight W., Executive Secretary	1846	1
Perry, Oliver H., Secretary of State	1854	1
Peters, John S., Lieut. Governor	1827	4
Peters, John S., Governor	1831	2
Phelps, Elisha, Comptroller	1830	4
Phelps, Noah A., Secretary of State	1842	2
Philbrick, John D., Supt Common Schools	1855	2
Pinney, Rufus G., Comptroller	1850	3
Pitkin, William, Treasurer	1678	1
Pitkin, William, Deputy Governor	1754	12
Pitkin, William, Governor	1766	3
Plant, David, Lieutenant Governor	1823	4
Platt, Orville H.,† Secretary of State	1857	1
Pomeroy, Ralph, Comptroller	1789	2
Pond, Charles H., Lieut. Governor	1850	3
Pond, Charles H., Governor	1853	1
Porter, John, Comptroller	1794	12
Prentis, Edward, Treasurer	1856	1
Rider, Hiram, Treasurer	1838	4
Robertson, John B., Secretary of State	1847	2
Robinson, L. F., Executive Secretary	1849	1
Saltonstall, Gurdon, Governor	1707	17
Sedgwick, Albert,* School Fund Commiss'r	1854	5
Seymour, Thomas H., Governor	1850	3
Smith, Henry D., Treasurer	1850	1
Smith, John Cotton,* Lieut. Governor	1811	2
Smith, John Cotton,* Governor	1813	4

Spencer, Isaac, Treasurer	1818	16
Sperry, Nehemiah D., Secretary of State	1855	2
Stanley, Caleb, Secretary of State	1709	3
Stanley, Nathaniel, Treasurer	1749	6
Stoddard, Ebenezer, Lieut. Governor	1833	4
Stearns, Edwin, Treasurer	1852	2
Talcott, John, Treasurer	1652	7
Talcott, John, (Jr,) Treasurer	1659	19
Talcott, Joseph, Deputy Governor	1724	—
Talcott, Joseph, Governor	1724	17
Talcott, Joseph, Treasurer	1755	14
Thomas, James, Comptroller	1819	11
Tomlinson, Gideon, Governor	1827	4
Toucey, Isaac, Governor	1846	1
Treadwell, John, Lieut. Governor	1798	11
Treadwell, John, Governor,	1809	2
Treat, Robert, Deputy Governor	1676	17
Treat, Robert, Governor	1683	13
Trumbull, Jonathan, Deputy Governor	1766	3
Trumbull, Jonathan, Governor	1769	15
Trumbull, Jonathan, (Jr,) Lieut. Governor	1796	2
Trumbull, Jonathan, (Jr,) Governor	1798	11
Trumbull, Gurdon, Sch. Fund Commissioner	1850	1
Trumbull, Joseph, Governor	1849	1
Trumbull, J. Hammond, State Librarian	1854	2
Tyler, Daniel P., Secretary of State	1844	2
Wadsworth, James, Comptroller	1786	2
Warner, Samuel L., Executive Secretary	1853	1
Waldo, Loren P., Sch. Fund Commissioner	1852	1
Webster, John, Deputy Governor	1655	1
Webster, John, Governor	1656	1
Weed, Hiram, Secretary of State	1850	(died)
Welles, Thomas, Treasurer	1639	5
Welles, Thomas, Secretary of State	1640	8
Welles, Thomas, Deputy Governor	1654	4
Welles, Thomas, Governor	1655	2
Welles, Gideon, Comptroller	1835	3
White, Jabez L., Treasurer	1842	2
Whiting, William, Treasurer	1641	7
Whiting, Joseph, do.	1679	3
Whiting, John, do.	1718	21
Wildman, Frederick S., Treasurer	1857	1*
Winthrop, John, Deputy Governor	1658	1
Winthrop, John, Governor	1657	9
Winthrop, Fitz John, Governor	1698	9
Wolcott, Roger, Deputy Governor	1741	9
Wolcott, Roger, Governor	1750	4
Wolcott, Oliver,* Lieut. Governor	1786	10

Wolcott, Oliver,* Governor	1796	2
Wolcott, Oliver, (Jr,)* Comptroller	1788	1
Wolcott, Oliver, (Jr,)* Governor	1817	10
Wyllys, George, Deputy Governor	1641	1
Wyllys, George, Governor	1642	1
Wyllys, Hezekiah, Secretary of State	1712	23
Wyllys, George, do. do.	1735	61
Wyllys, Samuel, do. do.	1796	14

* Chosen from Litchfield co. † Natives of the co. but residing elsewhere.

Superior Court and Supreme Court of Errors.

CHIEF JUSTICES.

[Previous to 1784, the Deputy Governors were the Chief Justices.]

	First chosen.	No. years.
Samuel Huntington, Norwich	1784	1
Richard Law, New London	1785	4
Eliphalet Dyer, Windham	1789	4
Andrew Adams, Litchfield	1793	5
Jesse Root, Coventry	1798	9
Stephen Mix Mitchell, Wethersfield	1807	7
Tapping Reeve, Litchfield	1814	1
Zephaniah Swift, Windham	1815	4
Stephen Titus Hosmer, Middletown	1819	14
David Daggett, New Haven	1833	1
Thomas S. Williams, Hartford	1834	13
Samuel Church, Litchfield	1847	7
Henry M. Waite, Lyme	1854	2
William L. Storrs, Hartford	1856	in office.

ASSOCIATE JUDGES.

	First chosen.	No. years
William Pitkin, Hartford	1711	2
Richard Christophers, New London	1711	21
Peter Burr, Fairfield	1711	7
Samuel Eells, Milford	1711	29
John Haynes, Hartford	1713	1
Jonathan Law, Milford	1715	9
John Hamlin, Middletown	1716	6
Joseph Talcott, Hartford	1721	1
Matthew Allyn, Windsor	1723	9
John Hooker, Farmington	1723	9

James Wadsworth, Durham	1725	27
Roger Wolcott, Windsor	1732	9
Joseph Whiting, New Haven	1732	13
Elisha Williams, Wethersfield	1740	3
William Pitkin, Hartford,	1741	13
Ebenezer Silliman, Fairfield	1743	23
John Bulkley, Colchester	1745	8
Samuel Lynde, Saybrook	1752	3
Daniel Edwards, Hartford	1753	10
Roger Wolcott, Jr. Windsor	1754	5
Jonathan Trumbull, Lebanon	1754	(declined)
Joseph Fowler, Lebanon	1754	6
Benjamin Hall, Wallingford	1759	7
Robert Walker, Stratford	1760	12
Matthew Griswold. Lyme	1765	4
Eliphalet Dyer, Windham	1766	23
Roger Sherman, New Haven	1766	23
William Pitkin, Hartford	1769	20
Wm. Samuel Johnson, Stratford	1772	1
Samuel Huntington, Norwich	1773	11
Richard Law, New London	1784	1
Oliver Ellsworth, Windsor	1785	4
Andrew Adams, Litchfield	1789	4
Jesse Root, Coventry	1789	9
Charles Chauncey, New Haven	1789	4
Erastus Wolcott, East Windsor	1789	3
Jonathan Sturges, Fairfield	1792	13
Benjamin Huntington, Norwich	1792	6
Ashur Miller, Middletown	1793	2
Stephen Mix Mitchell, Middletown	1795	12
Jonathan Ingersoll, New Haven	1798	8
Tapping Reeve, Litchfield	1798	16
Zephaniah Swift, Windham	1801	14
John Trumbull, Hartford	1801	18
William Edmond, Newtown	1805	14
Nathaniel Smith, Woodbury	1806	13
Jeremiah G. Brainard, New London	1806	23
Simeon Baldwin, New Haven	1806	12
Roger Griswold, Lyme	1807	2
John Cotton Smith, Sharon	1809	2
Calvin Goddard, Norwich	1815	3
Stephen Titus Hosmer, Middletown	1815	3
James Gould, Litchfield	1816	3
John T. Peters, Hartford	1818	16
Asa Chapman, New Haven	1818	7
William Bristol, New Haven	1819	7
James Lanman, Norwich	1826	3
David Daggett, New Haven	1826	7
Thomas S. Williams, Hartford	1829	5

Clark Bissell, Norwalk	1829	10
Samuel Church, Litchfield	1833	14
Jabez W. Huntington, Litchfield	1834	6
Henry M. Waite, Lyme	1834	20
Roger M. Sherman, Fairfield	1839	3
William L. Storrs, Hartford	1840	16
Joel Hinman, New Haven	1842	in office.
William W. Ellsworth, Hartford	1847	"
David C. Sanford, New Milford	1854	"
Thomas B. Butler, Norwalk	1855	"
Origen S. Seymour, Litchfield	1855	"
John D. Park, Norwich	1855	"
Loren P. Waldo, Tolland	1855	"
Charles J. McCurdy, Lyme	1856	"

COMMISSIONERS OF THE SUPERIOR COURT.

[Appointed by the Court for the term of two years. This office was created in 1854.]

Birdsey Baldwin, Cornwall.
J. H. Beach, Plymouth.
Seth P. Beers, Litchfield.
Frederick D. Beeman, Litchfield.
Merritt Bronson, New Hartford.
Edward Carrington, Colebrook.
William Cothren, Woodbury.
George L. Fields, Watertown.
Wait Garrett, New Hartford,
Joseph I. Gaylord, Goshen.
Albert N. Hodge, Roxbury.
Carlos Holcomb, New Hartford.
John H. Hubbard, Litchfield.
P. K. Kilbourn, Litchfield.
Leister Loomis, Barkhamsted.
Charles P. Lyman, Barkhamsted.
Stephen D. Mann, New Hartford.
John G. Mitchell, Salisbury.
William L. Ransom, Litchfield.
John G. Reid, Kent.
Jhon H. Russell, Salisbury.
Henry S. Sanford, New Milford.
Edward W. Seymour, Litchfield.
Nathaniel Smith, Woodbury.
Oliver A. G. Todd, New Milford.
John S. Turrell, New Milford.
George Wheaton, Cornwall.
Walter R. Whittlesey, Salisbury.

Justices of the Peace for the County of Litchfield,

RESIDING IN THE TOWN OF LITCHFIELD.

[Complete Roll, from the organization of the County to the present time. Until 1851, all Justices of the Peace in Connecticut were appointed annually by the Legislature. They are now elected by the People for the term of two years.]

First chosen.	
1774	Andrew Adams
1796	John Allen
1828	Joseph Adams
1836	E. S. Abernethy
1847	Charles Adams
1762	Isaac Baldwin
1781	Abraham Bradley
1803	Nathan Bassett
1810	Asa Bacon
1817	Seth P. Beers
1817	Jonathan Buel
1819	James Birge
1820	Isaiah Bunce
1828	Joseph Birge
1835	Joseph Birge, Jr.
1836	Samuel P. Bolles
1839	William Bassett
1840	Ozias B. Bassett
1840	Francis Bacon
1845	Samuel G. Braman
1846	Frederick D. Beeman
1846	Samuel Brooker, Jr.
1847	Frederick Buel
1847	Philip S. Beebe
1850	Charles O. Belden
1850	David Benton
1851	Chester G. Birge
1851	Junius Burgess
1854	Charles C. Buel
1856	William Bissell

First chosen.	
1753	Timothy Collins
1812	Levi Catlin
1836	Dan Catlin
1838	Edward Camp
1838	Edward Cowles
1839	Ralph G. Camp
1840	Cyrus Catlin
1846	Samuel Church
1846	Garner Curtis
1847	Phineas W. Camp
1847	Walter Coe
1858	John Catlin
1798	Julius Deming
1842	Stephen Deming
1838	Samuel H. Dudley
1858	Orson Emons
1849	Amos Farnsworth
1854	Henry Frisbie
1858	Royal A. Ford
1818	Nathaniel Goodwin
1832	Leonard Goodwin
1838	Chester C. Goslee
1838	Julius Griswold
1841	John Garnsey
1849	Albin Guild
1849	Henry B. Graves
1851	Edward Garnsey
1856	George Garnsey
1752	Thomas Harrison
1808	Uriel Holmes

First chosen.

1808 Uriel Holmes
1817 Jabez W. Huntington
1820 Ephraim S. Hall
1820 Elihu Harrison
1828 Asa Hopkins
1835 William Harrison
1838 Edward Hopkins
1843 G. H. Hollister
1845 Norman Hall
1846 Alanson Hall
1852 John H. Hubbard
1854 Levi Heaton
1854 George A. Hickox
1830 Truman Kilbourn
1835 Putnam Kilbourn
1846 Homer Kilbourn
1858 P. K. Kilbourn
1802 Seth Landon
1819 Ozias Lewis
1836 Abner Landon
1852 A. S. Lewis
1788 James Morris
1803 Roger Marsh
1809 Phineas Miner
1842 Augustus Morey
1846 Lemuel O. Meafoy
1849 Samuel A. Merwin
1854 Garry H. Minor
1858 Jacob Morse, Jr.
1843 Isaac Newton
1847 William Norton
1849 William Newton
1847 John A. Oviatt
1804 Mark Prindle
1836 A. J. Pickett
1837 Edward Pierpont
1838 James M. Pierpont

First chosen.

1838 Manly Peters
1847 Leonard Pierpont
1849 Ithamar Page
1844 Frederick W. Plumb
1846 Prentice Parkhurst
1851 Christopher C. Palmer
1783 Tapping Reeve
1819 Stephen Russell
1858 William L. Ransom
1754 Elisha Sheldon
1772 Reuben Smith
1779 Jedediah Strong
1797 Moses Seymour
1808 Aaron Smith
1808 Peter Sherman
1823 Enos Stoddard
1824 David C. Sanford
1826 Simeon Sanford
1829 Origen S. Seymour
1840 Henry Skilton
1843 Wm. L. Smedley
1827 Truman Smith
1847 Daniel B. Stoddard
1850 George A. Smith
1856 Abraham C. Smith
1856 Edward W. Seymour
1858 Newton Smith
1792 Uriah Tracy
1807 Benjamin Tallmadge
1844 Stephen Trowbridge
1845 Uri Taylor
1848 Oliver A. G. Todd
1759 Jacob Woodruff
1768 David Welch
1793 John Welch
1800 Frederick Wolcott
1804 Roger N. Whittlesey

First chosen.		First chosen.	
1814	Morris Woodruff	1840	Jason Whiting
1826	Hugh P. Welch	1845	James B. Woodruff
1832	George C. Woodruff	1845	Douglas Watson
1837	Enoch J. Woodruff	1847	Isaac B. Woodruff
1840	Charles L. Webb	1850	Tomlinson Wells

Court of Probate.

DISTRICT OF LITCHFIELD.

JUDGES.

[District organized in 1747. Judges appointed annually by the Legislature until 1851. Since elected annually by the People.]

		Appointed.	No. years.
Ebenezer Marsh,	of Litchfield	1747	25
Oliver Wolcott	"	1772	24
Frederick Wolcott	"	1796	41
Elisha S. Abernethy	"	1837	1
Phineas Miner	"	1838	2
Ralph G. Camp	"	1840	2
Elisha S. Abernethy	"	1842	2
Ralph G. Camp	"	1844	2
Elisha S. Abernethy	"	1846	1
Charles Adams	"	1847	3
Oliver A. G. Todd	"	1850	1
Henry B. Graves	"	1851	1
Oliver A. G. Todd	"	1852	1
George C. Woodruff	"	1853	1
Charles Adams	"	1854	3
George C. Woodruff	"	1857	1
Charles Adams	"	1858	in office.

CLERKS.

Isaac Baldwin,	Litchfield	1747	25
Hosea Hulbert	"	1772	2
Nath'l Brown Beckwith	"	1774	1
Samuel Lyman	"	1775	4
Oliver Wolcott, Jr.	"	1779	2
Thomas Gold	"	1781	5

		First appointed.	No. years.
Frederick Wolcott	"	1786	10
Roger Skinner	"	1796	10
Aaron Burr Reeve	"	1806	2
Elijah Adams	"	1808	1
Jabez W. Huntington	"	1809	20
Phineas Miner	"	1829	8
George C. Woodruff	"	1837	3
Francis Bacon	"	1840	2
Reuben M. Woodruff	"	1842	2
Douglas Watson	"	1844	1
William E. Dickinson	"	1845	1
Philip Wells	"	1846	1
George C. Woodruff	"	1847	4
Buel Sedgwick	"	1851	1
George C. Woodruff	"	1852	2
Charles O. Belden	"	1854	1
P. K. Kilbourn	"	1855	3
Edward W. Seymour	"	1858	in office

Court of Common Pleas.

COUNTY OF LITCHFIELD.

[Previous to 1819, this Court consisted of one Presiding Judge and four Associate Judges, called "Justices of the Quorum." From 1819 to 1839, there were but two Associate Judges, instead of four. From 1839 till the abolition of the Court in 1855, there were no Associate Judges—the County Commissioners being their successors.]

CHIEF JUDGES.

William Preston, Woodbury	1751	3
John Williams, Sharon	1754	19
Oliver Wolcott, Litchfield	1773	19
Daniel Sherman, Woodbury	1786	5
Joshua Porter, Salisbury	1791	17
Aaron Austin, New Hartford	1808	8
Augustus Pettibone, Norfolk	1816	14
David S. Boardman, N. Milford	1831	5
William M. Burrall, Canaan	1836	2
Ansel Sterling, Sharon	1838	1
Calvin Butler, Plymouth	1839	1
Ansel Sterling, Sharon	1840	2

	First appointed.	No. years.
William M. Burrall, Canaan	1842	2
Abijah Catlin, Harwinton	1844	2
Elisha S. Abernethy, Litchfield	1846	1
Holbrook Curtis, Watertown	1847	2
Hiram Goodwin, Barkhamsted	1849	1
Charles B. Phelps, Woodbury	1850	1
Hiram Goodwin, Barkhamsted	1851	1
Charles B. Phelps, Woodbury	1852	2
Hiram Goodwin, Barkhamsted	1854	1

ASSOCIATE JUDGES.

Thomas Chipman, Salisbury	1751	2
John Williams, Sharon	1751	3
Samuel Canfield, New Milford	1751	4
Ebenezer Marsh, Litchfield	1751	21
Joseph Bird, Salisbury	1753	1
Noah Hinman, Woodbury	1754	5
Elisha Sheldon, Litchfield	1754	7
Increase Moseley, Woodbury	1755	25
Roger Sherman, New Milford	1759	3
Daniel Sherman, Woodbury	1761	25
Bushnell Bostwick, New Milford	1762	14
Joshua Porter, Salisbury	1772	19
Samuel Canfield, New Milford	1777	13
Jedediah Strong, Litchfield	1780	11
Heman Swift, Cornwall	1786	16
Aaron Austin, New Hartford	1790	18
Nathan Hale, Caanan	1791	18
David Smith, Plymouth	1791	23
D. N. Brinsmade, Washington	1804	16
Judson Canfield, Sharon	1808	7
Birdsey Norton, Goshen	1809	3
Augustus Pettibone, Norfolk	1812	4
Uriel Holmes, Litchfield	1814	3
Moses Lyman, Jr., Goshen	1815	2
Oliver Burnham, Cornwall	1816	2
Cyrus Swan, Sharon	1817	2
Martin Strong, Salisbury	1817	12
John Welch, Litchfield	1819	10
William M. Burrall, Canaan	1829	7
Morris Woodruff, Litchfield	1829	10
Hugh P. Welch, Litchfield	1836	3

United States Senators elected from Litchfield county.

	First chosen.	No. years.
Uriah Tracy, Litchfield	1796	11
Elijah Boardman, New Milford	1821	died in office.
Perry Smith, New Milford	1836	6
Truman Smith, Litchfield	1849	5

Members of Congress elected from Litchfield County.

Uriah Tracy, Litchfield	1793	3
Nathaniel Smith, Woodbury	1795	4
John Allen, Litchfield	1797	2
John Cotton Smith, Sharon	1800	6
Benjamin Tallmadge, Litchfield	1801	16
Uriel Holmes, Litchfield	1817	1
Ansel Sterling, Sharon	1821	4
Orange Morwin, New Milford	1825	4
Jabez W. Huntington, Litchfield	1829	5
Phineas Miner, Litchfield	1834	1
Lancelot Phelps, Colebrook	1835	4
Truman Smith, Litchfield	1839	8
Origen S. Seymour, Litchfield	1851	4
William W. Welch, Norfolk	1855	2

Members of the Council.

Elisha Sheldon, Litchfield	1761	18
Oliver Wolcott, Litchfield	1771	15
Andrew Adams, Litchfield	1781	9
Jedediah Strong, Litchfield	1789	1
Heman Swift, Cornwall	1790	12
Tapping Reeve, Litchfield	1792	1
Aaron Austin, New Hartford	1794	24
Nathaniel Smith, Woodbury	1799	6
John Allen, Litchfield	1800	6
John Cotton Smith, Sharon	1809	1
Judson Canfield, Sharon	1809	6
Frederick Wolcott, Litchfield	1810	9
Noah B. Benedict, Woodbury	1816	2
Elijah Boardman, New Milford	1817	1

Senators

FOR LITCHFIELD COUNTY—ELECTED BY GENERAL TICKET.

[Under the Constitution of 1818, Senators are elected in place of Members of the Council, or Assistants.]

	Chosen.	No. years.
Frederick Wolcott, Litchfield	1819	4
Elijah Boardman, New Milford	1819	2
Orange Merwin, New Milford	1824	4
Seth P. Beers, Litchfield	1824	1
John Welch,[1] Litchfield	1825	3
Samuel Church, Salisbury	1825	3
Homer Boardman, New Milford	1828	2

UNDER THE DISTRICT SYSTEM.

[Fifteenth District.]

Phineas Miner, Litchfield	1830	2
William G. Williams, N. Hartford	1832	2
Theron Rockwell, Colebrook	1834	2
James Beebe, Winchester	1836	2
Andrew Abernethy, Harwinton	1838	2
Lambert Hitchcock, Barkhamsted	1840	2
Martin Webster, Torrington	1842	1
Israel Coe, Torrington	1843	1
Abijah Catlin, Harwinton	1844	1
William Beebe, Litchfield	1845	1
Lucius Clarke, Winchester	1846	1
Gideon Hall, Jr., Winchester	1847	1
Roger H. Mills, New Hartford	1848	1
Francis Bacon, Litchfield	1849	1
Samuel W. Coe, Winchester	1850	1
Charles Adams, Litchfield	1851	1
Warren Phelps, Colebrook	1852	1
Elliot Beardsley, Winchester	1853	1
John Boyd, Winchester	1854	1
Charles O. Belden, Litchfield	1855	1
Gideon H. Hollister, Litchfield	1856	1
George D. Wadhams, Torrington	1857	1
Reuben Rockwell, Colebrook	1858	1
Sheldon Osborne, Harwinton	1859	1

County Officers.

HIGH SHERIFFS.

	First chosen.	No. years.
Oliver Wolcott	1751	21
Lynde Lord	1772	29
John R. Landon	1701	18
Moses Seymour, Jr.,	1819	6
Ozias Seymour	1825	9
Albert Sedgwick	1834	1
Charles A. Judson	1835	3
Albert Sedgwick	1838	16
Leverett W. Wessells	1854	in office.

COUNTY TREASURERS.

John Catlin,	Litchfield,	1751	10
Elisha Sheldon	"	1761	18
Reuben Smith	"	1779	22
Julius Deming	"	1801	13
Abel Catlin	"	1814	28
Charles L. Webb	"	1842	in office.

COUNTY CLERKS.

Isaac Baldwin	1751	42
Frederick Wolcott	1793	43
Origen S. Seymour	1836	8
Gideon H. Hollister	1844	2
Origen S. Seymour	1846	1
Gideon H. Hollister	1847	3
Elisha Johnson	1850	1
Frederick D. Beeman	1851	in office.

NOTARIES PUBLIC.

[Appointed by the Governor for two years.]

Uriah Tracy
Frederick Wolcott
Seth P. Beers
David C. Sanford
Nathan Cooley
George C. Woodruff
O. S. Seymour
J. K. Averill
G. H. Hollister
Francis Bacon
George W. Beers
P. K. Kilbourn
Samuel P. Bolles
Jacob Kilbourn
E. L. Houghton
Francis E. Harrison.

Borough of Litchfield.

[Incorporated in 1818.]

PRESIDENTS.

	First chosen.	No. years.
Frederick Wolcott	1818	2
Uriel Holmes	1820	4
William Buel	1824	14
Phineas Miner	1838	1
Joseph Adams	1839	3
Josiah G. Beckwith	1842	11
Garwood Sanford	1853	1
Henry B. Graves	1854	2
P. K. Kilbourn	1856	1
Frederick D. Beeman	1857	1
John H. Hubbard	1858	1

TREASURERS.

	First chosen.	No. years.
William Buel	1818	6
Phineas Miner	1824	14
Josiah G. Beckwith	1838	4
Abel Catlin	1842	4
Charles L. Webb	1846	7
Chauncey M. Hooker	1853	3
Henry Ward	1856	1
Edward W. Seymour	1857	2

CLERKS.

	First chosen.	No. years.
Joseph Adams	1818	5
Seth P. Beers	1823	1
Joseph Adams	1824	14
Sylvester Galpin	1838	4
Stephen Trowbridge	1842	4
P. K. Kilbourn	1846	7
Albert Stoddard	1853	1
P. K. Kilbourn	1854	2
Henry W. Buel	1856	1
David E. Bostwick	1857	2

[Borough Officers—Continued.]

BAILIFFS.

[In the order of their election.]

Abel Catlin
Asa Bacon
Seth P. Beers, (declined.)
Samuel Buel
Ezekiel Lewis
Oliver Goodwin
Stephen Deming
Samuel P. Bolles
Leonard Goodwin
David C. Sanford, (declin'd)
Frederick Deming
Jonathan Carrington
William Deming
Ebenezer W. Bolles
Erastus A. Lord
James C. Wadsworth
Sylvester Galpin
David C. Bulkley
William R. Buel
William Lord
Augustus P. Hinman
A. S. Lewis
Wm. H. Crossman
Edward P. Cheney
George H. Baldwin
Wm. F. Baldwin

Town Officers.

TREASURERS.

	Chosen.	No. years.
John Bird	1721	15
Joseph Bird	1736	2
John Buel	1738	13
William Marsh	1751	4
Supply Strong	1755	8
Joshua Garrett	1763	5
Reuben Smith	1768	2
Abraham Bradley	1770	6
William Stanton	1776	resigned.
Samuel Lyman	1776	1
Reuben Smith	1777	6
Abraham Bradley	1783	4
Moses Seymour	1787	2
Ebenezer Marsh	1789	1
Timothy Skinner	1790	2
Abraham Bradley	1792	2
Benjamin Tallmadge	1794	7
Ebenezer Marsh	1801	2
James Gould	1803	8
Samuel Buel	1811	25
Isaac Lawrence	1836	5
William F. Baldwin	1841	3

George Dewey	1844	1
George C. Woodruff	1845	1
Francis Bacon	1846	1
George C. Woodruff	1847	4
Frederick D. Beeman	1851	3
Stephen Trowbridge	1854	1
Lemuel O. Meafoy	1855	1
William F. Baldwin	1856	in office.

CLERKS.

John Marsh	1721	9
John Bird	1730	5
Joseph Bird	1735	1
John Bird	1736	2
Joshua Garrett	1738	4
Isaac Baldwin	1742	31
Jedediah Strong	1773	16
Moses Seymour	1789	37
Elihu Harrison	1826	10
Samuel P. Bolles	1836	4
Sylvester Galpin	1840	1
Samuel P. Bolles	1841	13
Charles O. Belden	1854	1
George A. Hickox	1855	3
George H. Baldwin	1858	in office.

SELECTMEN.

Chosen.	
1737	Allen, Daniel 1
1735	Baldwin, David 2
1782	Baldwin, Isaac 2
1758	Barns, Abel 2
1846	Beach, Heman 1
1777	Beach, Miles 1
1748	Beach, Samuel 1
1778	Beebe, Bezaleel 3
1825	Beebe. William 4
1847	Beckwith, Josiah G. 6
1841	Benton, David 2
1826	Bird, John 2
1727	Bird, Joseph 9
1770	Bird, Seth 4
1811	Birge, James 10
1745	Birge, Joseph 1
1817	Birge, Joseph 1?
1751	Bissell, Isaac 2

Ceosen.	
1843	Bissell, William 2
1853	Blakeslee, Fred'k M. 3
1832	Bolles, Samuel P. 1
1803	Bradley, Aaron 9
1773	Bradley, Abraham 13
1777	Buel, Archelus 1
1846	Buel, Frederick 1
1833	Buel, George M. 2
1726	Buel, John 12
1811	Buel, Jonathan 5
1802	Buel, Norman 6
1746	Buel, Peter 4
1756	Buel, Solomon 3
1744	Catlin, John 5
1821	Catlin, Levi 5
1748	Catlin, Thomas 2
1838	Coe, William 2
1763	Collins, Timothy 2

1815 Clark, Peck 1
1758 Culver, Nathaniel 1
1731 Culver, Samuel 5
1841 Curtis, Eli 3
1791 Deming, Julius 1
1827 Deming, Stephen 1
1836 Dewey, George 2
1757 Farnham, John 2
1851 Frisbie, Henry 3
1834 Frisbie, Levi 2
1844 Garnsey, Edward 3
1833 Garnsey, John 3
1790 Garnsey, Noah? 4
1737 Garrett, Joshua 11
1736 Gay, John 2
1754 Gibbs, Benjamin 2
1841 Gilbert, Truman 6
1738 Gillett, Joseph 3
1747 Goodwin, Abraham 3
1795 Goodwin, Nathaniel 9
1846 Goslee, Henry R. 1
1757 Grant, Josiah 1
1825 Griswold, Benjamin 2
1725 Griswold, Jacob 9
1822 Griswold, Julius 4
1839 Griswold, Henry S. 2
1827 Guild, Gad 1
1810 Hall, Ephraim S., 7
1784 Harrison, Elihu 2
1828 Harrison, Roswell 2
1746 Harrison, Thomas 3
1830 Harrison, William 4
1854 Heaton, Levi 1
1830 Hopkins, Asa 1
1845 Jones, Charles 1
1847 Kenney, Murray 1
1746 Kilbourn, Abraham 7
1792 Kilbourn, David 3
1746 Kilbourn, James 3
1782 Kilbourn, Jesse 2
1722 Kilbourn, Joseph 1
1740 Kilbourn, Joseph, Jr. 3
1840 Kilbourn, Norman 1
1832 Kilbourn, Putnam 3
1799 Kirby, Ephraim 4
1836 Landon, Abner 10
1753 Landon, Daniel 4
1798 Landon, John 1
1785 Landon, Seth 2
1792 Lewis, Ozias 5
1817 Lewis, Ozias, Jr. 9
1854 Lewis, A. S. 1
1768 Lord, Lynde 2
1816 Lord, Phineas 6
1857 Marsh, Andrew W. 1
1821 Marsh. David 1
1740 Marsh, Ebenezer 13
1799 Marsh, James, 2d 7
1721 Marsh, John 5
1755 Marsh, John 10
1785 Marsh, Roger 2
1747 Marsh, William 5
1737 Mason, Joseph 3
1761 Mason, Joseph, Jr. 1
1762 Marvin, Reynold 2
1756 McNiel, Archibald 8
1779 McNiel, Archibald, Jr. 3
1819 Merwin, Samuel A. 2
1858 Minor, Garry H. 1
1847 Morse, Jacob 1
1857 Morse, Jacob, Jr. 2
1817 Moss, Philo 5
1846 Moss, Stephen 1
1786 Murray, Philemon 1
1831 Newton, Isaac 5
1846 Newton, William 3
1770 Osborn, John 4
1838 Oviatt, John A. 3
1845 Parkhurst, Prentice 1
1843 Peck, Sidney 2
1833 Pickett, Rufus 2
1836 Pierpont, Edward 2
1738 Phelps, Edward 7
1754 Plumb, Ezra 5
1769 Prindle, Mark 2
1815 Russell, Stephen 7
1780 Sanford, Jonah 2
1743 Sanford, Joseph 3
1817 Sanford, Simeon 7
1801 Sanford, Stephen, 2d 1
1835 Sedgwick, Albert 1
1825 Seymour, Charles 1
1797 Seymour, Samuel 6
1754 Sheldon, Elisha 3

1805 Sherman, Peter 7
1784 Skinner, Timothy 1
1803 Smith, Aaron 8
1855 Smith, Abraham C. 4
1857 Smith, Anson C. 2
1852 Smith, George A. 2
1776 Smith, Reuben 1
1778 Stoddard, Bryant 2
1857 Stoddard, Daniel B. 2
1820 Stoddard, Enos 4
1783 Stoddard, James 1
1780 Stoddard John 1
1743 Stoddard, Moses 2
1784 Stone, Heber 8
1851 Stone, Willis 2
1820 Woodruff, Morris 2
1770 Strong, Jedediah 13
1744 Strong, Supply 4
1754 Taylor, Ebenezer 3
1838 Tuttle, Isaac 1
1832 Tuttle, William 3
1737 Walker, Josiah 1
1738 Webster, Benjamin 5
1846 Webster, Lyman 1
1822 Webster, Reuben 2
1769 Welch, David 9
1799 Welch, John 4
1833 Wells, Tomlinson 5
1828 Wessells, Ashbel 3
1818 Westover, David 2
1840 Whiting, Jason 1
1787 Whittlesey, Roger N. 7
1761 Wolcott, Oliver 7
1760 Woodruff, Jacob 5
1843 Woodruff, Reuben M. 2
1849 Woodward, Sherman P. 3
1836 Wright, Samuel 2

FIRST CONSTABLES AND COLLECTORS.

	Chosen.	No. years.
Jacob Woodruff	1756	4
Asa Hopkins	1760	5
Nathaniel Goodwin	1765	5
Uriah Catlin	1770	1
Jonathan Mason	1771	1
John Marsh, 3d,	1772	2
David Stoddard	1774	1
William Stanton	1775	1
David Stoddard	1776	1
Timothy Skinner	1777	1
Asahel Strong	1778	4
Timothy Skinner	1782	1
Heber Stone	1783	1
Roger Newton Whittlesey	1784	1
Nathaniel Smith, 2d	1785	1
David Stoddard	1786	1
Samuel Seymour	1787	1
John Phelps	1788	1
Ozias Lewis	1789	2
Samuel Seymour	1791	2
James Stone	1793	1
Nathaniel Smith, 2d	1794	2
James Stone	1796	3
Ozias Seymour	1799	2
Dan Harrison	1801	1

Ozias Lewis, Jr.	1802	1
Joseph Adams	1803	2
Reuben Webster	1805	1
Dan Harrison	1806	2
James Stone	1808	3
Jacob Kilbourn	1811	3
Samuel Wright	1814	2
Charles Buel	1816	6
Eliada Peck	1822	1
Charles Buel	1823	5
Jacob Kilbourn	1828	4
Albert Sedgwick	1832	2
Seth Catlin	1834	2
Alanson Hall	1836	1
Augustus Morey	1837	1
Benjamin Kilbourn	1838	3
William Lord	1841	2
Leverett W. Wessells	1843	1
William F. Baldwin	1844	2
Leverett W. Wessells	1846	1
William F. Baldwin	1847	5

[This joint office was abolished in 1852. A. S. Lewis, Esq., has since held the office of Collector.]

CONSTABLES.

Chosen.		Chosen.	
1788	Adams, Andrew, Jr. 2	1347	Brooker, Samuel, Jr 2
1803	Adams, Joseph 6	1853	Candee, John B. 2
1754	Baldwin, Abner 9	1776	Catlin, Alexander 1
1844	Baldwin, William F. 7	1784	Catlin, David 3
1805	Barnard, Brainard 1	1749	Catlin, John 5
1838	Beach, Heman 1	1827	Catlin, Seth 10
1855	Birge, Chester G. 1	1770	Catlin, Uriah 2
1798	Birge, Joseph 4	1828	Carter, Lyman 7
1802	Bishop, Amos 3	1836	Chadwick, Abiather 2
1820	Benton, David 2	1854	Cheney, Edward P. 1
1839	Birge, Albert H. 2	1846	Churchill, Daniel C. 1
1840	Bissell, Henry B. 1	1802	Clark, Daniel 1
1738	Bissell, Isaac, Jr. 5	1844	Clark, Job 1
1837	Blakeslee, Asa 1	1795	Collins James 1
1816	Buel, Charles 14	1852	Crossman, William H. 7
1838	Buel, Charles S. 5	1726	Culver, Samuel 1
1767	Bradley, Abraham 3	1790	Emons, Phineas 7
1856	Bradley, George 3	1846	Ensign, William M. 1
1852	Burgess, William L. 3	1847	Ford, Royal A. 1

1846 Frisbie, Frederick 1
1806 Frisbie, Levi 3
1839 Garnsey, Elijah M, 2
1853 Garnsey, George 2
1819 Garnsey, John 2
1784 Garnsey, N. 5
1805 Garnsey, Samuel 2
1733 Garrett, Joshua 6
1789 Garrett, Joshua 3
1738 Gay, John 5
1728 Gibbs, Benjamin 1
1852 Gilbert, William H. 1
1721 Goodrich, William 1
1742 Goodwin, Abraham 2
1759 Goodwin, Nathaniel 14
1792 Goodwin, Nathaniel 3
1777 Goodwin, Solomon 2
1832 Goslee, Chester C. 4
1855 Goslee, Thomas C. 2
1755 Grant, Jehiel 2
1782 Grant, Jesse 1
1722 Griswold, Jacob 1
1853 Griswold, Lucius 1
1830 Hall, Alanson 8
1835 Hall, Salmon C. 1
1795 Harrison, Dan 14
1847 Harrison, Rollin H. 3
1838 Harrison, Simeon G. 1
1746 Hopkins, Asa 14
1807 Hopkins, Asa 1
1757 Hosford, Benjamin 1
1755 Hosford, David 1
1812 Humaston, Sherman
1839 Judd, Jesse L. 2
1838 Kilbourn, Benjamin 3
1808 Kilbourn, Jacob 23
1857 Kilbourn, Homer 2
1857 Lake, Peter 1
1770 Landon, Daniel, jr. 4
1744 Landon, James 5
1836 Landon, Sherman 3
1790 Lewis, Ozias 2
1841 Lord, William 2
1737 Marsh, George 1
1795 Marsh, James 5
1773 Marsh, Ebenezer 2
1818 Marsh, Jared 1
1772 Marsh, John 5?
1849 Marsh, John 2
1829 Marsh, Kirby 7
1771 Marsh, Solomon 1
1826 Marsh, Tracy 1
1841 McNiel, Charles 2
1725 Mason, Joseph 1
1769 Mason, Jonathan 6
1736 Mather, Timothy 1
1849 Merwin, Frederick S. 3
1841 Merwin, Samuel A. 5
1836 Morey, Augustus 3
1850 Morse, Jacob Jr. 4
1777 Morse, Levi 5
1857 Munger, George 2
1817 Northrop, Abner 7
1835 Norton, William 1
1724 Orton, Samuel 1
1805 Page, David, Jr. 1
1841 Parkhurst, Prentice 1
1820 Peck, Eliada 10
1844 Peck, Edward O. 6
1852 Peck, George 1
1853 Peck, Joseph C. 5
1841 Pickett, Rufus 1
1849 Pierpont, Andrew J. 3
1842 Pierpont, George 3
1842 Pierpont, George B. 3
1782 Phelps, John 12
1846 Pratt, Henry M. 1
1805 Ray, David 6
1854 Richards, Henry B. 1
1817 Russell, Emanuel 3
1794 Sanford, Stephen 2d, 9
1830 Sedgwick, Albert 4
1853 Sedgwick, Buel 1
1799 Seymour, Ozias 9
1785 Seymour, Samuel 5
1777 Skinner, Timothy 4
1787 Smith, Eli 2
1809 Smith, George 2
1724 Smith, Nathaniel 1
1781 Smith, Nathaniel 2d, 12
1845 Smith, Rufus 3
1775 Stanton, William 1
1773 Stoddard, Briant 5
1774 Stoddard, David 8
1838 Stoddard, Daniel B. 2
1850 Stoddard, Homer 2

1787 Stoddard, James 5
1782 Stone, Heber 4
1793 Stone, James 10
1779 Stone, Reuben 2
1847 Stone, Lewis 1
1778 Strong, Asahel 5
1857 Taylor, Isaac 2
1837 Taylor, Phineas 1
1780 Tracy, Uriah 1
1830 Turner, David P. 1
1723 Walker, Josiah 1
1731 Webster, Benjamin 2
1838 Webster, Lyman 1
1805 Webster, Reuben 1
1842 Wadhams, Charles D. 8
1788 Welch, John 5
1779 Whittlesey, Roger N. 8
1839 Whittlesey, William H. 2
1842 Wessells, Leverett W. 2
1846 Wetmore, John, Jr. 1
1820 Wilmot, Eli 1
1844 Woodruff, Edward 4
1816 Woodruff, Enoch J. 5
1750 Woodruff, Jacob 7
1813 Woodruff, James 3
1830 Woodruff, Nathaniel 1
1825 Woodward, Henry B. 1
1808 Woodward, Reuben S. 4
1851 Wright, Everett H. 1
1811 Wright, Samuel 13
1796 Wright, Jonathan, 2d, 2

LISTERS, OR RATE-MAKERS.

]From 1721 to 1819. At the latter date, Assessors were substituted—the duties of the two offices being much the same.]

Chosen.
1771 Adams, Andrew 2
1811 Adams, Elijah 1
1802 Adams, Joseph 12
1789 Allen, John 2
1722 Allen, Nehemiah 1
1794 Ames, Cheney 1
1791 Baldwin, Horace 1
1742 Baldwin, Isaac 31
1780 Baldwin, Isaac, Jr, 5
1810 Baldwin, Isaac, 2d 1
1736 Baldwin, John 1
1776 Baldwin, Phineas 6
1784 Baldwin, William 3
1735 Baldwin, Nathaniel 1
1768 Barnard, Samuel 2
1750 Barns, Abel 3
1783 Barns, Amos 4
1775 Barns, Moses 1
1782 Barns, Timothy 1
1779 Beach, Miles 1

Chosen.
1775 Beach, Laban 1
1764 Beach, Zophar 2
1818 Beebe, William 1
1778 Benton, Ebenezer 2
1808 Benton, Ebenezer, Jr, 1
1807 Bolles, Ebenezer
1818 Birge, Albert 1
1758 Birge, Benjamin 1
1793 Birge, James 4
1723 Bird, John 6
1775 Bird, Seth 2
1762 Bidwell, Stephen 1
1803 Bishop, Amos 2
1805 Bishop, Calvin 1
1782 Bishop, Luman 2
1771 Bishop, Sylvanus 3
1736 Bissell, Isaac, Jr. 9
1810 Bissell, John 1
1796 Bradley, Aaron 2
1776 Bradley, Abraham 9

1804 Bradley, Comfort 2
1817 Bradley, Lemuel 2
1781 Bradley, Phineas 1
1786 Bradley, Zina 2
1774 Buel, Archelus 1
1801 Buel, Charles 8
1799 Buel, Jonathan 4
1789 Buel, Norman 7
1775 Buel, Peter 2
1806 Buel, Samuel 7
1763 Buel, Solomon 2
1777 Burgess, James, Jr. 1
1787 Camp, Abel, Jr. 2
1782 Catlin, Alexander 1
1789 Catlin, Bradley 2
1783 Catlin, David 1
1801 Catlin, Horace 1
1752 Catlin, John 3
1763 Catlin, Thomas 4
1794 Catlin, Thomas, Jr. 3
1791 Chase, Lot 8
1817 Chase, Philo 3
1766 Clark, Elisha 1
1812 Clark, Peck 1
1812 Coe, Levi 1
1806 Clemons, Abel 1
1760 Clemons, John, Jr. 3
1761 Collins, John I
1766 Collins, Timothy 1
1757 Collins, Oliver 1
1796 Collins, William 2
1774 Comstock, Calvin 11
1755 Culver, Nathaniel 3
1723 Culver, Samuel 1
1787 Deming, Julius 2
1814 Deming, Frederick 1
1806 Dennison, Chauncey 1
1817 Dewey, George 1
1779 Dickinson, Michael 1
1786 Dickinson, Oliver 1
1799 Dutton, Thomas 1
1791 Emons, Arthur, jr. 1
1770 Emons, Arthur 4
1797 Emons, Phineas I
1803 Ensign, Isaac 3
1773 Ensign, Samuel 1
1730 Fairbanks, Jonathan 2
1767 Farnham, Gad 2
1774 Farnham, Nathan, 1
1778 Farnham, Seth, 1
1791 Foot, Timothy, Jr. 3
1804 Frisbie, Jonathan 1
1811 Frisbie, Levi 1
1813 Garnsey, John 2
1781 Garnsey, Noah 2
1767 Garnsey, Nathan 4
1727 Garrett, Joshua 8
1781 Garrett, Joshua, Jr. 2
1818 Garrett, Daniel 1
1817 Galpin, Sylvester 1
1728 Gay, John 2
1759 Gibbs, Benjamin 1
1781 Gibbs, Caleb 1
1779 Gibbs, Lemuel 1
1794 Gibbs, Reuben 1
1819 Gilbert, Abner 1
1799 Gilbert, Calvin 4
1816 Gilbert, James 1
1807 Glazier, John 1
1736 Gillett, Joseph 1
1727 Goodwin, Abraham 2
1753 Goodwin, Nathaniel 16
1812 Goodwin, Oliver 5
1777 Goodwin, Solomon 3
1818 Goodwin, Thomas 1
1803 Goslee, Solomon 3
1801 Gould, James 1
1800 Grannis, Gurdon 2
1812 Grannis, Thomas 1
1796 Grant, Ambrose 1
1785 Grant, Charles 4
1746 Grant, Jehiel 6
1736 Grant, Josiah 1
1761 Grant, Josiah jr. 1
1782 Grant, Jesse 3
1737 Grant, Thomas 8
1814 Green, Samuel 1
1813 Griswold, Benjamin 1
1780 Guitteau, Judson 2
1802 Gunn, Samuel 1
1811 Hall, David 2
1799 Hall, Ephraim S. 3
1806 Hand, S. P. 1
1795 Harrison, Dan 3
1790 Harrison, Elihu 1
1761 Harrison, Ephraim 3

1757 Harrison, Gideon 2
1767 Harrison, Lemuel 4
1811 Harrison, Roswell 2
1744 Harrison, Thomas 2
1801 Harrison. Simeon 3
1742 Hibbard, Reuben 2
1796 Holmes, Uriel 2
1826 Hopkins, Asa 1
1781 Hopkins, Harris 2
1807 Hopkins, William 1
1724 Hosford, Benjamin 2
1752 Hosford, David 3
1778 Hosford, John 1
1803 Humaston, Asaph 1
1780 Humaston, John Jr. 1
1784 Humaston, Noah 2
1816 Humaston, Sherman 2
1818 Humpherville, Lemuel 1
1754 Kilbourn, Abraham 4
1767 Kilbourn, David 8
1802 Kilbourn, Jacob 1
1811 Kilbourn, Jeremiah 1
1781 Kilbourn, Jesse 3
1725 Kilbourn, Joseph 1
1724 Kilbourn, Joseph Jr. 1
1800 Kilbourn, Levi 2
1792 Kilbourn, Orange 4
1743 Landon, Daniel 3
1793 Landon, Daniel 2d, 1
1774 Landon, Seth 7
1811 Landon, Seth Jr. 2
1803 Landon, Zophar 3
1722 Lee, Thomas 1
1808 Lewis, Luke 1
1780 Lewis, Ozias 1
1816 Lewis, Ozias Jr. 1
1770 Linsley, Edward 6
1783 Lord, Daniel 1
1776 Lord, Lynde 1
1811 Marsh, Aaron 1
1728 Marsh, Ebenezer 1
1736 Marsh, George 2
1791 Marsh, James 3
1771 Marsh, John 1
1802 Marsh, Isaac 2
1793 Marsh, Nathaniel 1
1771 Marsh, Roger 2
1789 Marsh, Roger Jr. 1
1788 Marsh, Samuel 3
1763 Marsh, Solomon 2
1805 Marsh, Thomas 1
1745 Mason, John 1
1768 Mason, Jonathan 5
1752 Mason, Joseph 2
1758 McNeile, Alexander 4
1776 McNeile, Archibald, Jr. 2
1779 McNiele, Isaac 4
1799 McNeile, Samuel 2
1809 Merwin, Samuel A. 3
1727 Mitchell, Nathan 1
1748 Moody, Adonijah 2
1756 Morris, James 3
1784 Morris, James Jr. 1
1775 Moss, Amos 1
1790 Moss, David 1
1774 Moss, Levi 3
1814 Moss, Philo 1
1818 Northrop, A. 1
1801 Norton, Miles 10
1798 Osborn, Eliada 1
1788 Osborn, Jacob 3
1785 Osborn, Jeremiah 2
1761 Osborn, John 6
1777 Osborn, John Jr 2
1792 Parker, Joseph 2
1809 Page, David 2
1770 Palmer, Ambrose 4
1784 Parmelee, Amos 2d, 2
1769 Parmelee, Jehiel 4
1762 Parmelee, Thomas 2
1778 Parmelee, Thomas jr. 1
1782 Parsons, Eliphaz 1
1813 Philips, Gideon 1
1780 Phelps, Edward Jr. 1
1787 Phelps, John 1
1797 Phelps, Samuel Jr. 2
1806 Pierpont, James 3
1778 Plumb, E. 2
1804 Plumb, Samuel
1757 Prindle, Mark 1
1796 Ranney, Stephen 1
1814 Ray, David 1
1781 Reeve, Tapping 1
1806 Riley, James 1
1788 Rowe, Daniel 1
1810 Russell, Stephen 3
1810 Sanford, Ebenezer 1
1773 Sanford, Jonah 1
1759 Sanford, Oliver 5
1810 Sanford, Simeon 2

1779 Sanford, Solomon 1
1765 Sanford, Stephen 1
1795 Sanford, Stephen 2d 4
1818 Seymour, Charles 1
1774 Seymour, Moses 6
1800 Seymour, Moses Jr. 2
1803 Seymour, Ozias 2
1781 Sheldon, Samuel 1
1782 Shether, Samuel 1
1798 Skinner, Roger 2
1778 Skinner, Timothy 3
1779 Smedley, Ephraim Jr. 1
1783 Smedley, Gideon 1
1796 Smedley, Nathan 3
1797 Smith, Aaron 3
1767 Smith, Charles 3
1788 Smith, Charles 2
1780 Smith, Eli 2
1805 Smith, Hicks 1
1769 Smith, John 1
1762 Smith, Nathaniel 1
1790 Smith, Nathaniel 2d, 6
1817 Smith, Simeon 2
1807 Smith, Solomon 1
1752 Smith, Stephen 2
1781 Stanley, Frederick 1
1806 Spencer, Samuel W. 2
1768 Stewart, Nathan 2
1795 Stewart, William 1
1809 Stoddard, Briant Jr. 5
1778 Stoddard, Daniel 4
1817 Stoddard, Enos 1
1774 Stoddard, John 1
1785 Stoddard, James 6
1779 Stone, Heber 3
1810 Stone, Noah 2d, 1
1775 Stone, Reuben 3
1799 Stone, Thomas 1
1816 Stone, Solomon 1
1764 Stone, Stephen 3
1773 Strong, Jedediah 6
1726 Strong, Supply 8
1790 Tallmadge, Benjamin 1
1775 Taylor, Zebulon 1
1799 Tomlinson, Noah 1
1782 Tracy, Uriah 6
1809 Trowbridge, Thomas 1
1804 Trumbull, Ezekiel 1
1808 Turner, Isaac 5
1802 Turner, Thomas 1
1813 Wadsworth, Henry 2
1785 Wallace, Richard 2
1792 Waugh, James 2
1790 Waugh, Samuel 4
1746 Webster, Benjamin 7
1814 Webster, Claudius 1
1766 Webster, Timothy 1
1766 Webster, Justus 2
1766 Welch, David 2
1788 Welch, John 3
1808 Wessells, George B. 1
1776 Wetmore, Joseph 1
1785 Whittlesey, Roger N. 2
1805 Wilmot, John 2
1810 Woodruff, Enoch J, 3
1746 Woodruff, Jacob 4
1813 Woodruff, James 2
1807 Woodruff, Morris 2
1728 Woodruff, Nathaniel 1
1804 Woodruff, William 1
1813 Wooster, Henry 1
1792 Wolcott, Frederick 4
1779 Wright, Jonathan 3
1817 Wright, Samuel 1
1758 Vaill, Joseph 3
1807 Vaill, Benjamin 2

*** The offices of Assessor and Board of Relief were created by the Constitution of 1818—at which date the office of Lister terminated. The lists of Selectmen, Constables and Grand Jurors are designed to embrace all who have been chosen, from the organization of the town in 1721 to the present time—with the year of the first election of each, and the number of times each was elected.

ASSESSORS.

1857 Ames, William B. 1
1830 Beebe, William 1
1836 Benton, David 2
1838 Benton, D. L. 2
1819 Birge, James 9
1823 Birge, Joseph 1
1836 Birge, Harvey 2
1845 Booth, Charles 1
1833 Buel, Frederick 5
1823 Buel, Salmon 4
1840 Buel, Samuel 1
1846 Buel, William R. 1
1846 Bunnell, Ephraim K. 3
1841 Burgess, Junius 4
1827 Catlin, Levi 2
1836 Clemons, Abel H 2
1851 Coe, Walter 1
1858 Cooke, George 1
1832 Cooke, Roger 1
1830 Curtis, Eli 7
1857 Curtis, George 2
1845 Emons, Ethiel 1
1836 Ensign, Samuel M. 1
1853 Ford, Royal A. 1
1852 French, Asahel 1
1849 Frisbie, Henry 1
1830 Frisbie, Levi 3
1838 Frisbie, Sherman 3
1858 Fuller, Cyrus S. 1
1855 Garnsey, George 2
1840 Garnsey, John 1
1838 Garnsey, Noah 2
1849 Gibbs, Frederick 2
1827 Gilbert, Aaron C.
1831 Goslee, Chester C. 1
1838 Goslee, Henry R. 3
1851 Griswold, Henry S. 2
1849 Griswold, Lyman 2
1849 Hall, Alanson 2
1819 Hall, Ephraim S. 9
1846 Hall, Norman 1
1839 Hopkins, Edward 1
1851 Hopkins, Wm. L. 1
1852 Hull, Eben 1
1841 Jones, Charles 5
1835 Keeler, Daniel 1
1840 Kenney, Leonard 1
1844 Landon, Sherman 2
1854 Moulthrop, E. P. 1
1829 Marsh, David 5
1835 Merwin, Samuel M 1
1857 Morey, Augustus 2
1849 Morse, Jacob, Jr 1
1847 Moss, Lewis H.
1819 Moss, Philo 7
1841 Newton, Ransom 2
1843 Newton, William 2
1846 Oviatt, John A. 1
1841 Page, Ithamar 3
1841 Peck, Sidney 2
1827 Pickett, Rufus 1
1855 Pierpont, Andrew J. 2
1823 Pierpont, James M. 2
1857 Potter, Garry G. 2
1835 Ray, William 1
1829 Russell, Stephen 1
1819 Seymour, Samuel 9
1834 Skilton, Henry 1
1852 Smedley, Frederick 1
1847 Smith, Anson C. 4
1855 Smith, George A. 2
1833 Smith, Simeon 1
1853 Steele, Henry 1
1843 Stoddard, Daniel B. 1
1847 Stone, Truman 1
1853 Taylor, Uri 1
1843 Tompkins, Lucius 3
1834 Tuttle, William 2
1828 Webster, Reuben 1
1844 Wheeler, Christopher 3
1851 Wheeler, Charles D. 3
1836 Wells, Tomlinson 4
1840 Whittlesey, Frederick 1
1848 Woodward, S. P. 1

BOARD OF RELIEF.

1841 Abernethy, Elisha S. 1
1844 Ames, Rufus 2
1829 Bacon, Asa 1
1839 Baldwin, Nehemiah 2
1838 Barber, Elizur 1
1838 Barnard, Benton 2
1838 Bassett, William 1
1840 Beach, Theron 1
1845 Beckwith, Josiah G. 1
1829 Beebe, William 2
1847 Benton, David 2
1853 Birge, Chester G. 1
1837 Birge, Joseph Jr. 1
1840 Bissell, Nathaniel 1
1851 Bissell, William 2
1834 Bolles, Samuel P. 2
1836 Bostwick, Joel 1
1838 Braman, Samuel G. 2
1844 Brooker, Samuel Jr. 1
1839 Buel, George S. 1
1819 Buel, Jonathan 9
1858 Clarke, Alvah 1
1816 Coe, William 2
1828 Cooke, Roger 1
1836 Curtis, Eli 1
1841 Curtis, Garner B. 5
1842 Dewey, George 1
1854 Ford, Royal A.
1828 Garnsey, John 1
1823 Garrett; Daniel 6
1847 Gibbs, Frederick 2
1853 Gilbert, George 1
1832 Goodwin, Oliver 2
1853 Griswold, Darius P. 1
1846 Griswold, Henry S. 1
1849 Griswold, Lucius 2
1853 Griswold, Lyman S. 1
1841 Guild, Albin 3
1836 Guild, Gad 1
1855 Guild, P. Gould 4
1847 Guild, Jeremiah 2
1841 Hall, Alanson 4
1835 Hall, David 1
1851 Hall, Norman 1
1846 Hand, Hiram J. 4
1831 Harrison, Elihu 1
1846 Hopkins, Edward 1
1844 Hopkins, Wm. L. 1
1837 Jones, Cahrles 1
1842 Kilbourn, Putnam 3
1857 Kilbourn, William P. 2
1847 Landon, Abner 2
1849 Lord, William 1
1819 Marsh, David 11
1840 Marsh, Aaron 1
1837 Merwin, Samuel M. 1
1838 Moss, Stephen 2
1849 Moss, Linus G. 3
1853 Loveland, James L. 1
1845 Newton, William 1
1850 Odell, William 1
1842 Pickett, Alanson J. 1
1849 Pickett, Rufus 2
1845 Page, Ithamar 1
1847 Pierpont, Edward 4
1846 Potter, Miner 1
1828 Russell, Stephen 2
1837 Stoddard, Enos 1
1841 Stoddard, Harmon 1
1828 Sanford, Simeon 4
1835 Skilton, Henry 1
1845 Stone, Truman 1
1849 Stone, Willis 2
1858 Taylor, Phineas 1
1819 Welch, John 9
1855 Wells, Tomlinson 3
1837 Westover, David 3
1854 Whiting, Jason 1
1840 Whittlesey, Jabez 1
1836 Wilmot, Eli 1
1819 Woodruff, Morris 12
1844 Wright, Samuel 1

GRAND JURORS.

1810 Adams, Elijah 2
1802 Adams, Joseph 6
1777 Allen, Cornelius1
1740 Allen, Daniel 1
1727 Allen, Nehemiah 1
1788 Allen, John 1
1858 Alvord, Chauncey H. 1
1837 Ames, Rufus 3
1852 Ames, William B 1
1779 Atwater, Abel 2
1808 Baldwin, Abner 1
1739 Baldwin, David Jr. 4
1782 Baldwin. Isaac Jr. 2
1812 Baldwin, Isaac 1
1826 Baldwin, Harmon 1
1733 Baldwin, Nathaniel 1
1779 Baldwin, Phineas 5
1734 Baldwin, Samuel 1
1780 Baldwin, Stephen 1
1803 Baldwin, James 1
1800 Baldwin, William 1
1807 Bacon, Asa 1
1779 Barnard, Samuel 1
1754 Barns, Abel 1
1772 Barns, Enos 1
1791 Barns, Enos Jr, 1
1743 Barns, Daniel 1
1844 Beach, George 1
1825 Beach, Enos 1
1838 Beach, Isaac C. 1
1778 Beach, Laban 1
1773 Beach, Miles 2
1789 Beard, Lewis 1
1781 Beebe, Bezaleel 1
1735 Beebe, James 1
1807 Beebe, William 2
1836 Benedict, Andrew 4
1820 Benton, Amos 1
1833 Benton, David 5
1772 Benton, Ebenezer 1
1808 Benton, Ebenezer jr .2
1780 Benton, Nathaniel 1
1793 Bidwell, Elijah 1
1778 Bidwell, Stephen 1
1807 Bidwell, Stephen 3
1801 Bishop, Amos 4
1770 Bishop, Noah 2
1833 Bishop, Samuel 4
1776 Bishop, Seth 1
1804 Bishop, Sylvanus 1
1756 Bissell, Isaac 1
1817 Bissell, John 1
1839 Bissell, Harmon 2
1813 Bissell, Nathaniel 2
1855 Bissell, William 1
1786 Birge, James 2
1728 Birge, Joseph 4
1725 Bird, John 1
1723 Bird, Joseph 4
1786 Bird, Seth 1
1851 Blake, Edward W 1
1818 Blakeslee, Isaiah 1
1803 Bolles, Ebenezer 5
1829 Bolles, Eben W. 5
1792 Bradley, Aaron 1
1811 Bradley, Comfort 1
1826 Bradley, Elihu 1
1812 Bradley, Joseph 1
1773 Bradley, Leaming 2
1746 Bradley, Phineas 2
1755 Bradley, Zina 1
1809 Brace, James 2
1770 Buel, Archelus 1
1840 Buel, Andrew 1
1847 Buel, Charles S. 1
1782 Buel, David 1
1799 Buel, Norman 5
1768 Buel, Peter 1
1804 Buel, Salmon 2
1751 Buel, Solomon 2
1837 Bulkley, David C. 2
1788 Bull, Asa 2
1830 Burgess, Ezra 2
1839 Burgess, Junius 2
1838 Bunnell, Ephraim K. 1
1779 Camp, Abel jr. 3
1827 Camp, Ralph G. 2
1799 Catlin, Abel 2d, 2
1853 Catlin, Henry 1
1846 Catlin, John 1
1785 Catlin, Theodore 1

1769 Catlin, Uriah 1
1731 Catlin, John 4
1737 Catlin, Thomas 2
1805 Carter, Samuel 1
1761 Chamberlain, Moses 1
1793 Chase, Lot 1
1813 Clark, Peck 1
1846 Clock, Samuel 1
1831 Coe, Walter 1
1771 Collins, Charles 1
1783 Collins, John 1
1721 Colkins, John 1
1776 Comstock, Calvin 2
1789 Crampton, Elon 1
1757 Culver, Benjamin 2
1753 Culver, Nathaniel 1
1825 Curtis, Eli 2
1852 Curtis, Garner B. 1
1856 Curtis, Levi 1
1800 Dare, George 1
1782 Deming, Julius 1
1831 Dewey, George
1775 Dickinson, Reuben 1
1807 Dodge, Stephen 1
1794 Doolittle, Benjamin 1
1757 Easton, Eliphalet 1
1775 Emons, Arthur 1
1786 Emons, Phineas 2
1781 Emons, Russell 1
1846 Ensign, Charles A. 1
1811 Ensign, Isaac 2
1780 Ensign, Samuel 1
1807 Ensign, Samuel jr. 2
1778 Farnham, Gad 1
1849 Farnham, John 2
1855 Farnham, Leman H. 1
1768 Farnham, Seth 2
1804 Foote, Timothy 1
1858 Fuller, Cyrus S. 1
1783 Galpin, Amos 3
1841 Garnsey, Edward 3
1854 Garnsey, John 1
1771 Garnsey, Noah 1
1830 Garnsey, Noah 3
1822 Garrett, Daniel 1
1748 Garrett, Joshua 2
1788 Garrett, Joshua 2
1726 Gay, John 1
1758 Gibbs, Benjamin 3
1780 Gibbs, Benjamin jr. 1
1832 Gibbs, Birdsey 1
1780 Gibbs, Caleb 2
1844 Gibbs, Frederick 1
1751 Gibbs, Henry 2
1778 Gibbs, Lemuel 1
1805 Gibbs, Medad 1
1799 Gibbs, Moor 1
1796 Gibbs, Noah 1
1835 Gibbs, Willis 3
1771 Gibbs, Zebulon 1
1854 Gibbud, Harris B. 1
1802 Gilbert, Calvin 1
1855 Gilbert, George 1
1808 Gilbert, James 3
1858 Gilbert, William H. 1
1731 Goodwin, Abraham 1
1811 Goodwin, Erastus 1
1806 Goodwin, Medad 1
1801 Gould, James 1
1800 Grannis, G. 2
1804 Grannis, Robert 1
1808 Grannis, Thomas 1
1816 Grant, Charles 1
1752 Grant, Ebenezer 1
1747 Griswold, Elijah 2
1838 Griswold, Henry S. 1
1802 Green, Samuel 1
1724 Griswold, Jacob 1
1820 Griswold, Benjamin 8
1810 Griswold, John 1
1811 Griswold, Julius 2
1847 Griswold, Lucius 1
1809 Grove, Thomas F. 1
1829 Guild, Gad 2
1851 Guild, Jeremiah 4
1842 Hall, Alanson 2
1824 Hall, David 4
1765 Hall, Benjamin 1
1760 Hall, Gilbert 1
1839 Hall, Norman 2
1801 Harrison, Elias 1
1775 Harrison, Elihu 1
1770 Harrison, Ephraim 1
1760 Harrison, Gideon 1
1743 Hibbard, Reuben 1
1801 Hinsdale, Elias 1
1799 Holmes, Uriel 1
1822 Hopkins, Asa 2
1795 Hopkins, Joseph H 3
1820 Hopkins, Orange 1

1813 Horton, Elisha 2
1730 Hosford, Benjamin 1
1759 Hosford, David 2
1810 Hoyt, Levi 1
1823 Hubbard, Jacob 2
1847 Hull, Eben 2
1849 Humaston, A. P. 2
1849 Humaston, Noah 1
1819 Humphreville, Albro M. 1
1847 Humphreville, L. 1
1811 Huntington, Daniel 1
1842 Johnson, Horace 3
1833 Jones, Charles 1
1780 Judd, Jesse 1
1761 Kilbourn, Abraham 1
1781 Kilbourn, David 3
1753 Kilbourn, Elisha 1
1789 Kilbourn, Jacob 4
1801 Kilbourn, James 1
1799 Kilbourn, Jeremiah 1
1773 Kilbourn, Jesse 2
1730 Kilbourn, Joseph 2
1742 Kilbourn, James 1
1798 Kilbourn, Levi 2
1793 Kilbourn, Lewis 1
1827 Kilbourn, Norman 4
1830 Kilbourn, Putnam 3
1825 Keeler, Daniel 1
1780 King, David 1
1779 Kirby, Ephraim 2
1809 Lamson, Daniel 7
1844 Landon, Abner 1
1746 Landon, Daniel 4
1776 Landon, Daniel jr. 1
1765 Landon, David 1
1737 Landon, James 1
1785 Landon, Nathan 3
1778 Landon, Seth 3
1803 Landon, Seth jr, 2
1831 Landon, Sherman 1
1804 Law, Benedict A. 1
1846 Law, Willis 1
1727 Lee, Thomas 1
1798 Lewis, Daniel W. 1
1808 Lewis, Luke 2
1773 Lewis, Ozias 4
1815 Lewis, Ozias jr. 4
1755 Linsley, Abel 1
1775 Linsley, Edward 1
1757 Linsley, Joseph 3
1854 Lord, William 1
1817 Loveland, Clark 1
1856 Loveland, James L. 1
1844 Loveland, Lewis 1
1840 Loveland, Nathaniel G. 1
1813 Mansfield, John 1
1804 Marsh, Elisha 1
1770 Marsh, Ebenezer 1
1798 Marsh, James 4
1747 Marsh, John 3
1771 Marsh, John 1
1801 Marsh, Jonathan 1
1802 Marsh, Isaac 1
1805 Marsh, Ozias 1
1790 Marsh, Roger jr. 1
1848 Mar3h, Linus 5
1849 Marsh, Solomon 2d, 2
1804 Marsh, Thomas 1
1735 Marsh, William 4
1751 McNeile, Alexander 4
1842 Mase, Solomon 1
1796 Mason, Elisha 2
1745 Mason, Joseph 1
1756 Mason, Joseph jr. 1
1844 Meafoy, Lemuel O. 1
1837 Merriman, Reuben 1
1844 Merwin, Samuel A. 1
1823 Merwin, Samuel M. 3
1834 Morey, Augustus 1
1886 Morris, Arvil 1
1774 Moss, Amos 2
1836 Moss, Jacob 1
1840 Moss, James H. 1
1786 Moss, John 1
1783 Moss, Levi 1
1856 Newbury, Joseph A. 3
1810 Norton, Ambrose 1
1802 Norton, Miles 5
1815 Moulthrop, William 1
1725 Norton, Samuel 2
1757 Orton, Samuel jr. 1
1738 Osborn, Benjamin 1
1750 Osborn, Benjamin jr. 1
1801 Osborn, Eliada 1
1790 Osborn, Jacob 2
1757 Osborn, John 3
1784 Page, Jonathan 1
1840 Palmer, Christopher C. 1
1793 Parker, Joseph 2
1785 Parmelee, Amos 1

1775 Parmelee, Jehiel 1
1732 Parmelee, Jonathan 1
1774 Peck, Abijan 1
1772 Peck, Benjamin 3
1788 Peck, Elijah 1
1852 Perkins, Charles L. 3
1746 Phelps, Edward 1
1760 Phelps,, Edward jr. 1
1808 Pickett, Ebenezer 2
1820 Pickett, Rufus 4
1725 Pier, Thomas 1
1760 Pierce, John 5
1848 Pierpont, Andrew J. 2
1795 Pierpont, James 3
1829 Pierpont, James M. 1
1744 Plumb, Ezra 2
1851 Pond, Seth 1
1787 Potter, Israel 1
1855 Pratt, Francis H. 4
1755 Prindle, Mark 2
1797 Ray, William 1
1776 Riggs, Jeremiah 5
1723 Root, Samuel 1
1744 Rossiter, Jonathan 2
1804 Sanford, Daniel 1
1821 Sanford, David C. 2
1738 Sanford, Joseph 1
1774 Sanford, Jonah 1
1775 Sanford, Moses 1
1827 Sanford, Nathan 2
1773 Sanford, Oliver 1
1793 Sanford, Stephen 2d, 1
1823 Seymour, Charles 1
1826 Seymour, Origen S. 2
1790 Seymour, Samuel 4
1805 Seymour, Ziba 2
1857 Sharp, Homer 2
1797 Skinner, Roger 2
1775 Skinner, Timothy 2
1756 Smedley, Ephraim 4
1782 Smedley, Gideon 1
1806 Smedley, Nathan 1
1796 Smith, Aaron 1
1762 Smith, Abiel 1
1849 Smith, Anson C. 2
1771 Smith, Charles 1
1784 Smith, Charles jr, 1
1781 Smith, Eli 3
1796 Smith, Jacob jr. 2
1755 Smith, Josiah 1
1845 Smith, Nathan D.
1791 Smith, Nathaniel 2d, 1
1817 Smith, Reuben 1
1821 Smith, Simeon 1
1806 Smith, Solomon 1
1750 Smith, Stephen 4
1798 Spencer, Samuel W. 1
1758 Stanley, Timothy jr. 1
1856 Stephens, Seymour 1
1786 Stewart, Nathan 2
1791 Stoddard, Briant 2
1816 Stoddard, Briant jr. 1
1803 Stoddard, Daniel 1
1833 Stoddard, Daniel B. 1
1806 Stoddard, Gideon 1
1826 Stoddard, Harmou 1
1853 Stoddard, Homer 3
1798 Stoddard, James 1
1732 Stoddard, Moses 2
1783 Stoddard, Moses 2
1823 Stone, Alvah 4
1806 Stone, James 2
1817 Stone, John 1
1829 Stone, Leman 1
1770 Stone, Noah 1
1776 Stonc, Reuben 1
1816 Stone, Solomon 1
1761 Stone, Stephen 2
1795 Stone, Thomas 3
1836 Stone, Willis 1
1771 Strong, Asahel 1
1749 Strong, Josiah 2
1727 Strong, Supply 2
1736 Sutliff, John 1
1761 Taylor, Ebenezer 1
1836 Taylor, Phineas 1
1755 Taylor, Zebulon 1
1781 Thomas, Joseph 1
1833 Trowbridge, Stephen 3
1803 Trowbridge, Thomas 3
1806 Todd, Ebenezer 1
1797 Todd, Eli 1
1803 Tuttle, Nathan 1
1815 Turner, Jacob 1
1837 Turner, Lucius S. 1
1780 Turner, Titus 1
1771 Tryon, John 1
1804 Vaill, Benjamin 1
1752 Vaill, Joseph 2
1835 Warner, A. W. 1

1821 Warren, Horace 1
1756 Warner, Reuben 2
1800 Ward, William 1
1791 Washburn, William 3
1807 Waugh, James 1
1754 Waugh, Robert 2
1801 Waugh, Samuel 3
1787 Wadsworth, Elijah 1
1728 Walker, Josiah 1
1734 Webster, Benjamin 2
1777 Webster, Benjamin 1
1807 Webster, Claudius 1
1839 Webster, Lyman 1
18ñ4 Webster, Reuben 1
1763 Wlch, David 2
1819 Welch, Garry P. 1
1837 Wetmore, Elihu 2
1782 Wetmore, Joseph 1
1835 Whittlesey, Frederick 1
1839 Whittlesey, Jabez 1
1777 Whittlesey, Roger N. 5
1857 Wheeler, Charles D. 1
1847 Williams, Robert 2
1808 Wilmot, Eli 1
1787 Woodcock, Samuel 3
1851 Woodruff, Edward 4
1816 Woodruff, Enoch J. 3
1828 Woodruff, George C. 3
1794 Woodruff, James, 1
1753 Woodruff, Benjamin 1
1763 Woodruff, Charles 2
1812 Webster, Truman 2
1758 Woodruff, Nathaniel 1
1808 Wooster, Lemuel 1
1791 Wright, Jonathan 2d 3
1767 Wessells, Lawrence 4

Prosecuting Attornies
FOR THE COUNTY OF LITCHFIELD

[KING'S ATTORNIES.]

Samuel Pettibone, Goshen.
J. Whitney, Canaan.
Reynold Marvin, Litchfield.
Andrew Adams, Litchfield.

[STATE'S ATTORNIES.]

Andrew Adams, Litchfield.
Tapping Reeve, Litchfield.
John Canfield, Sharon.
John Allen, Litchfield.
Uriah Tracy, Litchfield.
Daniel W. Lewis, Litchfield.
Uriel Holmes, Jr., Litchfield.
Elisha Sterling, Salisbury.
Seth P. Beers, Litchfield.
Samuel Church, Salisbury (and Litchfield.)
Leman Church, Canaan.
David C. Sanford, N. Milford (and Litchfield.)
John H. Hubbard, Salisbury (and Litchfield.)
Julius B. Harrison, New Milford.
Gideon Hall, Winchester.
Charles F. Sedgwick, Sharon, (now in office.)

Corporations in Litchfield.

PHŒNIX BRANCH BANK.

[Incorporated in 1814.]

PRESIDENTS.

Benjamin Tallmadge	1814	12
James Gould	1826	7
Asa Bacon	1833	14
Theron Beach	1846	6
George C. Woodruff	1852	—

CASHIERS.

James Butler	1814	7
Austin Kilbourn	1821	5
Henry A. Perkins	1826	2
Charles Spencer	1828	10
Theron Beach	1838	1
Gustavus F. Davis	1839	12
Henry R. Coit	1851	—

DIRECTORS.

[From 1814 to 1859—in the order of their election.]

Benjamin Tallmadge
Frederick Wolcott
Aaron Smith
James Gould
Henry Wadsworth
Elisha Sterling
Solomon Rockwell
Morris Woodruff
Samuel Buel
Seth P. Beers
Joseph Battell
Ithamer Canfield
William Buel
Jabez W. Huntington
David Foot
Erastus Hodges
Charles L. Webb
David S. Boardman
Erastus Lyman
Daniel Bacon
Ozias Seymour
Asa Bacon
David C. Sanford
Origen S. Seymour
Samuel P. Bolles
Seth Thomas
Theron Beach
Elihu Harrison
John C. Coffing
Charles Deming
George C. Woodruff
William C. Sterling
E. Champion Bacon
Benjamin Deforest
Oliver Goodwin
Gustavus F. Davis
Lemuel Hurlbut
John Deforest
David C. Whittlesey
Jason Whiting
Gideon H. Hollister
William H. Thompson
Samuel Church
Henry W. Buel
Edward W. Seymour
David L. Parmelee
Abraham C. Smith

LITCHFIELD SAVINGS BANK.

[Incorprated in 1850.]

PRESIDENTS.

George C. Woodruff	1850	3
Josiah G. Beckwith	1853	3
Edwin B. Webster	1856	—

VICE PRESIDENTS.

Samuel P. Bolles	1850	1
Josiah G. Beckwith	1851	2
Samuel P. Bolles	1853	3
Stephen Trowbridge	1856	2
Jason Whiting	1858	—

SECRETARIES AND TREASURERS.

Gustavus F. Davis	1850	1
Samuel P. Bolles	1851	1
Henry R. Coit	1852	—

DIRECTORS.

[From 1850 to 1859—in the order of their election.]

Seth P. Beers
Charles L. Webb
Josiah G. Beckwith
Charles Adams
Edwin B. Webster
Theron Beach
Gideon H. Hollister
Oliver Goodwin
William F. Baldwin
Jason Whiting
Frederick D. McNiel
Jesse L. Judd
Abraham C. Smith
Chauncey M. Hooker
Henry W. Buel.

LITCHFIELD BANK,

[Incorporated in 1856—organized in 1857.]

PRESIDENTS.

William H. Crossman	1857	1
Josiah G. Beckwith	1858	—

CASHIERS.

Edward L. Houghton	1857	1
Frederick E. Harrison	1858	—

RECEIVERS, { ABIJAH CATLIN, F. E. HARRISON.

LITCHFIELD MUTUAL FIRE INSURANCE COMPANY.

[Incorporated in 1833.]

PRESIDENTS.

Phineas Miner	1833	2
William Buel	1835	6
William Beebe	1841	10
Josiah G. Beckwith	1851	—

SECRETARIES.

Leonard Goodwin	1833	1
Sylvester Galpin	1834	7
Jason Whiting	1841	—

TREASURERS.

Oliver Goodwin	1833	22
George C. Woodruff	1855	—

DIRECTORS.

[From 1833 to 1859—in the order of their election.]

Phineas Miner
Oliver Goodwin
Charles L. Webb
Leonard Goodwin
Samuel P. Bolles
Origen S. Seymour
Albert Sedgwick
George C. Woodruff
Tomlinson Wells
Sylvester Galpin
Jonathan Carrington
Apollus Warner
Wm. M. Burrall
David C. Sanford
Frederick Wolcott
William Buel
Elihu Harrison
Joseph Adams
Ebenezer W. Bolles
John M. Holley
Richard Smith
Jason Whiting
Lewis Smith
Lucius Bradley
Israel Coe
Stephen Trowbridge
William Beebe
Samuel G. Braman
Josiah G. Beckwith
George D. Wadhams
William H. Thompson
Leman W. Cutler
David C. Whittlesey
Stephen Deming
Robbins Battell
A. S. Lewis
Sheldon Osborne
Seth P. Beers
Abijah Catlin
Charles Adams
Philip S. Beebe

LITCHFIELD FEMALE ACADEMY.

[Incorporated in 1827.]

PRESIDENTS.

Frederick Wolcott	1827	10
William Buel	1837	9
Seth P. Beers	1846	8
Samuel P. Bolles	1854	declined.
Josiah G. Beckwith	1854	—

SECRETARIES.

Truman Smith	1827	1
John P. Brace	1828	4
Leonard Goodwin	1832	3
Elihu Harrison	1835	2
Origen S. Seymour	1837	4
Sylvester Galpin	1841	3
Samuel P. Bolles	1844	10
Henry R. Coit	1854	1
Chauncey M. Hooker	1855	—

TREASURERS.

William Buel	1827	19
Josiah G. Beckwith	1846	8
Henry W. Buel	1854	—

TRUSTEES.

Frederick Wolcott
James Gould
William Buel
Phineas Miner
Seth P. Beers
Jabez W. Huntington
Truman Smith
John P. Brace
John R. Landon
Daniel Sheldon
Leonard Goodwin
Oliver Goodwin
Elihu Harrison
Origen S. Seymour
Samuel Buel
Samuel P. Bolles
Sylvester Galpin
Jason Whiting
J. G. Beckwith
Albert Sedgwick
Charles Adams
Gideon H. Hollister
Henry W. Buel
William Deming
Henry R. Coit
David E. Bostwick
Frederick D. McNiel
Chauncey M. Hooker
Stephen Deming
George C. Woodruff

LITCHFIELD COUNTY HISTORICAL AND ANTIQUARIAN SOCIETY,

[Incorporated in 1856.]

PRESIDENT.

Seth P. Beers, Litchfield,	1856	—

VICE PRESIDENTS.

George C. Woodruff, Litchfield,	1856	—
John Boyd, Winchester,	1856	—
Charles F. Sedgwick, Sharon,	1856	—
Abijah Catlin, Harwinton,	1856	—
Charles B. Phelps, Woodbury,	1856	dead.
William Cothren, Woodbury,	1858	—

SECRETARY.

Payne Kenyon Kilbourn, Litchfield,	1856	—

TREASURER.

Charles Adams, Litchfield,	1856	—

AUDITOR,

Edwin B. Webster, Litchfield,	1856	—

DIRECTORS.

David L. Parmelee
Herman L. Vaill
D. E. Bostwick
George C. Woodruff
James Richards
P. K. Kilbourn
J. G. Beckwith.

LITCHFIELD COUNTY AGRICULTURAL SOCIETY.

[Incorporated in 1818.]

OFFICERS FOR THE YEAR 1858–'9

PRESIDENT,

JOHN M. WADHAMS, Goshen.

VICE PRESIDENTS,

Royal A. Ford, Litchfield.
George C. Hitchcock, Washington.
Nathan Hart, Jr., Cornwall.

CORRESPONDING SECRETARY,

J. G. Beckwith, Litchfield.

RECORDING SECRETARY,

William F. Baldwin, Litchfield.

TREASURER,

E. W. Seymour, Litchfield.

LITCHFIELD VIGILANT SOCIETY.

[Organized in 1828.]

PRESIDENTS.

	Chosen.	No. years.
Stephen Russell	1828	4
Enos Stoddard	1832	2
Truman Kilbourn	1834	2
Norman Kilbourn	1836	2
Putnam Kilbourn	1838	3
Luman Bishop	1841	3
Murray Kenney	1844	4
Daniel B. Stoddard	1848	1
Prentice Parkhurst	1849	1
Willis Stone	1850	1
George Kenney	1851	2
William P. Kilbourn	1853	3
Daniel B. Stoddard	1856	1
Sherman C. Keeler	1857	—

SECRETARIES.

Enos Stoddard	1828	4
William Coe	1832	5
Willis Stone	1837	2
Leonard Kenney	1839	1
Lucius Wilmot	1840	2
Daniel B. Stoddard	1842	2
Lucius Wilmot	1844	5
Henry M. Pratt	1849	2
Edward Woodruff	1851	3
Homer Stoddard	1854	3
H. L. Kenney	1857	—

TREASURERS.

William Coe	1828	5
Putnam Kilbourn	1833	1
Leonard Kenney	1834	3
Daniel B. Stoddard	1837	2
Luman Bishop	1839	2
Harmon Stoddard	1841	1
Garry G. Potter	1842	2
Prentice Parkhurst	1844	5
Daniel B. Stoddard	1849	5
David Kenney	1854	3
George Bradley	1857	—

Institutions, Societies, etc.

THE ELM PARK COLLEGIATE INSTITUTE.

A Boarding School for Boys.

CORNER OF NORTH AND PROSPECT STREETS, LITCHFIELD.

REV. JAMES RICHARDS, *D. D.*, *Superintendent.*
English and Philosophical Teacher, & Lecturer on History and Physical Geography.

JAMES RICHARDS, JR., *A. B.*,
Professor of Ancient Languages and Mathematics.

D. M. COE,
Assistant Teacher of Mathematics.

W. POWELLE,
Instructor in French.

R. VON SCHMIEDEBERG,
(of Cornwall,)
Instructor in German.

BOARD OF VISITORS—1859.

G. C. WOODRUFF,	CYRUS CATLIN,
WM. DEMING,	P. K. KILBOURN,
HENRY W. BUEL,	CHARLES ADAMS.

THE WOLCOTT INSTITUTE.

A Boarding School for Boys.

SOUTH STREET, LITCHFIELD.

REV. D. G. WRIGHT, *M. A.*, RECTOR.*

OFFICERS FOR THE YEAR 1859.

SETH P. BEERS, *President.*
JOSIAH G. BECKWITH, *Secretary.*
WM. F. BALDWIN, *Treasurer.*

E. B. WEBSTER, H. N. HUDSON, WM. F. BALDWIN, J. G. BECKWITH, E. W. SEYMOUR,	*Directors.*

* While this work was in press, Mr. Wright resigned. The vacancy is not filled.

ELM-PARK COLLEGIATE INSTITUTE—LITCHFIELD.

REV. JAMES RICHARDS, D. D., SUPERINTENDENT.

THE GOULD SEMINARY.

A Boarding and Day School for Young Ladies.

North-street, Litchfield.

MISS HARRIETTE STYLES, Principal.
MISS WOODWARD, Assistant Principal.

SPRING HILL,

LITCHFIELD, CONN.

THIS Institution is now open for the reception of patients afflicted with Nervous Diseases.

The design is to give the household as much the character of the family circle as possible, and to combine with this the most thorough medical treatment and supervision.

The retired and healthful nature of the situation renders it well adapted to the purpose, and the House has been fitted up in the most complete manner for this special object.

Terms according to the accommodations required in each case.

For further particulars, enquiries may be made of

H. W. BUEL, *M. D.*

Connecticut Mining Company.

[Office in Seymour's Building, South-street, Litchfield.]

Officers for 1858–'9.—(Capital $200,000.)

GEORGE G. WEST, President.
JOHN W. BUELL, Secretary.
H. H. K. ELLIOTT, Assistant Secretary.
I. M. ASHTON, Treasurer.

DIRECTORS.

I. W. Mickel, C. R. Moore,
L. Wheeler, John W. Buell,
W. H. Crossman, H. Daley,
J. S. Fisher, A. B. Curtiss,
G. G. West.

LITCHFIELD COUNTY MEDICAL SOCIETY.

President—H. M. KNIGHT, *M. D.*, Salisbury.

Secretary—D. E. BOSTWICK, *M. D.*, Litchfield.

Fellows, { D. B. W. Camp, *M. D.*, 1858.
George Seymour, *M. D.*, 1859.

Roll of Representatives from Litchfield.

[First represented in the Legislature in 1740.]

1740.	May.	Joseph Bird,	Ebenezer Marsh.
	October.	John Bird,	John Buel.
1741.	May.	Ebenezer Marsh,	John Buel.
	October.	Ebenezer Marsh,	Samuel Culver.
1742.	May.	Ebenezer Marsh,	Jacob Griswold.
	October.	Ebenezer Marsh,	Jacob Griswold.
1743.	May.	Ebenezer Marsh,	John Bird.
	October.	Ebenezer Marsh,	Joseph Bird.
1744.	May.	Ebenezer Marsh,	Joseph Bird.
	October.	Edward Phelps,	Joseph Bird.
1745.	May.	Edward Phelps,	Joseph Bird.
2d.	May.	Ebenezer Marsh,	Isaac Baldwin.
	October.	Edward Phelps,	Joseph Bird.
1746.	May.	Ebenezer Marsh,	Joseph Bird.
	October.	Ebenezer Marsh,	Joseph Bird.
1747.	May.	Thomas Harison,	Joseph Sanford.
	October.	Thomas Harrison.	Joseph Sanford.
1748.	May.	Ebenezer Marsh,	John Bird.
	October.	Ebenezer Marsh,	John Bird.
1749.	May.	Ebenezer Marsh,	Joseph Bird.
	October.	Ebenezer Marsh,	Thomas Harrison.
1750.	May.	Ebenezer Marsh,	Thomas Harrison.
	October.	Ebenezer Marsh,	Thomas Harrison.
1751.	May.	Ebenezer Marsh,	Thomas Harrison.
	October.	Ebenezer Marsh,	Thomas Harrison.
1752.	May.	Ebenezer Marsh,	Thomas Harrison.
	October.	Joseph Kilbourn,	Benjamin Webster.
1753.	May.	Joseph Kilbourn,	Benjamin Webster.
	October.	Thomas Harrison,	Benjamin Webster.
1754.	May.	Ebenezer Marsh,	Benjamin Webster.
	October.	Ebenezer Marsh,	Thomas Harrison.
1755.	May.	Peter Buel,	Benjamin Webster.
	October.	Ebenezer Marsh,	Elisha Shelden.
1756.	May.	Ebenezer Marsh,	Peter Buel.
	October.	Ebenezer Marsh,	Peter Buel.
1757.	May.	Ebenezer Marsh,	Peter Buel.
	October.	Ebenezer Marsh,	Elisha Shelden.
1758.	May.	Ebenezer Marsh,	Elisha Shelden.
	October,	Ebenezer Marsh,	Elisha Shelden.
1759.	May.	Jacob Woodruff,	Elisha Shelden.
	October.	Ebenezer Marsh,	Elisha Shelden.
1760.	May.	Ebenezer Marsh,	Elisha Shelden.
	October.	Ebenezer Marsh,	Elisha Shelden.
1761.	May.	Ebenezer Marsh,	Elisha Shelden.
	October.	Ebenezer Marsh,	Isaac Baldwin.
1762.	May.	Ebenezer Marsh,	Isaac Baldwin.
	October.	Ebenezer Marsh,	Isaac Baldwin.
1763.	May.	Ebenezer Marsh,	Isaac Baldwin.
	October.	Ebenezer Marsh,	Isaac Baldwin.
1764.	May.	Ebenezer Marsh,	Isaac Baldwin.
	October.	Ebenezer Marsh,	Oliver Wolcott.
1765.	May.	Ebenezer Marsh,	Isaac Baldwin.
	October.	Ebenezer Marsh,	Isaac Baldwin.
1766.	May.	Ebenezer Marsh,	Isaac Baldwin.
	October.	Ebenezer Marsh,	John Marsh.
1767.	May.	Oliver Wolcott,	John Marsh.
	October.	Ebenezer Marsh,	John Marsh.
1768.	May.	Ebenezer Marsh,	John Marsh.
	October.	Oliver Wolcott,	Jacob Woodruff.
1769.	May.	Ebenezer Marsh,	Abraham Kilbourn.
	October.	Ebenezer Marsh,	Abraham Kilbourn.
1770.	May.	David Welch,	Abraham Kilbourn.

	October.	Oliver Wolcott,	Abraham Kilbourn.
1771.	May.	Ebenezer Marsh,	John Marsh.
	October.	Jedediah Strong,	Lynde Lord.
1772.	May.	Jedediah Strong,	Lynde Lord.
	October.	Jedediah Strong,	John Marsh.
1773.	May.	Jedediah Strong,	David Welch.
	October.	Jedediah Strong,	David Welch.
1774.	May.	Jedediah Strong,	John Marsh.
	October.	Jedediah Strong,	David Welch.
1775.	May.	Jedediah Strong,	David Welch.
	October.	Jedediah Strong,	Abraham Bradley.
1776.	May.	Jedediah Strong,	Abraham Bradley.
	October.	Jedediah Strong,	Andrew Adams.
1777.	May.	Jedediah Strong,	Andrew Adams.
	October.	Jedediah Strong,	Andrew Adams.
1778.	May.	Jedediah Strong,	Andrew Adams.
	October.	Jedediah Strong,	Andrew Adams.
1779.	May.	Jedediah Strong,	Andrew Adams.
	October.	Jedediah Strong,	Andrew Adams.
1780.	May.	Jedediah Strong,	Andrew Adams.
	October.	David Welch	Andrew Adams.
1781.	May.	Jedediah Strong,	Andrew Adams
	October.	Jedediah Strong,	Bezaleel Beebe.
1782.	May.	Jedediah Strong,	Bezaleel Beebe.
	October.	Jedediah Strong,	Isaac Baldwin.
1783.	May.	Jedediah Strong,	Bezaleel Beebe.
	October.	Abraham Bradley,	Isaac Baldwin, Jr.
1784.	May.	Ebenezer Marsh,	Isaac Baldwin.
	October.	Ebenezer Marsh,	Isaac Baldwin, Jr.
1785.	May.	Jedediah Strong,	Abraham Bradley,
	October.	Ebenezer Marsh,	Jedediah Strong.
1786.	May.	Ebenezer Marsh,	Jedediah Strong.
	October.	Ebenezer Marsh,	Jedediah Strong.
1787.	May.	Ebenezer Marsh,	Ebenezer Benton.
	October.	Ebenezer Marsh,	Jedediah Strong.
1788.	May.	Ebenezer Marsh,	Jedediah Strong.
	October.	Ebenezer Marsh,	Uriah Tracy.
1789.	May.	Jedediah Strong,	Uriah Tracy.
	October.	Tapping Reeve,	Uriah Tracy.
1790.	May.	Ebenezer Marsh,	Uriah Tracy.
	October.	Julius Deming,	Uriah Tracy.
1791.	May.	Julius Deming,	Uriah Tracy.
	October.	Ephraim Kirby,	Uriah Tracy.
1792.	May.	Ephraim Kirby,	Uriah Tracy.
	October.	Solomon Marsh,	Bezaleel Beebe.
1793.	May.	John Allen,	Uriah Tracy.
	October.	Bezaleel Beebe,	John Allen.
1794.	May.	Ephraim Kirby,	John Allen.
	October.	Ephraim Kirby,	John Allen.
1795.	May.	Ephraim Kirby,	John Allen.
	October.	Moses Seymour,	Bezaleel Beebe.
1796.	May.	Moses Seymour,	John Allen.
	October.	Moses Seymour,	John Allen.
1797.	May.	Moses Seymour,	Ephraim Kirby.
	October.	Moses Seymour,	Ephraim Kirby.
1798.	May.	James Morris,	Julius Deming.
	October.	Moses Seymour,	Ephraim Kirby.
1799.	May.	Moses Seymour,	Ephraim Kirby.
	October.	Ephraim Kirby,	John Welch.
1800.	May.	Ephraim Kirby,	John Welch.
	October.	Ephraim Kirby,	James Morris.
1801.	May.	Moses Seymour,	Ephraim Kirby.
	October.	Moses Seymour,	John Welch.
1802.	May.	James Morris,	Frederick Wolcott.
	October.	Moses Seymour,	Ephraim Kirby.
1803.	May.	James Morris,	Frederick Wolcott.
	October.	James Morris,	Uriel Holmes.
1804.	May.	James Morris,	Uriel Holmes.
	October.	James Morris,	Uriel Holmes.

1805.	May.	James Morris,	Uriel Holmes.
	October.	James Morris,	Uriel Holmes.
1806.	May.	Moses Seymour,	Norman Buel.
	October.	Uriel Holmes,	Aaron Bradley.
1807.	May.	Uriel Holmes,	Aaron Bradley.
	October.	Uriel Holmes,	Aaron Bradley.
1808.	May.	Aaron Bradley,	Aaron Smith.
	October.	Nathaniel Goodwin,	Aaron Smith.
1809.	May.	Nathaniel Goodwin,	Aaron Smith.
	October.	Nathaniel Goodwin,	Aaron Smith.
1810.	May.	Moses Seymour,	Aaron Bradley.
	October.	Moses Seymour,	Aaron Bradley.
1811.	May.	Aaron Smith,	Moses Seymour
	October.	Moses Seymour,	Aaron Smith.
1812.	May.	Aaron Smith,	Moses Seymour.
	October.	Morris Woodruff,	Aaron Smith.
1813.	May.	Aaron Smith,	Morris Woodruff.
	October.	Aaron Smith,	Morris Woodruff.
1814.	May.	Aaron Smith,	Morris Woodruff.
	October.	Uriel Holmes,	Morris Woodruff.
1815.	May.	William Beebe,	Morris Woodruff.
	October.	William Beebe,	Jonathan Buel.
1816.	May.	William Beebe,	Jonathan Buel.
	October.	William Beebe,	Jonathan Buel.
1817.	May.	Jonathan Buel,	Ephraim S. Hall.
	October.	Jonathan Buel,	Ephraim S. Hall.
1818.	May.	Stephen Russell,	Ephraim S. Hall.
	October.	Stephen Russell,	Phineas Lord.
1819.	May.	John Welch,	Phineas Lord.
1820.	May.	John Welch,	Seth P. Beers.
1821.	May.	Seth P. Beers,	John Welch.
1822.	May.	Seth P. Beers,	John Welch.
1823.	May.	Seth P. Beers,	Phineas Miner.
1824.	May.	David Marsh,	Morris Woodruff.
1825.	May.	David Marsh,	Morris Woodruff.
1826.	May.	Morris Woodruff,	Reuben Webster.
1827.	May.	Phineas Miner,	William Beebe.
1828.	May.	Jabez W. Huntington,	William Beebe.
1829.	May.	Phineas Miner,	Morris Woodruff.
1830.	May.	Stephen Russell,	Morris Woodruff.
1831.	May.	Stephen Russell,	Truman Smith.
1832.	May.	Truman Smith,	Elihu Harrison.
1833.	May.	William Beebe,	Asa Hopkins.
1834.	May.	Stephen Russell,	Truman Smith.
1835.	May.	Phineas Miner,	Elihu Harrison.
1836.	May.	Morris Woodruff,	Phineas Lord.
1837.	May.	Morris Woodruff,	Phineas Lord.
1838.	May.	Samuel Buel,	William Ray.
1839.	May.	Samuel Buel,	William Ray.
1840.	May.	Frederick Buel,	E. Champion Bacon.
1841.	May.	Frederick Buel,	E. Champion Bacon.
1842.	May.	Origen S. Seymour,	Enos Stoddard.
1843.	May.	Origen S. Seymour,	Enos Stoddard.
1844.	May.	Elisha S. Abernethy,	Dan Catlin.
1845.	May.	Charles Adams,	Dan Catlin.
1846.	May.	David Marsh,	George Seymour.
1847.	May.	David Marsh,	George Seymour.
1848.	May.	Samuel P. Bolles,	William L. Smedley.
1849.	May.	Origen S. Seymour,	Christopher Wheeler.
1850.	May.	Origen S. Seymour,	Christopher Wheeler.
1851.	May.	George C. Woodruff,	Thomas M. Coe.
1852.	May.	Josiah G. Beckwith,	William Newton.
1853.	May.	Josiah G. Beckwith,	William Newton.
1854.	May.	Frederick Buel,	Samuel P. Bolles.
1855.	May.	Philip S. Beebe,	Samuel Brooker, Jr.
1856.	May.	Josiah G. Beckwith,	Garry H. Minor.
1857.	May.	Josiah G. Beckwith,	Edward Pierpont.
1858.	May.	Henry B. Graves,	William Bissell.
1859.	May.	Edward W. Seymour,	William Bissell.

NATIVE AND RESIDENT GRADUATES,

INCLUDING THOSE WHO HAVE RECIVED HONORARY DEGREES.

NOTE.—This list is not designed to embrace the names of such as have received medical degrees only—though some of the number have received the M. D. in ADDITION to other degrees. In the first column, the * indicates that the person whose name is given on the same line, was BORN in this town. The figures in the same column denote the number of years the individual lived in Litchfield. The figures in the second column, indicate the year of graduation. The † after the name, indicates an honorary degree. The name of the college is given immediately after that of the graduate.

*	1848	Edward P. Abbe, Yale, clergyman in Massachusetts.
*	1848	Frederick R. Abbe, Yale, " "
10	1825	Elisha S. Abernethy, Yale, lawyer—now resides in Bridgeport.
30	1760	Andrew Adams, LL. D., Yale, Chief Justice of Connecticut.
26	1791	John Allen,† Yale, lawyer and member of Congress.
*	1840	John W. Allen,† Yale, lawyer of Cleveland, Ohio; member of Congress.
48	1793	Asa Bacon, Yale, an eminent lawyer—died in New Haven in 1857.
*	1833	E. Champion Bacon, Yale, lawyer, legislator—died at Seville, Spain, 1845.
*	1838	Francis Bacon, Yale, lawyer, Senator, Major General.
3	1850	Leonard W. Bacon, Yale—present pastor of the First Church, Litchfield.
*	1776	Ashbel Baldwin, Yale, formerly Rector of St. Michael's, Litchfield.
*	1810	Charles A. Baldwin, Williams, lawyer in State of New York—died 1818.
65	1735	Isaac Baldwin, Yale, lawyer, legislator, clerk of the courts ; died in 1805.
*	1774	Isaac Baldwin, Jr, Yale, lawyer and legislator; died in Pompey, N. Y., 1830.
*	1801	Isaac Baldwin. 3d, Yale, lawyer—died in 1844,
*	1801	Samuel S. Baldwin, Yale, lawyer—died in 1854.
9	1766	George Beckwith, Yale, pastor of the church in South Farms.
30	1827	Josiah G. Beckwith, M. D., Union, a practicing physician in this town.
16	1797	Lyman Beecher, D. D., Yale, former pastor of the 1st Church in this town.
*	1833	Charles Beecher, Bowdoin, now pastor in Georgetown, Mass,
16	1822	Edward Beecher, D. D., Yale, late President Illinois College; author, etc.
16	1828	George Beecher, Yale, died while pastor of a church in Chilicothie, Ohio.
*	1834	Henry Ward Beecher, Amherst, pastor of Plymouth Church, Brooklyn.
*	1843	Thomas K. Beecher, Illinois, now pastor in Elmira, N. Y.
16	1833	William H. Beecher,† Yale, formerly pastor in Midnletown, etc.
16	1842	Frederick D. Beeman, Yale, lawyer, and clerk of the courts.
—	1800	Amos Benedict, Yale, lawyer—died in this town in 1816.
*	1846	Andrew D. Benedict, Kenyon, Episcopal clergyman,
*	1847	Samuel Benedict, Trinity, late Ass't Rector Trinity church, N. Haven.
*	1846	Alfred H. Beers, M. D., Trinity, physician in Buffalo, N. Y.
*	1839	George W. Beers, Trinity, member of the Bar, Litchfield.
*	1786	John Bird, Yale, lawyer in Litchfield & Troy, N. Y.; member of congress.
*	1851	Edward Bissell, Yale, lawyer in Fondulac, Wisconsin.
*	1849	Oscar Bissell, Yale, pastor of a church in Westminster, N. H.
*	1853	William Bissell, M. D., Yale, physician in Salisbury.
*	1833	Noah Bishop, Yale, pastor of a church in or near Springfield, Ohio.
*	1812	John P. Brace, Williams, teacher, author, editor.
*	1846	Charles Loring Brace, Yale, author, Secretary Children's Aid Soc., N. Y.
6	1850	Jonathan Brace,† D. D., Yale, now pastor of a church in Milford.
3	1843	John J. Brandagee, Yale, former Rector of St. Michael's, Litchfield.
*	1812	Solyman Brown, Yale, dentist, author, clergyman, New York city.
30	1836	Frederick Buel, Yale, Agent American Bible Society, California.
15	1826	William P. Buel, M. D., Yale, physician on California steamer.
*	1844	Henry W. Buel, M. D., Yale, physician in his native town.
*	1805	David Buel, Jr., Williams, of Troy, N. Y., lawyer, Judge, regent univ'ty.
12	1836	Joshua D. Berry, Middlebury, late President Shelby College, Ky.
?	1832	Amos B. Beach, Union, late Rector St. Paul's, Bantam Falls.
*	1827	Horace Bushnell, D. D., Yale, pastor North Church, Hartford; author, etc.
10	1833	David Butler, D. D.,† Washington, former Rector St. Michael's.
42	1787	Joseph E. Camp, Yale, pastor church in Northfield.
*	1822	Albert B. Camp, Yale, pastor in Bridgewater, Ashby, Mass., etc.
*	1786	Lynde Catlin, Yale, merchant, and President Merchants' Bank, N. York.
*	1839	John Catlin, Yale, teacher, &c., resides in Northfield.
60	1751	Judah Champion, Yale, 2d pastor of the first church in this town.
27	1780	Amos Chase, Dartmouth, pastor church in South Farms.
9	1803	Samuel Church, LL. D., Yale, chief justice of Connecticut.

*	1844	John Churchill,† Yale, now pastor of a church in Woodbury.
54	1718	Timothy Collins, Yale, first pastor of the first church in this town.
*	1758	Ambrose Collins, Yale, went a missionary to the Indians, and died.
—	1758	Thomas Davies, Yale, former Rector of St. Michael's.
*	1811	William Deming, Yale, resides in his native town.
—	1829	George C. V. Eastman, Middlebury, Rector of church in Bantam Falls.
9	1822	Samuel Fuller, D. D., Union, late President Kenyon College, Ohio.
*	1759	Fisher Gay, Yale, colonel revolutionary army; legislator, magistrate.
47	1791	James Gould, LL. D., Yale, Judge Sup. Court, principal Law School.
*	1827	George Gould, Yale, of Troy, N. Y., now Judge Supreme Court, N. York.
*	1824	James R. Gould, Yale, lawyer, died in Augusta, Georgia, 1830.
*	1816	William T. Gould, Yale, Judge Court of Oyer and Terminer, Augusta, Ga.
*	1839	John M. Grant, Yale, colporteur in Maryland, &c.
*	1844	Wm. H. Guernsey, Yale, clergyman; died in Savannah, Ga., 1850.
*	1849	Luther B. Hart, Union, late pastor Baptist church, North Norfolk.
7	1820	Laurens P. Hickok, D. D., Union, now Vice President Union college.
7	1851	George A. Hickox, Trinity, now a practicing lawyer in this town.
16	1840	Gideon H. Hollister, Yale, lawyer, clerk of the courts, senator.
32	1784	Uriel Holmes, Jr., Yale, lawyer, judge, member of congress.
*	1816	Uriel Holmes, Jr., Yale, died July 3, 1818, while member Theo. Sem. And.
8	1784	Lemuel Hopkins,† M. D., Yale, poet, &c.
11	1794	Dan Huntington, Yale, former pastor of the first church in this town.
*	1822	Charles P. Huntington, Harvard, now Judge Superior Court, Boston, Ms.
27	1806	Jabez W. Huntington, Yale, lawyer, judge, member of congress, senator.
*	1824	William P. Huntington, Harvard, pastor in Mass. and Illinois; artist, etc.
6	1843	George J. Harrison, Union, now congregational minister in Milton.
40	1792	Isaac Jones, Yale, minister of St. Michael's parish.
3	1791	Benjamin Judd, Yale, pastor in Milton.
*	1837	James Kilbourn, Yale, pastor in Bridgewater, Middle Haddam, & Illinois.
15	1840	John Kilbourn, Yale, teacher in State of New York.
*	1853	P. K. Kilbourn,† Union, author of this volume.
*	1787	Ephraim Kirby,† Yale, lawyer, judge, author of "Kirby's Reports."
*	1844	Wm. H. Lewis,† D. D., Kenyon, Rector of Holy Trinity church, Brooklyn.
—	1788	Daniel W. Lewis, Yale, lawyer, state's attorney.
6	1770	Samuel Lyman, Yale, removed to Springfield, Mass.; member of congress.
*	1783	Lynde Lord. Jr., Yale, died in his native town in 1813.
*	1812	Stephen Mason, Williams, former pastor in Washington, now in Michigan.
50	1748	Reynold Marvin, Yale, lawyer, king's attorney; died here, July 30, 1802.
*	1786	Samuel Marsh, Yale, lawyer in his native town, and in Norfolk, Va.
*	1786	Truman Marsh, Yale, Rector of St. Michael's 27 years; died here in 1851.
*	1775	James Morris, Yale, teacher, magistrate, legislator, captain; died 1820.
*	1803	James Morris, jr., Yale, tutor University of Georgia; d. in Sunbury, Ga.
*	1804	Reuben S. Morris, Yale, lawyer; died in Utica, N. Y., in 1832.
*	1838	Dwight Morris, Union, lawyer in Bridgeport, judge of probate, legislator.
*	1775	Benjamin Osborn, Dartmouth, pastor in Tinmouth, Vt.; author. d. 1818.
*	1779	Isaac Osborn, Dartmouth, farmer, teacher, deacon; died in Litchfield 1826.
*	1779	Jeremiah Osborn, Dartmouth, farmer, died in Litchfield in 1829.
*	1784	Jacob Osborn, Dartmouth, farmer and teacher, died in Litchfield in 1821.
*	1784	Ethan Osborn, Dartm'th, pastor Fairfield, N. J., 54 yrs; d. in his 100th yr.
13	1729	Solomon Palmer, Yale, Rector of St. Michael's; d. in this town in 1771.
?	1750	Benjamin Palmer, Yale, died in 1780.
*	1853	John M. Peck, D. D.,† Harvard, Baptist pastor in Illinois; author; d. 1858.
*	1853	Wm. G. Peck,† Trinity, (also at West Point,) Prof. Mat. Colum. Col., N. Y.
*	1842	James Peck, Union, merchant at La Crosse, Wisconsin.
6	1807	Amos Pettingill, Harvard, pastor church in South Farms—1816 to 1822.
*	1837	John H. Pettingill, Yale, District Secretary Am. Board—Albany, N. Y.
*	1804	John Pierpont, Yale, clergyman in Boston, author, lecturer, poet.
25	1813	Charles Perkins, Yale, lawyer, died in London, (Eng.,) Nov 18, 1856, Æ 64.
50	1763	Tapping Reeve, LL. D., Princeton, chief justice of Connecticut.
*	1802	Aaron Burr Reeve, Yale, lawyer in Troy, N. Y., died in 1809.
*	1829	Tapping Burr Reeve, died in Litchfield in 1829.
—	1833	James Richards, D. D., Union, now Principal Elm Park Col. Institute.
—	1858	James Richards, jr., Princeton, Professor Ancient Lan. and Mat. in do.
*	1831	Rollin Sanford, Yale, merchant in Brooklyn, N. Y.; candidate for congress.
*	1797	Horatio Seymour, LL. D., Yale, lawyer, U. S. Senator from Vt 12 years.
*	1824	Origen S. Seymour, Yale, member of congress, judge Superior Court.
*	1853	Edward W. Seymour, Yale, lawyer, member present House of Represent's.
25	1730	Elisha Sheldon, Yale, legislator and judge; died in Litchfield in 1779.
*	1800	Elisha Sheldon, M. D., Yale, died in 1832; buried in Litchfield.

* — Richard Skinner, LL. D.,† Middlebury, Governor and chief justice of Vt.
25 1790 Aaron Smith, Yale, lawyer, legislator and merchant; d. in this town in 1834.
7 1806 Lucius Smith, Yale, merchant, colonel in war with Gt. Britain, clergyman.
45 1757 Reuben Smith, Yale, physician, magistrate, county treasurer; died in 1804.
35 1815 Truman Smith, Yale, lawyer, member of congress, U. S. Senator.
* 1761 Jedediah Strong, Yale, member continental congress, legislator, etc.
3 1823 John S. Stone, D. D., Union, former Rector of St. Michael's.
— 1838 Benjamin W. Stone, Trinity, " " " "
* 1857 Storrs O. Seymour, Yale, now a student of theology.
* 1822 William Sheldon, Yale, merchant, died in France in 1826.
10 1844 Benjamin L. Swan,† Yale, now pastor of a church in Stratford.
52 1773 Benjamin Tallmadge, Yale, member of congress 16 years.
* 1830 Benjamin Tallmadge, jr.† Yale, Lieut. U. S. N.; d. off Gibraltar in 1830.
* 1811 Frederick A. Tallmadge, Yale, Recorder N. Y. city, member of congress.
28 1778 Uriah Tracy, Yale, lawyer, member of congress, U. S. Senator, General.
* 1778 Joseph Vaill, Dart'th, pastor in Hadlyme; d. 1838 after a ministry of 58 yrs.
* 1824 Hermon L. Vaill, Yale, pastor in East Lyme; also Seneca Falls, N. Y.
* 1848 Louis F. Wadsworth, Trinity, lawyer in N. Y. city, Dep. Clerk Assembly.
* 1837 Charles Wadsworth, D. D., Union, pastor Arch st. church, Philadelphia.
* 1795 Holland Weeks, Dartmouth, pastor in Waterbury, and in Vermont.
? 1809 William R. Weeks, D. D., Princeton; d. 1848, Æ. 66.
* 1778 John Welch, Yale, merchant, judge, legislator; died in 1844.
* 1805 William Welch, Yale, captain U. S. A.; died in the public service in 1811.
* 1827 William H. Welch, Yale, late chief justice of Minnesota Territory.
46 1747 Oliver Wolcott, LL. D., Governor, Signer Declaration of Independence.
* 1778 Oliver Wolcott, jr, LL. D., Yale, Governor, Secretary U. S. Treasury, etc.
* 1786 Frederick Wolcott, Yale, lawyer, legislator, judge of probate.
* 1779 Ezekiel Woodruff, Yale, lawyer, Adjutant revolutionary army.
* 1849 Curtis T. Woodruff, Yale, Rector Episcopal church in Woodbury.
* 1825 George C. Woodruff, Yale, lawyer, legislator, judge of probate.
* 1857 George M. Woodruff, Yale, now a law student in Cambridge, Mass.
* 1830 Lewis B. Woodruff, Yale, now a Judge Superior Court, New York city.
* 1809 Simeon Woodruff, Yale, clergyman, settled at the West.
* 1836 Lucius H. Woodruff. Yale, teacher in Insane Retreat, Hartford; d. in 1852.
* 1803 Samuel Whittlesey, Yale, pastor at Washington and elsewhere.
2 1851 Junius M. Willey, Trinity, Rector of St. Michael's; now in Waterbury.

Physicians who have Practiced in Litchfield.

NOTE.—The * designates natives of this town. ‡ Those who received the M. D.

Timothy Collins, from Guilford, the first clergyman and physician in the town, preached and practiced here from 1721 till his death in 1777.
Thomas Little, from Taunton, came here about 1747—died in Northfield of old age.
Seth Bird,* b. Jan. 4, 1733-'4; died in this town in 1804.
Daniel Huntington, practitioner and druggist; d. in Woodbury Feb. 19, 1819.
Phineas Bradley, practitioner and druggist; became Ass't P. M. Gen'l U. States.
Samuel Catlin,* b. Nov. 6, 1739; lived to old age, and died in his native town.
Hosea Hulbert,‡ removed to Fairfield county.
Daniel Sheldon,‡ a native of Hartford, practiced here from 1781 until his death.
Phineas Smith.* b. Oct. 27, 1759; lived and died in his native town.
Comfort Bradley,* lived and died in native town.
Partridge Parsons,* b. Aug. 22, 1763, d. in Pen Yan, N. Y., May 9, 1846, aged 83.
Robert Catlin,* surgeon, b. March 29, 1773: d. in his native town in 1823.
Abel Catlin,* b. March 18, 1770: died in his native town January 13, 1856.
John M. West,‡ died in this town July 27, 1836, aged 47.
Reuben S. Woodward,‡ died in Northfield in 1849, aged 83.
Isaac Marsh,* died in Cornwall, Sept. 1, 1829, aged 53.
Joseph Parker, died in South Farms, Feb. 6, 1830, aged 70.
William Buel,*‡ President State Medical Soc., d. in this town, Oct. 15, 1851, Æ. 84.
Samuel Buel,*‡ died in this town, July 10, 1854, aged 72.
Alanson Abbe,‡ now resides in Boston.
Manly Peters,‡ now resides in Knoxville, Tennessee.
Norman Landon,*‡ died in this town in 1830.
John W. Russell,*‡ now resides in Mount Vernon. Ohio.
Josiah Barnes,‡ now resides in Buffalo, N. Y.

Moses A. Lee,‡ died while Professor in the Medical College at Pittsfield, Mass.
Anson Wildman, practitioner and druggist: present residence unknown.
John S. Wolcott,‡* (son of the last Gov. Wolcott,) died in this town in 1844.
Reuben M. Woodruff,*‡ died in this town April 29, 1849, aged 38.
Charles Vaill,*‡ now resides in Rochester, N. Y.
Garry H. Minor,‡ a native of Woodbury, now resides in South Farms.
Benjamin Welch, jr.,‡ from Norfolk, now resides in Salisbury.
Caleb Ticknor,‡ died in New York, Sept. 7, 1840, aged 36.
Samuel R. Childs,‡ now resides in Saratoga Springs.
William Deming, jr.,*‡ now resides in Lenox, Mass.
James K. Wallace,* now a practitioner at Bantam Falls.
George Seymour,*‡ now a practicing physician in this village.
A. Sidney Lewis,*‡ " " "
Eliada Osborn,*‡ " " "
David E. Bostwick,*‡ " " "
Orson Buel,* (botanic,) " " "
D. B. W. Camp,*‡ " " Northfield.

Physicians born in Litchfield but who practiced elsewhere.

[Not included in either of the foregoing Lists.]

Judah Champion Landon, (son of J. R. Landon, Esq.) died in Kentucky a few years.
John Ward Birge, now of Utica, N. Y.
Levi Moulthrop, died in early manhood at Rockford, Illinois.
Timothy Pierce, died at the South.
Clark Sanford, settled in Stamford and died there.
John Stoddard emigrated westward.
Asa Barnes, settled in Virginia.
Burr Reeve Abbe, Boston, Mass.
Charles W. Grant, now resides at Iona, near Newburgh, N. Y.
Aaron W. Gibbs, now of Chicago, Illinois.
Samuel Catlin, jr, formerly of Watertown: now in Michigan.
Egbert Guernsey, author, Professor, and practitioner, New York city.
Ozias Lewis, jr, of Kosciusco, Mississippi.
Isaac W. Russell, died in Mount Vernon, Ohio.
Joseph W. Camp, late of Bristol—now of Wisconsin.
Fred'k B. Woodward, former physician in Woodbury—now Rector ch. in Bethany.
Asa C. Woodward, now of Bethany.
Elijah A. Woodward, now of Madison, Wisconsin.
Warren Smith, died in Stillwater, N. Y., Nov. 1805.
Ephraim Smedley, of North East, Pennsylvania.
Abel Brace, of Catskill, N. Y.—late coroner of Green co.
Henry Holmes, of Hartford—Health Officer, Alms House Physician, Coroner.
George Bissell, late of Dutches county, N. Y., now of California.
Charles J. Kilbourn, of Stanfordville, Dutches co., N. Y.; died in this town in 1852.
James B. Kilbourn, of Hinds county, Miss.; died there in 1837.
Washington Irving Wright, surgeon in the U. S. Army.
Oliver Wolcott, died in California in 1856. A son of Colonel Oliver S., he was the last of the Wolcotts in the line of the three Governors. His remains were brought to Litchfield for interment.
Joseph Hall, died recently at North East, Penn.
Augustus Bissell, Pennsylvania.
Daniel H. Moore, died in New Haven in 1849.
Walter Peck, died in Goshen Nov. 8, 1834, aged 24.
Horatio M. Baldwin, died in Binghamton, N. Y., in 1842.
Marcus M. Wood, of Greene, Chenango county, N. Y.
Henry Pierpont, of Naugatuck.
Charles H. Webb, of Woodbury.
Zephaniah Webb, of New York city.
Moses M. Seymour, of Painesville, Ohio.

Town of Litchfield.

THE town of Litchfield is situated near the geographical centre of the County of Litchfield, of which it is the shire town or seat of justice. It is claimed, (by those who have from time to time sought to divide it,) that it is the largest township in the State—being eight miles north and south, by nine miles east and west. It is 32 miles west of Hartford, 35 mile north-westerly from New Haven, and about 100 miles north-easterly from New York. It is bounded north by Cornwall, Goshen and Torrington; south by Bethlem, Watertown and Plymouth; east by Harwinton, from which it is separated by the Naugatuck river; and west by Warren and Washington. The Naugatuck, Shepaug and Bantam rivers, and some of their branches, pass through the town, affording an abundance of water-power. Bantam Lake, which lies wholly in this town, is the largest lake in the State, covering an area of 900 acres. The Little Pond covers about 15 acres; and Cranberry Pond is still smaller. Mount Tom Pond lies partly in Washington and partly in this town. The surface of the town is gently rolling, here and there breaking into abrupt ridges or bluffs. The highest of these is Mount Tom, some six miles south-west of the village, which reaches an altitude of 700 feet above the river at its base, or, according to President Dwight, 1500 feet above the level of tide-water. From Prospect Mountain, about four miles west of the Court House, may be seen the Cattskill mountains, west of the Hudson. A large proportion of the land in the vallies and on the hill-sides, is easily tilled, and yields abundant crops. The balance is profitably used for meadow, pasturage and wood-land. Some of the most beautiful and diversity landscapes in New England, are to be met with in this town. In 1800, the total amount of the Grand List of Litchfield was $107,164 27—of which sum $51,687 67 was for the First Society; $26,882 02 for South Farms; $14,740 45 for Northfield; $13,855 13 for Milton. In 1810, there were in the town 4087 acres of plow-land; 7298 acres of meadow and clear pasture; 966 acres of boggy meadow that was mowed; 294 acres do. not mowed; other meadow 1312 acres; 9343 acres bush pasture; 4408 acres first rate wood-land; 3789 acres 2d rate do.; 4756 acres 3d rate do. Since that date, the plow-land, meadow and cleared pasture, have greatly increased; while the area of wood-land has decreased in a like ratio. Wood is now so scarce and high in our borough market, that some of our people have already commenced burning Pennsylvania mineral coal.

Litchfield contains four incorporated Ecclesiastical Societies and twenty-eight School Districts. The societies are, Litchfield, South Farms, Northfield, and Milton.

The Naugatuck Railroad runs through the entire length of the township from north to south—the Litchfield Station being about four miles from the Court House.

The population of Litchfield in 1756, was 1,366; in 1774, it was 1,554; in 1800, it was 4,287; in 1810, it was 4,639. From this time, the tide of emigration began to set so strongly westward that our population commenced decreasing. In 1820, the census-taker gave us 4,610; while in 1850, our population was but 3,987.

In hotly contested elections, more than 1,000 votes have been polled in this town.

Though the population of the Town has thus decreased, the Borough has gradually increased its numbers, and has been constantly improving in rural beauty.

In 1848-'9 the New England Mining Company commenced mining for copper in the "Pitch," four miles south-east of this village; and about the same time, another company with the famous P. T. Barnum at its head, began digging in the same vicinity. Both these companies were unsuccessful. Barnum, in his examination before his creditors in New York, put down as one item of loss, "$10,000 sunk in a Litchfield copper mine."

In other parts of the town, however, miners have met with better success. About two miles north-east of the village, on the form of Mr. Beach, a shaft has been sunk 25 feet in depth, by Messrs. Sedgwick and Buell. The vein or lode is 14 feet in width, composed of pure quartz, with a slight mixture of felspar. In this vein is found a very pure gray Copper Ore, yielding by analysis 79 1-2 per cent. of copper. A bevel has been driven 140 feet, which whe completed, will intersect the vein at 50 feet in depth. In this vein are also found great quantities of small pure garnets, which are as yet too small to be made valuable as articles of commerce. This vein, bearing nearly a north and south direction, can be traced for a distance of three miles. On the farm of Mr. Gilbert, half a mile from this location, was recently found an old shaft, 15 feet deep, which is supposed to have been sunk long before the Revolution. This has been cleaned out, and sunk 30 feet upon a small vein of iron and copper running together. The quantity of copper found is not yet sufficient to render the digging profitable—the mine having been but partially developed.

The lands of the Connecticut Mining Company, on Prospect Mountain, promise an abundant return for funds invested and labor performed. Disinterested parties who have visited these lands, and others who have analyzed and smelted their copper, nickel and silver ores, pronounce the per centage of pure metal to be much greater than that of some the celebrated English mines. The enterprize is this company deserves and will receive a rich reward.

Litchfield Borough Corporation.

At the May Session of the Legislature of this State, 1818, the inhabitants of this village presented their memorial, praying for a Borough Charter. In their petition they state that "the houses are as contiguous as they are in many of our cities; that the Public Schools, which for many years have been established in this village, make a great addition to its ordinary population;" that on account of their local situation and compact settlement, they are, as they conceive, in an unusual degree exposed to injury from fire," &c. The application was successful; and the petitioners and their associates, residing within the limits prescribed, "were constituted and declared to be forever thereafter, a body corporate in fact and in name, by the name of the *Corporation of the Village of Litchfield.*" The powers vested in the corporation were similar to those of the ordinary borough charters of this state, viz., to levy taxes for the purchase of fire-engines, fire-hooks, ladders, and such other improvements as should be deemed necessary to protect the village against fires; to order and direct in all matters relating to side-walks, shade-trees, and the sinking of public wells and pumps; to restrain cattle, sheep, and geese from running at large in the public highways; and to pass such by-laws and regulations, with suitable penalties attached, as might, from to time, be thought necessary for the attainment of the objects contemplated in the charter. The officers designated in the act of incorporation, were, a *President*, *Treasurer*, and *Clerk*, (who were in all cases to be chosen by ballot,) a *Collector of Taxes*, and a number of *Fire-Wardens* not to exceed ten, together with such other officers not enumerated as should be necessary to carry the by-laws and the provisions of the charter into effect. In case the collector should refuse or neglect to collect the tax according to the tenor of the warrant committed to him, the President must "issue his warrant directed to the Sheriff of the county of Litchfield, or his deputy, to distrain the sums or rates neglected by such collector to be collected, to be paid out of the estate of said collector." The Assessors were to be appointed by the County Court.

The first meeting of the inhabitants of the Borough under the charter, was held on the 17th of June, 1818, at which the following officers were elected, viz., Hon. FREDERICK WOLCOTT, President; Dr. WILLIAM BUEL, Treasurer; and JOSEPH ADAMS, Clerk. A committee of five was appointed to prepare a code of By-Laws for the Borough, viz. Seth P. Beers, Julius Deming, Asa Bacon, Phineas Miner, and Ozias Lewis. At an adjourned meeting holden on the 20th of June, it was voted to choose a Bailiff by ballot; and Dr. Abel Catlin was elected to that office. Benjamin Tallmadge, Asa Bacon and Charles L. Webb, were appointed a Committee of Inspection; and Ashbel Marsh was chosen Key Keeper.

These gentlemen constituted the first list of officers of our corporation. It is sad to note the inroads which death has made in their ranks in the lapse of forty years. The President, Treasurer, Clerk, and Bailiff, together with Messrs. Deming, Miner, Tallmadge and Bacon, are all with the dead.

At the regular annual meeting in September, 1818, Judge Wolcott was re-elected President; Dr. Buel, Treasurer; and Mr. Adams, Clerk; Messrs. Roger Cook, Ambrose Norton, Moses Seymour, Jr., Oliver Goodwin and James Trowbridge, were chosen Fire Wardens. At an adjourned meeting, Asa Bacon, Esq., was chosen Bailiff; Charles L. Webb, Leonard Goodwin, Jonathan Carrington, and Ambrose Norton, Assistant Bailiffs; and Leonard Goodwin, Collector.

The first Board of Assessors consisted of Erastus Lyman, Esq., Gen. Morris Woodruff, and John N. Guun, Esq. The amount of the Grand List of the Borough, Oct., 1818,) as returned by the Assessors, was $128,913.65.

In 1820, the Hon. Uriel Holmes was elected President of the Borough. In 1824, he was succeeded by Dr. William Buel, who held the office for twelve years. His successors have been the Hon. Phineas Miner, Joseph Adams, Esq., Dr. J. G. Beckwith, Garwood Sanford, Henry B. Graves, and P. K. Kilbourne, F. D. Beeman, and John H. Hubbard.

In 1823, the second general assessment of the village was made by Samuel Seymour, Frederick Wolcott, and Jonathan Carrington, Esqrs., (gentlemen appointed for that purpose by the County Court,) and did not differ materially in amount from that made in 1818. The assessment of 1835 amounted to $140,627; that of 1853, to $143,525; showing a gradual increase in the actual value of the real estate of our village, from the date of its incorporation to the present time.

The village now (1859) contains something over 200 dwellings, stores, offices, and shops; 4 houses of Public Worship, three of which have chapels annexed; a Court House, Jail, and County House; two Banks, one Savings Bank, one weekly newspaper, three Hotels, an Insurance Office, three Public Halls in addition to the Town Hall and Court Room, three High Schools, (one for young ladies and two for young gentlemen;) also, it is the residence of five clergymen, seven physcians, and ten lawyers, exclusive of those who have summer residences here.

Professor BENJAMIN SILLIMAN, LL. D., of Yale College, in 1820, published in his Journal of Science, an account of a Journey through New England. Of this village he says:

"Litchfield Hill is a beautiful spot. One principal street, (intersected, however, by some cross streets,) extends more than a mile in length, and contains a collection of very handsome houses, with gardens and court-yards. The houses and appendages are generally painted white; and it is rare to see so considerable a number of houses in a country town, where nearly all apparently belong to the gentry. In *England*, such a town would be a wonder; and here, connected as it is with the rich agricultural country which surrounds it, swelled into beautiful hills and scooped into luxuriant vallies, everywhere crowned with lively verdure and with cultivated fields—it presents a very interesting and gratifying spectacle."

COUNTY OFFICERS, PROFESSIONAL MEN, MERCHANTS, &c.,

RESIDING IN THE BOROUGH OF LITCHFIELD—1859.

HIGH SHERIFF.—Leverett W. Wessells.
DEPUTY SHERIFF.—Edward O. Peck.
COUNTY CLERK.—Frederick D. Beeman.
COUNTY TREASURER.—Charles L. Webb.

JUSTICES OF THE PEACE.—Charles Adams, John H. Hubbard, Henry B. Graves, George C. Woodruff, P. K. Kilbourn, Edward W. Seymour, Frederick D. Beeman, Wm. L. Ransom, G. A. Hickox.

MEMBERS OF THE BAR.—Seth P. Beers, (retired from practice,) Origen S. Seymour, (Judge Superior Court,) George C. Woodruff, John H. Hubbard, Gideon H. Hollister, Henry B. Graves, George W. Beers, William L. Ransom, E. W. Seymour, Frederick D. Beeman, George A. Hickox.

PHYSICIANS.—Josiah G. Beckwith, A. S. Lewis, George Seymour, David E. Bostwick, Henry W. Buel, Eliada Osborn. Orson Buel, Botanic.

CLERGYMEN.—Leonard W. Bacon, pastor 1st congregational church; H. N. Hudson, Rector St. Michael's church; James Richards, D. D., Principal Elm-Park Collegiate Institute; Joshua D. Berry, Rector Episcopal church, Plymouth; William Howard, pastor 1st Methodist church.

MERCHANTS.—Charles L Webb, J. G. Beckwith, W. F. & G. H. Baldwin, Silas N. Bronson, Wm. Wheeler, C. Rinehart, Charles F. Bishop, Theodore S. Sedgwick, A. C. Smith, George Munger, Frederick D. McNiel, Wm. H. Braman, L. O Meafoy, Wm. Munson, Henry W. Adams, Samuel Clock. Thomas H. Richards, Edward Coe.

DENTISTS.—E. W. Blake, Edward Crossman.

Daguerreotypist—Jesse L. Judd.

Jewellers.—Reuben Merriman, Christian Rinehart.

Furniture Ware-house.—David C. Bulkeley.

Dealer in Stoves, &c.—Garwood Sanford.

Meat-Markets.—Robert Merriman, Egbert T. Warner.

The professional men now residing in other parts of the town are—Rev. David L. Parmelee, pastor congregational church in South Farms; Rev. George J. Harrison, minister congregational church in Milton; Rev. J. R. Williams, Rector St. Paul's, Bantam Falls, and Trinity, Milton; Rev. Jackson Ganun, pastor of the Baptist church in Bantam Falls; Rev. Hermon L. Vaill, retired congregational minister. Dr. Garry H. Minor, South Farms; Dr. D. B. W. Camp, Northfield; Dr. James K. Wallace, Bantam Falls.

[Of the 14 practicing physicians in this town thirty years ago, (1829,) two only remain among us, Dr. Beckwith, of this village, and Dr. Minor, of South Farms.]

[From the Litchfield Monitor.]

LITCHFIELD, March 29th, 1785.—"Died on the 27th inst., in this town, Mrs. Sarah McNeil, wife of Capt. Archibald McNeil, in the 73d year of her age. She shared largely in the vicissitudes of fortune. In her native country she was brought up under easy affluent circumstances. In crossing the Atlantic they were shipwrecked, lost their only child, and an affluent fortune. By the Divine blessing upon their indefatigable industry, they procured a handsome interest. To her, emphatically, belonged that character of a virtuous woman, Prov. xxxi. She was very steady and devout in her attendance upon divine worship and ordinances—was exemplary pious, and hopefully died in the Lord. Her works do follow her."

Temperance in Litchfield Seventy Years Ago.

[Said to have been the earliest Temperance Organization in the world.]

"So many are the avenues leading to human misery, that it is impossible to guard them all. Such evils as are produced by our own folly and weakness are within our power to avoid. The immoderate use which the people of this State make of Distilled Spirits, is undoubtedly an evil of this kind. It is obvious to every person of the smallest observation, that from this pernicious practice follows a train of evils difficult to be enumerated. The morals are corrupted, property is exhausted, and health destroyed. And it is most sincerely to be regretted that from a mistaken idea that distilled spirits are necessary to laboring men, to counteract the influence of heat, and give relief from severe fatigue, that a most valuable class of citizens have been led to contract a habit of such dangerous tendency. Hence arises the inability to pay public taxes, to discharge private debts, and to support and educate families. Seriously considering this subject, and the frowns of Divine Providence in denying many families in this part of the country the means of a comfortable subsistance the present year, by failure of the principal crops of the earth; we think it peculiarly the duty of every good citizen to unite his efforts to reform a practice which leads so many to poverty, distress, and ruin. Whereupon we do hereby associate, and mutually agree, that hereafter we will carry on our business without the use of distilled Spirits as an article of refreshment, either for ourselves, or those whom we employ, and that instead thereof, we will serve our workmen with wholesome food, and common simple drinks of our own production.

Ephraim Kirby,
Timothy Skinner,
David Buel,
Julius Deming,
Benjamin Tallmadge,
Uriah Tracy,
Ebenezer Marsh,
Moses Seymour,
Samuel Marsh,
James Stone,
Samuel Seymour,
Daniel Sheldon,
Ozias Lewis,
Lawrence Wessells,
Elijah Wadsworth,
Alexander Catlin,
Reuben Smith,
Lynde Lord,
Archibald McNeil,
Abraham Bradley,
I. Baldwin, Jr.,
T. Reeve,
Collier & Adam,
Tobias Cleaver,
Amos Galpin,
Thomas Trowbridge,
S. Shethar,
Solomon Buel,
Bryant Stoddard,
Abraham Peck,
Frederick Wolcott,
Nathaniel Smith 2d,
John Allen,
John Welch,
Arthur Emmons.

By Necessity and on Principle, in consequence of little experiment and much observation, I have effectually adopted and adhered to the salutary plan herein proposed during several months past, and am still resolved to persevere until convinced that any alteration will be productive of some greater good, whereof at present I have no apprehensions whilst Human Nature remains the same.

Litchfield, 9*th May*, 1789. J. STRONG."

Slavery in Litchfield.

From sixty to eighty years ago, many of the wealthy people in this town owned negro slaves. Some were voluntarily emancipated by their owners; while others were liberated by the laws which have from time to time been passed on the subject. In 1800, the census shows only seven slaves in this town. The 'institution' is now extinct among us, though some who were born slaves are still living here.

The following document, executed by the first Governor Oliver Wolcott, we find on our town records:

"Know all men by these presents, that I, OLIVER WOLCOTT, of Litchfield, in the state of Connecticut, in expectation that my negro servant man, *Cæsar*, will, by his industry, be able to obtain a comfortable subsistence for himself, and that he will make a proper use of the freedom which I hereby give him, do discharge, liberate, and set free, him, the said *Cæsar*, and do hereby exempt him from any further obligations of servitude to me, my heirs, and from every other person claiming any authority over him, by, from, or under me. And that my said servant, whom I now make free, as aforesaid, may be known hereafter, by a proper cognomen, I hereby give him the name of *Jamus*, so that hereafter he is to be known and distinguished by the name of *Cæsar Jamus*. As witness my hand and seal, in Litchfield, November twenty-third day, A. D. 1786.

OLIVER WOLCOTT. [L. S.]

In presence of
MARY ANN WOLCOTT,
FREDERICK WOLCOTT.

VIEW OF THE CENTENNIAL CELEBRATION AT LITCHFIELD—1851.

LITCHFIELD COUNTY CENTENNIAL CELEBRATION.

On the 13th and 14th days of August, 1851, the One Hundredth anniversary of the organization of Litchfield County was celebrated with appropriate ceremonies in this village. A Committee of Arrangements had been previously appointed in each town in the county—that for Litchfield consisting of the Hon. Samuel Church, George C. Woodruff, Esq.. Rev. David L. Parmelee, Hon. William Beebe and Jonathan Buel, Esq. The following gentlemen composed the Central Committee, viz., Hon. Seth P. Beers, (Chairman,) Hon. Origen S. Seymour, G. H. Hollister, Edwin B. Webster and Wm. H. Thompson, Esqrs., all of Litchfield: Col. Robbins Battell, of Norfolk, Hon. David C. Sanford, of New Milford, and Rev. Jonathan Lee, of Salisbury.

An immense crowd of returning emigrants from the county, and others, were present. The great Tent belonging to Yale College was spread on the West Park, under which the public services took place—consisting of an Historical Address, by the Hon. Samuel Church, LL. D., of Litchfield, the then Chief Justice of the State; a Discourse, no 'The Age of Homespun,' by the Rev. Horace Bushnell, D. D., of Hartford, a native of Litchfield; and a Poem, by the Rev. John Pierpont, of Medford, Mass. also a native of this town.

The following were the Officers of the Day:

Gen. DANIEL B. BRINSMADE, of Washington, President.
Gen. R. C. Abernethy,
Hon. Roger H. Mills,
John Buckingham, Esq.,
Hon. Charles B. Phelps,
Hiram Goodwin, Esq.,
} Vice Presidents.
Major-General William T. King, of Sharon, Chief Marshall.
Col. William F. Baldwin, of Litchfield, and 21 others, Marshals.

On the second day of the celebration, addresses were made under the Tent by the Hon. Messrs. Daniel S. Dickinson, Amasa J. Parker, F. A. Tallmadge, David Buel, George W. Holley, George Gould, Henry Dutton, &c. Letters were read, songs and hymns were sung: old acquaintances were renewed, and new one formed; and, though friends and strangers came in thousands, the hospitality of our people proved abundant. The 13th and 14th of Augest, 1851, are days that will long be remembered in our local calender.

☞ The drawing on the opposite page, was made by Mr. Jules Busch, (a native of Dresden, Germany,) who, in 1851–'2, was a teacher of Drawing, etc., in this village. He was subsequently a Professor of the Fine Arts in the State Normal School. On his return from a visit to his native country in the autumn of 1858, he perished at sea, with 500 others, by the burning of the steamship Austria.

ZEBULON GIBBS' NARRATIVE.

[Zebulon Gibbs was born in Windsor Aug. 19, 1711; died in Litchfield Jan. 8, 1803.]

"Memoirs of Capt. Zebulon Gibbs.—Some memoirs of my life may not be uninteresting. I came to Litchfield in the year 1720, then being in my tenth year. There were then but three families living within the limits of Litchfield, viz., John Peck, Captain Jacob Griswold, and Ezekiel Buck. Said Griswold was taken by two Indians in the month of May, 1722, and carried as far as Canaan; and in the succeeding night, when the Indians were asleep, said Griswold took their guns and made his escape, and returned to the town next day—though he was followed by the Indians within sight of the houses then standing on the now town plat. In the same year, in the month of August, Joseph Harris was killed and scalped by the Indians. On the day that said Harris was killed, I was solicited by him to go with him out to the Plain west of the town, to drive his team; but as there was no guard going that day to that part of the town, I refused to go with him. He then went alone; but when the news came into town that Harris was killed, there was an alarm made, and the people rallied out in search of him, and I was the first who found him dead.

I am now the oldest man living in the county of Litchfield, save one. I attended the first funeral that was ever attended in this town, of a white person. I have been a mighty hunter in my early life; I have killed five Deer in this town in one day.

I went up to Ticonderoga in the late revolutionary war, with Colonel Hinman. I was active in the French War in the year 1756, till the year 1762. I was a conductor of teams and horses, by which means I obtained the title of Captain. I married about the age of 21, and lived with my wife 62 years, and she died—by whom I had nine children; three died young, and six lived to settle in the world in the marriage state. I have had 48 grandchildren, 133 great-grandchildren, and sundry of the 5th generation, but the number I cannot ascertain. I am now 91 years old. I have enjoyed a firm constitution. I was able the last summer to mow and reap, and very probably shall do some this season.

I cannot boast of holding many places of office and trust in this town, though I have been a Nuisance Committee above forty years, and have endeavored to be faithful in removing encroachments from the highways. But the young ones are now rising up, and think they know more than the old man: but I am alive yet, though I have experienced almost everything but death. ZEBULON GIBBS.

Litchfield, June 30, 1802."

The Press and Politics.

On Tuesday, December 21, 1784, was issued in this town the first number of "The Weekly Monitor, and American Advertizer," printed by Collier & Copp, "in the south end of the Court House." It contains only three Litchfield advertizements, viz.. 1. That of William Russell, Stocking Weaver, [from Norwich, England,] who announced that he was ready to make "worsted, cotton and linen Jacket and Breeches Patterns, men's and women's Stockings, Gloves, and Mitts." 2. That of Zalmon Bedient, Barber, who offers cash for human Hair, at his barber's shop "a few rods north of the Court House in Litchfield." 3. That of Cornelius Thayer, Brazier, who gives notice that he carries on business at the shop of Col. Miles Beach, in North street—at which shop the Jewelers' and Silversmith's business "is carried on as usual by said Beach."

The Monitor was continued for a period of 22 years: for 16 years of which, it had no rival in the town. It was printed on a sheet about one-third the present size of the Litchfield Enquirer—with course type, and coarse blue paper. A single compositor might have set the type in a single day for all the new matter which was contained in some of the weekly issues. Yet it is a most interesting epitome of the olden times. From it we are able to glean very many facts and events in the history of this town and county, which are preserved no where else. Until after the advent of the present century, both the town and county were federal in their politics; and the Monitor was was at once the organ and the oracle of the federal party in this region.

In August, 1805, two young printers—Messrs. Sellick Osborn and Timothy Ashley —came to this town and established THE WITNESS, a violent democratic newspaper. The Witness was edited by Mr. Osborn, who, though a man of talents and energy, was a most unscrupulous partizan and bitter satirist. Though there was a formidable minority of democrats in the township at this time, Litchfield Hill was the stronghold of Federalism. Tallmadge, Reeve, Wolcott, Deming, Gould, Tracy, Holmes, Allen, Aaron Smith, Rev. Messrs. Champion and Huntington, and indeed nearly all the leading men of the village, were Federalists, and looked upon Jefferson as an infidel and reprobate. Subsequent to the Presidential Election of 1800, (which resulted in the choice of Jefferson to the Presidency,) the partizan sermons and prayers of Messrs. Champion and Huntington of the congregational church had driven several of their church members (including Deacon Lewis) to Episcopacy. On one occasion, after a political sermon from Parson Huntington, his venerable colleague, Father Champion, prayed first and fervently for "*thy servant* the President of the United States" (John Adams;) and concluded thus—"And, O Lord! wilt thou bestow upon the Vice President (Jefferson) a double portion of Thy grace, *for Thou knowest he needs it!*" The summary withdrawal of so many members, caused the first church no little embarrassment. A formal expulsion was proposed; but some of them occupied high social positions, and others were nearly allied to remaining members. The matter was finally adjusted by a simple withdrawal of the "watch and fellowship" of the church from the the seceders. The feeling of hostility between federalists and democrats was such that prominent men living the same neighborhood refused to recognize each other when they met; federal ladies refused even to make formal calls at the houses of their democratic neighbors; and the children of federalists were forbidden to associate with those of the hated democrats. Such was the state of feeling on Litchfield Hill when The Witness opened its batteries on the ranks of Federalism. At first, its saults were treated with contempt. Osborn grew bolder, more bitter, and more personal—gathering up and parading before the public the foibles or follies (real or manufactured) of the principal men of the village, against whose honor no word of suspicion had before been breathed. Charges and insinuations of hypcrisy and crime were freely blended with the most scathing ridicule. This was "bearding the lion in his den." It was not long before Osborn was indicted, tried and convicted, of a libel on Julius Deming, Esq. Osborn and his partner, Ashley, were both subjected to a fine, in default of the payment of which, both were committed to the County Jail. Ashley was soon liberated; and Osborn *might* have been had he complied with the terms of the court. But, as he himself expressed it, "the only alternative offered him, was to have either his *body* or *mind* imprisoned, of course he remained in confinement." His friends regarded him as a martyr to his political fidelity. It was published far and wide through the columns of the democratic journals, that his health was sinking from confinement "in a damp and loathsome cell:" that a maniac charged with murder was thrust into the same cell with him, &c. On the 4th of July, 1806, a meeting of the democrats of Litchfield was held at Phelps' Hotel, at which a committee of three was appointed "to repair to the prison and learn the true situation of Mr. Osborn, and his treatment since his imprisonment, and to report at an adjourned meeting." At the adjourned meeting, on the 14th, the committee reported, in substance, that they had visited Mr. O. at the jail: that he was confined in the same room with two criminals, both charged with capital offences; that his room was formed of damp and ragged stone walls, in which the air was impure, stagnant and offensive, and so dark that it was difficult to distinguish one's features; that his friends were generally denied admission to his room, and could only have intercourse with him through the outer grate of the prison; that his health was failing, &c.. &c. From this date, the committee visited the prison from time to time, and issued their weekly bulletins through the columns of The Witness. In vain Sheriff Landon denied the truth of the com mittee's original report. The story of Osborn's persecutions went abroad over the land. The democracy of distant States held indignation meetings, at which Osborn was extolled, the Connecticut Courts denounced, and the Litchfield federalists execrated At length it was resolved to have a grand ovation in behalf of Osborn, at Litchfield—and the 6th of August was fixed upon for the celebration. The great day finally arrived, and with it came an immense concourse of democrats from this and other States. Day-break was greeted with the discharge of one gun at the head of North street, a responsive discharge an the flag-staff on the Public Green, and martial music until sun-rise. At Sun-Rise, 17 guns were fired—with martial music. At 11, the procession moved in the following order, viz.,

MILITARY—commanded by Major Stephen Ranney; Lieut. Swett, U. S. Officer stationed at Springfield, acting as Marshal, John M. Felder, as Adjutant, and Chauncey Hotchkiss, as Quarter-Master—consisting of

Cavalry, commanded by Captain Carter.
Band of Music.
Matross company from Danbury, commanded by Lieut. Ambler,
do. do. of this town, commanded by Capt. Bissell.
do. do. composed of boys, in white uniform.
Light Infantry, commanded by Captain Shethar.
Infantry, commanded by Captain Grannis.
do. commanded by Lieut. Stone.
do. commanded by Ensign Norton.
Two of the Committee of Arrangements.
Clergy and Orator,
General TIMOTHY SKINNER, President of the Day,
Moses Seymour, Esq., John Welch, Esq. Ozias Lewis, Esq, } Vice Presidents of the Day,
Six of the Committee of Arrangement,
Marshals of Connecticut and Vermont,
Collectors of New Haven and Middletown,
Citizens generally.

The procession passed under Osborn's prison window, with heads uncovered, each saluting the prisoner with a passing bow, and the military giving him a brigadier's salute. Notwithstanding the hatred with which many of the congregationalists regarded democracy, the society's committee had generously tendered the use of their meeting-house for the occasion. Thither the procession wended. The services in the church consisted of a prayer by the Rev. Asahel Morse, (Baptist,) of Suffield; Reading of the Declaration of Independence, by Jonathan Law, Esq,, of Cheshire; an Oration, by David Plant, Esq, of Stratford, [since member of congress and lieut. governor]: and an Address by Joseph L. Smith, Esq, of Litchfield.

Before the arrival of the procession at the church, an occurrence took place which created much ill-feeling and comment at the time. Messrs. Champion and Huntington entered the church, and were proceeding up the aisle toward the pulpit, when (according to Mr. Champion's statement,) he was seized near the shoulder by Joseph L. Smith, Esq, a member of the committee of arrangements, who pulled him around, saying—"You have no business here, and must go out of the house." Mr. C. replied, that he was an old man, and wished for liberty to sit in the pulpit, assuring him that he would make no disturbance. Mr. Smith grew more boisterous, and the two clergymen withdrew. Mr. Smith and his friends published a very different version of the story; while the federalists reiterated that Smith had at first boasted of the exploit, and declared that he would have called the military to his aid if it had been necessary in ejecting the intruders. Mr. Champion seems to have taken the matter very seriously. "I was much afflicted," he wrote, "at being cast out of the House of God, where I had worshipped almost 54 years, and could expect to be there but a few days more. These reflections crowded into my mind, when ejected and retiring from the place where God's honor had dwelt."

At the annual election in October, 1805, it may be remarked, not a single democrat had been chosen to the Legislature in Litchfield county; and the federalists had not been backward in taunting Osborn about the "revolution" which it was said he had boasted he would produce in this region. At the annual election in May, 1806, the tables had been partially reversed by the election of two democratic Representatives from Litchfield by a vote of 314 to 308. A portion of the democratic enthusiasm in behalf of Osborn, is attributable to an appreciation of his services in producing this result.

As an incident of the celebration, it is mentioned that during the day, a placard was displayed on the door of one of principal Hotels, bearing the significant words—"No DEMOCRATS ADMITTED HERE." Some gentlemen from a distance put up, as was their custom when this way, with an intimate friend, who chanced to be a rank federalist. He soon enquired if they had come to attend the celebration; and on being answered in the affirmative, he abruptly replied—"Then you cannot be accommodated at my house. As old friends, I should have been glad to see you; as democrats I want nothing to do with you!" Such was the spirit of the times.

When the services in the church were over, the procession was re-formed and proceeded to a large Bower which had been erected in the meadow on the south side of East street, nearly opposite the Jail, where a cold repast had been prepared by Capt. Phelps. Seventeen regular toasts were drank, accompanied by the discharge of cannon and music from the band. Among them were the following:

"Justice—May false witnesses, perjured judges, and packed juries, be banished from its courts."

"Selleck Osborn—Like Daniel in the lion's den, he is teaching his persecutors that the beasts cannot devour him." [3 cheers.]

"Liberty of the Press—Litchfield Jail its stronghold." [3 cheers.]

"The Political Clergy—If there were twenty Gods, perhaps some one might approve their services; but the ONE God wants no political pastors." [8 cheers.]

"The memory of our departed friend, Ephraim Kirby—His virtues will live while our memory lasts; his merits shall be known to posterity."

"Litchfield Jail—Our votes will level it as the ram's horns did the walls of Jericho." [6 cheers.]

The Witness complains that the name of Major Seymour was stricken from the roll of Justices of the Peace for this county, by the Legislature, (May 1807,) because of his participation in the 6th of August celebration.

In June 1807, The Witness gives the following summary of the suits against Messrs Osborn and Ashley, viz.:

"Fine and costs in libel suit with J. Deming, Esq.,	$346 46
For publishing case of Tallmadge & Wolcott vs. General Hart, with comments thereon, fine and costs,	605 98
For slandering Thomas Collier,	522 00
(Besides cost of complaint in favor of Mr. Ashley against Thomas G. Collier, which complaint the county court dismissed.)	
Aggregate,	$1,474 44

Osborn was not the only man involved in libel suits in those days. The Hon. Tapping Reeve, and Capt. Thomas Collier of the Monitor, were both indicted before the U. S. District Court at New Haven, for libeling President Jefferson; and the Rev. Dan Huntington, of this village, recovered $1,000 from Maj. Babcock, of the Hartford Mercury, a democratic paper.

The Witness was discontinued in the summer of 1807—having been published about two years. Selleck Osborn was a native of Danbury; and, after leaving Litchfield, published The Delaware Watchman, at Wilmington, Del. A volume of his Poems was published in Boston. He died in Philadelphia in 1826.

The Litchfield Monitor was discontinued in 1806—having been published by Mr. Collier for 22 years. Thomas Collier (son of Richard) was born in Boston, Feb. 20, 1760, and died in Binghamton, N. Y., 1844. On leaving this town, he resided for several years in Troy. In June, 1799, an orphan lad of 14 years, named John C. Wright, from Wethersfield, entered the Monitor Office as an apprentice, remained with Mr. Collier until of age, married his daughter Mary, and for some time published a paper in Troy. Having been admitted to the bar, he settled in Steubenville, Ohio, in the winter of 1809-'10; and in 1831, he removed thence to Cincinnati, where the venerable couple are still living. Mr. Wright has been State's Attorney, member of Congress, U. S. Attorney for the District of Ohio, and Judge of the Supreme Court. In 1834, he received the degree of Doctor of Laws from a Kentucky college.

The Litchfield Gazette was commenced in January, 1808, by Messrs. Charles Hosmer and Oliver Goodwin, both from Hartford. The Gazette was discontinued May 17, 1809. Mr. Hosmer returned to Hartford, where he is still engaged in mercantile business, and has been for many years the Recording Secretary of the Connecticut Historical Society. Mr. Goodwin remained in this village as a bookseller and stationer until his death in 1855.

Isaiah Bunce came to this town soon after, and commenced The Litchfield Journal, the name of which was changed to The Litchfield Republican in 1819—which, in turn, was succeeded by The Miscellany, a small quarto, in July, 1821. In September, 1822, Mr. Bunce commenced in this village the publication of The American Eagle, which he removed to New Haven in March, 1826. Mr. Bunce was a man of enterprize, and established a Bookstore, Reading Room, and Circulating Library; and was for a few years a Justice of the Peace.

The Litchfield County Post was established in 1826, by Stephen S. Smith, from Poultney, Vermont. He disposed of the establishment to Joshua Garrett, who, after publishing the Post for a few weeks, sold out to Henry Adams in 1829. Mr. Adams soon changed the name of the paper to THE LITCHFIELD ENQUIRER, which it still bears. After editing and publishing The Enquirer for about thirteen years, he was accidentally drowned, while fishing, by breaking through the ice of Bantam river, near the entrance of that stream into Bantam Lake. Mr. A. was a son of the late Joseph Adams, Esq., of this village, and was a talented and popular editor. His brother, Charles Adams, Esq., succeeded him in the publication of the Enquirer. From 1845 to 1853, the paper was conducted by P. K. Kilbourn. H. W. Hyatt and E. C. Goodwin afterwards successively became proprietors of the establishment. The present publishers are Messrs. Adams and Betts. The Enquirer is now in its 34th volume.

Nov. 3, 1833, Melzer Gardner, from Hartford, commenced The Litchfield Democrat, which was discontinued in September, 1834. Subsequently, while editing a paper in Richmond, Va., Gardner was shot on board a steamboat near that city, by a man to whom he had given offense by an article which he had published.

The Litchfield Sun was commenced by John M. Baldwin, (a native of this town,) in February, 1835; sold out to S. G. Hayes, of New Haven, in Sept. 1837, who discontinued it in April, 1839.

In January, 1840, Charles E. Moss & Co. commenced The Mercury, which was transferred to Josiah Giles in the following August. It was discontinued some time in 1842. The Mercury was soon succeeded by The Democratic Watchman, also published by Mr. Giles, which was discontinued in 1844.

In 1845, J. K. Averill commenced the New Milford Republican, at New Milford; in September, 1846, he removed his office to this village, and changed the name of his paper to the Litchfield Republican. W. F. & G. H. Baldwin, Albert Stoddard, and Franklin Hull, successively continued the publication of the Republican. In 1856, the office was removed to Falls Village, where the paper is still continued under the name of The Housatonic Republican.

All these papers, it should be remarked, were published weekly.

OUR PARKS.

Our East and West Parks, which now add so much to the beauty of our village, were graded, enclosed, and planted with trees, in the summer of 1836. During the preceding year, the subject had been considered by our citizens, in connection with several natives of this town residing in New York city, and the sum of $600 was readily subscribed for the object. On the 2d of January, 1836, a special town meeting was held—Roger Cook, Moderator, and George C. Woodruff, Clerk pro tem. At this meeting full permission was granted to the committee appointed by the subscribers of the fund to enclose and "improve as they shall see proper," that portion of the Green or Highway at present enclosed in the parks referred to. One of the most efficient and active members of the first Park Committee (and who, perhaps, did more than any other person in raising the Park Fund,) was the late Dr. J. S. Wolcott, of this village, a son of the last Gov. Wolcott.

On the 4th of October, 1858, the town voted that the inhabitants of this village 'have leave to construct, without expense to the town, a Park in the common ground between the East and West Parks, in such suitable place as a committee appointed by this meeting shall designate, in such way as shall not materially interfere with travel.'

The Litchfield Law School.

This institution was established in 1784, by TAPPING REEVE, Esq., (afterwards chief justice of the State, and LL. D.,) who was the sole Principal until 1798, when the Hon. JAMES GOULD, LL. D., became associated with him. This was the first institution of the kind in the country; and, as its conductors were learned and eminent men, it attained a wide-spread renown. From 1820, Judge Gould conducted the School alone for several years; when the Hon. Jabez W. Huntington became his assistant. In consequence of the failing health of Judge Gould. it was discontinued in 1833. Up to that time the number of students had been 1,024—every State then in the Union having been represented. Of this number, 15 became U. S. Senators; 50 members of Congress; 40 Judges of the higher State courts: 10 Governors of States; 5 members of the National Cabinet, (Messrs. Calhoun, Woodbury, Mason, Clayton and Hubbard;) 2 Judges Supreme Court United States, (Henry Baldwin and Levi Woodbury;) 1 Vice President of the United State, (John C. Calhoun;) and several Foreign Ministers—among whom is the Hon. John Y. Mason, our present Ambassador to France.

At the annual dinner of the "Story Association" of the Cambridge Law School, (Mass.,) in 1851, the following reference was made to our Law School. Mr. Loring, like scores of his fellow-students, married a Litchfield lady.

Judge Kent gave—

"*The first-born of the law schools of this country—the Litchfield Law School.* The Boston bar exhibits its rich and ripened fruits. By them we may judge of the tree and declare it good."

Hon. C. G. Loring, replied. He began with expressing his regret that there was no other representative from the Litchfield Law School present to respond to the complimentary but just notice of that institution.

"I do not remember, said he, to have ever been more forcibly reminded of my younger days, than when looking around upon our young friends in the midst of whom I stand. It recalls the time when I, too, was a student among numerous fellow students. It will, probably, be news to them and many others here, that thirty-eight years ago, which to many here seems a remote antiquity, there existed an extensive Law School in the state of Connecticut, at which more than sixty students from all parts of the country were assembled,—every State then in the Union, being there represented. I joined it in 1813, when it was at its zenith, and the only prominent establishment of the kind in the land.

The recollection is as fresh as the events of yesterday, of our passing along the broad shaded streets of one of the most beautiful of the villages of New England, with our inkstands in our hands, and our portfolios under our arms, to the lecture room of Judge Gould—the last of the Romans, of Common Law lawyers; the impersonation of its genius and spirit. It was, indeed, in his eyes, the perfection of human reason—by which he measured every principle and rule of action, and almost every sentiment. Why, Sir, his highest visions of poetry seemed to be in the refinement of special pleading; and to him, a *non sequitur* in logic was an offense deserving, at the least, fine and imprisonment—and a repetition of it, transportation for life. He was an admirable English scholar; every word was pure English, undefiled, and every sentence fell from his lips perfectly finished, as clear, transparent, and penetrating as light, and every rule and principle as exactly defined and limited as the outline of a building against the sky. From him, Sir, we obtained clear, well-defined, and accurate knowledge of the Common Law, and learned that allegiance to it was the chief duty of man, and the power of enforcing it upon others his highest attainment. From his lecture room we passed to that of the venerable Judge Reeve, shaded by an aged elm, fit emblem of himself. He was, indeed, a most venerable man, in character and appearance—his thick, gray hair parted and falling in profusion upon his shoulders, his voice only a loud whisper, but distinctly heard by his earnestly attentive pupils. He, too, was full of legal learning, but invested the law with all the genial enthusiasm and generous feelings and noble sentiments of a large heart at the age of eighty, and descanted to us with glowing eloquence upon the sacredness and majesty of law. He was distinguished, Sir, by that appreciation of the gentler sex which never fails to mark the true man, and his teachings of the law in reference to their rights and to the domestic relations, had great influence in elevating and refining the sentiments of the young men who were privileged to hear him. As illustrative of his feelings and manner upon this subject, allow me to give a specimen. He was discussing the legal relations of married women: he never called them, however, by so inexpressible a name, but always spoke of them as, "the better half of mankind," or in some equally just manner. When he came to the axiom that "a married woman has no will of her own;" this, he said, was a maxim of great theoretical importance for the preservation of the sex against the undue influence or coercion of the husband; but, although it was an inflexible maxim, in theory, experience taught us that practically it was found that they sometimes had wills of their own—MOST HAPPILY FOR US.

We left his lecture room, Sir, the very knight errants of the law, burning to be the defenders of the right and the avengers of the wrong; and he is no true son of the Litchfield School who has ever forgotten that lesson. I propose, Sir

The Memories' of Judge Reeve and Judge Gould,—among the first, if not the first founders of a National Law School in the United States—who have laid one of the corner stones in the foundation of true American patriotism, loyalty to the law.

SOUTH FARMS.

From 1740 to 1767, the people residing in the southern section made several unsuccessful applications to the Legislature—first, "to be annexed to the north society of Woodbury; second, to be allowed what were termed "winter privileges;" and, finally, to be set off as a distinct ecclesiastical society. In December, 1760, the inhabitants of South Farms, having obtained permission of the Legislature "to enjoy the privileges of a winter parish for three months in a year," asked the town to be released from a part of their tax for building the meeting-house on the Hill. Whereupon it was voted in town meeting, that "in case South Farms shall become a distinct ecclesiastical society within forty-five years, the town will pay back to said society the money advanced by said winter parishioners toward building said meeting-house." In 1761, the Legislature voted that the inhabitants of South Farms "be allowed to have the Gospel preached to them for four months in the winter season, and shall have liberty to build a meeting-house;" and three years later, they voted to build a winter house 35 feet long, 25 feet wide, with nine feet posts, "provided Justus Gibbs will do it for £70: 10."

In 1767, the society of South Farms was duly incorporated, and its inhabitants have since transacted their ecclesiastical and educational affairs separately from those residing in other portions of the town. The act of 1857, it should be remarked, restores to the *town* all business relating to *schools*. The first person buried in that part of the town, was Mr. James Stoddard, who was killed at the raising of a dwelling house. I have already given specimens of the orthography of certain portions of the town records. The records of South Farms's Society were by no means an *improvement* upon them. For instance, on the 14th of March, 1759, the society voted "to pay Charles Woodruff six shillings for *Bears* to carry ye dead." In 1769, it was voted "that we think the sealing ordinances are equally sacred, and any person that is qualified for one is qualified for both." In 1770, "voted that we approve of the church vote, viz., that conversion should not be a term for admission for church communion." In 1776, the town granted to Thomas Waugh, and his heirs forever, the right to use a certain burying ground in South Farms for *pasturing*, "provided he or they shall keep up and maintain convenient *bars* for the people to pass and repass for the purpose of burying their dead." In 1785, a new and commodious church was erected. In April of that year, the society voted that "the meeting-house committee shall have good right to furnish *Rum*, *Grindstones* and *Ropes*, sufficient for framing the meeting-house according to their best discretion," and in June, an overseer was appointed to direct the issue of liquor at the raising, and a vote at the same time was passed that said overseer "shall give two drams a day to the spectators, one a little before noon, and the other a little before night." The present church was built in 1844. The present pastor, Rev. David L. Parmelee, was settled in 1841.

President DWIGHT, of Yale college, (in his Travels,) gives the following interesting facts relative to this parish, and the Academy which formerly flourished there:

"Immediately above Watertown lies South Farms—the southern part of Litchfield. This parish is principally a collection of hills, which are high, moist, and excellent grazing ground. The surface is pleasant, the houses good farmers' dwellings, of which a little village is formed around the church. The inhabitants are industrious and thrifty; and distinguished for good morals, good order, and decency of deportment. A flourishing academy has been raised of late, almost solely by the efforts of James Morris, Esq., who is at once its founder and preceptor. This gentleman, soon after he had finished his education at Yale College, became an officer in the American army, in which he continued throughout the revolutionary war. After the peace, his parents and his patrimony being in this place, he was induced to establish himself here for life. At his return, he found the inhabitants less enlightened and less refined than those of many other parts of the state. What in this country is perhaps singular, they regarded him, both as a man liberally educated and as an officer, with suspicion and alienation. At the same time he perceived, with not a little mortification, that they were in many instances ignorant and vicious. As he had been absent from his early youth, his influence among them was to be created. With a disposiion, which cannot be enough commended, he determined to commence in form the work of a general reformation. After various experiments, sufficiently discouraging, among those who have arrived at middle age, he turned his attention to their children; and hoped by communicating to them the advantages of a well-directed education to furnish their minds with both knowledge and virtue, and thus to transform their character into amiableness and worth. For this benevolent purpose he founded the institution which I have mentioned. In this Academy it has, from the first, been the commanding object to inculcate the best principles of morality and religion, and to require of the students an unexceptionable deportment. The youths of both sexes, usually assembled here from various parts of the country, are in number from 40 to 70. Mr. Morris has had the satisfaction of seeing his expectations more than realized. Not only were the benefits of his design realized by the inhabitants of South Farms, but they are spread also through most parts of the country, and extensively through this and the neighboring states. This is one among the proofs furnished by experience of the power possessed by an individual, of spreading around him, if properly disposed, the best blessing of society."

St. Paul's Masonic Lodge.

The first Charter of this Lodge was obtained from the R. W. Joseph Webb, "Grand Master of Masons in America," then residing in Boston, and bears date June 1, 1781. It was granted on petition of the following persons, viz, Rev. James Nichols, John Watkins, Thomas Philips, Eaton Jones, Benjamin Hanks, John Collins, Noah Blakeslee, Wm. Durkee, Daniel Starr, John Colvill, Jonathan Kettle, Josiah Norton and Adino Hale—about half of whom belonged in this town, the remainder in Goshen and Harwinton. The first meeting of the Lodge was held June 13, 1781—the Rev. Ashbel Baldwin presiding as Master. The following other offieers were chosen—Benjamin Hanks, S. W.; Eaton Jones, J. W.; John Collins, Treasurer; and J. Kettle, Secretary. On the 15th of October, 1790, the Lodge received a new charter from the Grand Lodge of the State, in which it is designated as "St. Paul's Lodge, No. 11." It has numbered among its members some of our most eminent citizens.

The following the present officers of the Lodge:—David E. Bostwick, W. M.; F. D. Beeman, S. W.; Levi Curtis, J. W.; Charles L. Webb, Treasurer; Wm. H. Crossman, Secretary; Henry A. Hull, S. D.; George Munger, J. D.; Edward Crossman and George Horace Baldwin, Stewards; Sheldon Munger, Tyler.

TOWN DEPOSIT FUND.

This fund was derived from the Surplus Revenue in the Treasury of the United States, which, by an act of Congress passed in 1836, was distributed among the several states in proportion to their representation in that body. The share belonging to Connecticut was, by order of the Legislature, apportioned to the several towns in the state according to their population. The amount thus given to Litchfield was $11,444.50. The town appointed Isaac Lawrence to be Treasurer, and Theron Beach and George C. Woodruff to be Managers of the Town Deposit Fund. On the 9th of April, 1838, the town voted to appoint a committee of seven to direct in what manner the interest of the Fund should be divided among the several school districts of the town; and Messrs. Putnam, Kilbourn, James M. Pierpont, Dan Catlin, William Bassett, Edward Pierpont, Frederick Buel and O. S. Seymour, were appointed said committee. The Fund is invested in promissory notes, secured by mortgage, and in town orders. The annual interest is $686.67, which is appropriated to the support of schools.

MINERAL SPRING.

In August, 1820, James Pierce, Esq., announced in Silliman's Journal of Science that he had discovered a valuable Mineral Spring on the eastern slope of Prospect Mountain, in this town. The waters of the Pool (as it was called,) soon became celebrated for their medicinal virtues, and a House was erected near by for the accommodetion of visitors. In March, 1821, it is stated in Silliman's Journal that the waters of this spring had "effected cures of obstinate rheumatic complaints that had resisted ordinary remedies;" and that they had "been sent for weekly from Hartford, and were considered equal to those of the Stafford Spring." The Pool is now more often visited by the lovers of wild and picturesque scenery, than for its waters.

ILLUSTRIOUS GUESTS.—I have elsewhere referred to the visits of Washington and LaFayette to this town. In 1807, Jerome Bonaparte, with his young American wife, came 'with coach and four,' and put up at Catlin's Hotel. About 1820, the Hon. Martin Van Buren came here on a visit with his friend, Judge Skinner—spending the Sabbath, and attending Dr. Beecher's church. July 16, 1832, the Hon. John Quincy Adams arrived in town and spent the night here.

"LITCHFIELD, October 30th, 1797.—We the subscribers, having at our own expense, erected a Church in the Western Part of Litchfield, and being desirous of forming ourselves into an Episcopal Society, hereby lay before, request, and petition the meeting of the First Episcopal Society in said Litchfield, to give their consent to this request, and in future exempt us from paying taxes to the First Episcopal Society—upon condition of our organizing and taxing ourselves. All of which we submit to said meeting in brotherly love.

Isaac Kilbourn,
David Kilbourn,
Sylvanus Bishop,
Solomon Kilbourn,
John Landon,
Jesse Kilbourn,
John Tryon,
Heber Stone,
Orange Kilbourn,
James Kilbourn,
Nathaniel Smith 2d,
Levi Kilbourn,
Simeon Palmer,
Elisha S. Munger,
James Glass,
Horace Stone,
Samuel Denison,
James Lee,
Benjamin Johnson, Jr.,
Philander Westover,
Chauncey Kilbourn,
Heman Kilbourn,
John Kilbourn,
Benjamin Doolittle,
Reuben Smith 2d,
James Adams,
Newell Miller,
Remembrance Landon,
Arunah Blakeslee,
Jacob Kilbourn,
Frederick Hunt,
Samuel Woodcock,
Thaddeus Stocker,
Noah Stone, 2d,
Samuel Hazen,
Jesse Stoddard,
Jehial Gates,
Jonathan Bishop,
Joseph Burgess,
Benjamin Bissell, 3d,
Hicks Smith,
Chauncey Denison,
Phineas Smith,
David Westover,
Wait Smith,
Samuel Carter,
Abel Clemons,
Anson Smith,
Lumbert Johnson,
Daniel Haskins
David Kenney,
Joseph Westover,
Jeremiah Kilbourn,
Nathaniel Smith,
Milo Hunt,

A true Copy of Record.

N. B. The above petition was granted the 6th day of November, 1797.

SETH LANDON, *Society's Clerk.*"

Miscellaneous Items.

BENEFACTIONS.—The lot on which stands St. Michael's church, in South street, was the gift, in 1809, of Samuel Marsh, Esq., of Norfolk, Va., a native of this town.

The Town Clock in the tower of the first church, was presented to the society by the late Dr. Abel Catlin.

Mr. Nath'l Bosworth, (a member of the West Episcopal society of this town,) died in 1801, leaving a bequest of £100 for the purchase of a bell for the West Church. The bell purchased with this sum is still in use in St. Paul's church, Bantam.

In 1843, Messrs. Hugh P. and Garry Welch presented the Episcopal society in Milton with the bell which is now in use in the church of that parish.

Mr. Solomon Marsh, soon after the completion of the first Episcopal church-edifice in this village, presented that society with an Organ at a cost of $800.

Asa Hopkins, Esq., a native and resident of this town, died in 1838. In his will, he gave the use of his property to his wife during her life. At her decease, (after the payment of certain legacies,) he bequeathed the residue of his property to the congregational church and society in Northfield. Mrs. Hopkins died in 1855. The whole amount received by the said church and society, from Mr. Hopkins' estate, is $10,000.

EXECUTIONS.—It is believed that no native of Litchfield was ever convicted of murder; and that wilful murder was never committed by or upon a white man, within the limits of this town. In 1768, an Indian named John Jacob was hanged for the murder of another Indian. In November, 1795, Thomas Goss, of Barkhamsted, was executed for the murder of his wife. In these days he would have been acquitted on the ground of insanity. On the plea that his wife was a witch, he split her head open with an axe. Though at times apparently rational, he sometimes declared that he was the second Lamb of God—that he was brother of Jesus Christ—that he was the child born of the woman, mentioned in the Revelation of St. John, 'before whom the dragon stood ready to devour the child;' he forbid his counsel to apply for a reprieve; declared the sheriff could not hang him, &c. May 8, 1780, Barnet Davenport, aged 20 years, was executed for murder and arson in Washington. Residing as a laborer in the family of Caleb Mallory, he entered the sleeping room of Mr. and Mrs. Mallory at midnight and beat them to death with a club; and their little grandchild shared the same fate. After robbing the house and setting it on fire, the murderer fled, leaving two other persons asleep who perished in the flames. These persons, it is understood, were executed in Gallows Lane, in this village. Other convictions for capital crimes have taken place before our courts, but these are the only individuals who have ever suffered the extreme penalty of the law in this county.

JAMES WATSON, from this county, graduated at Yale college in 1776; was lieutenant of a revolutionary company raised chiefly in Litchfield. After the war, he settled in New York—became wealthy, was Speaker of the House, state Senator, Naval Officer, and U. S. Senator; and died in 1806. *Where was he born ?* The late Douglas Watson, Esq, (assistant clerk of our courts,) expressed to me his belief that he was born in this town. In a retired little grave-yard, about half a mile south of Bantam Lake, is a red sandstone tablet bearing the following inscription, viz., "To the Memory of Mr. John Watson, who died November 9, 1781, in the 74th year of his age. Berthyah Watson, his widow, died Jnne 24th, 1792, in the 85th year of her age. This monument is respectfully erected by James Watson, their youngest son." The Hon. James Watson died in New York in 1806.

Obituaries.

In Litchfield, April, 1773, Col. Ebenezer Marsh, Esq., aged 72.

In Litchfield, Dec. 3, 1805, Capt. William Stanton, aged 78—commander of a company in Sheldon's regiment of light dragoons in the Revolution, and for more than 40 years a resident of this town.

In Litchfield, July 30, 1802, Reynold Marvin, Esq., aged 78—King's Attorney for the county previous to the Revolution.

In Litchfield, June 6, 1821, Capt. Joseph Mansfield, aged 84—an officer in the regiments of colonels Meigs and Douglas in the Revolution. He was from New Haven, but settled in this town soon after the war.

At Spadre Bluffs, on the Arkansas river, near Little Rock, Aug. 1, 1822, Colonel Matthew Lyon, aged 75—a native of Wicklow county, Ireland. In 1761, at the age 14, he came to this country poor and friendless, and was sold to pay his passage, to Mr. Hugh Hannah, of Litchfield, (who is said to have lived at tlie time on the farm owned and occupied by the late Mr. Grant Wickwire, a mile south of Bantam Lake.) Mat. was rough and independent; and Hannah was a severe disciplinarian, and not unfrequently applied the rod to his refractory servant. At length an altercation ensued—Mat. threw a mallet at the head of his master, and fled. He was soon heard from in Vermont, where, among the hardy mountaineers, he became a leader. He was Deputy Secretary to the governor and council, clerk of the court of confiscation, Representative in the legislature, colonel of militia, editor of a newspaper, associate Judge of the Rutland county court, and, in 1796, was elected to Congress; and reelected in 1798. Removing to Kentucky in 1800, he was returned to Congress from that State from 1803 to 1810. He married a daughter of Gov. Chittenden of Vermont. His son, Chittenden Lyon, who was for eight years a member of congress from Kentucky, was one of the most popular men in that State; and from him Lyon county was named. Precisely how long Lyon lived in this town, is uncertain. In one of his addresses to his constituents, he says—" After living ten yenrs in Connecticut, from my 15th to my 25th year, I removed to a new settlement in Vermont." Were all of these 'ten years' spent in Litchfield? Hannah was living here eight or ten years after Lyon first took his seat in congress, and was fond of talking about him; attributing his success in life to the corporeal lessons which *he* had given him. The price paid by Hannah for Mat. was a pair of stags valued at £12—a fact which gave rise to many a coarse jest at the expense of the latter.

At Jackson, Mississippi Territory, Sept. 1827, Col. Stephen Ranney, U. S. A., aged 68—formerly for more than 20 years, a resident of Litchfield.

In Litchfield, Sept. 16, 1839, the Hon. Phineas Miner, aged 60—a distinguished member of the bar of this county, and late member of congress.

In Phelps, Ontario co., N. Y., July 17, 1841, Colonel David McNiel, aged 53—late a Judge of the court of common pleas for that county. He was a native of this town.

In Cazenovia, N. Y., May 14, 1842, Jesse Kilbourn, aged 64, a native of Litchfield. For more than 25 years he was in public life in that town—as Trustee and President of the corporation of Cazenovia, Postmaster, Representative, &c.

In St. Augustine, Florida, May 24 1846, Col. Joseph L. Smith, aged 70—formerly a colonel in the army, and more recently U. S. Judge of the Eastern District of Florida. From 1800 to 1817, (except a year or two,) he resided in this town. He married a daughter of the Hon. Ephraim Kirby.

In Geneseo, N. Y., Nov. 28, 1846, Samuel W. Spencer, Esq., aged 76—a native of Litchfield. He had been a magistrate, and Surrogate of Livingston county.

In Litchfield, January 19, 1852, Miss Sarah Pierce, aged 84. In 1792, she established the Litchfield Female Academy, which became one of the most celebrated institutions in the country. She remained connected with it until 1832—though for a few years previous, her nephew, John P. Brace, Esq., was the Principal. More than 2,500 young ladies and misses were members of the Academy. It was incorporated in 1827. The successors of Miss Pierce have been Misses Swift, Jones, Heyden, and others.

In Hartford, Nov. 10, 1858, the Hon. Amos M. Collins, aged 70—an eminent merchant and philanthropist. From 1843 to 1846, inclusive, he was Mayor of the city of Hartford. He was a son of Dea. Wm. Collins, and was born in Litchfield, March 30, 1788.

BIOGRAPHICAL ADDENDA.

CHILDS, Samuel R., *M. D.*, (son of Mr. Timothy Childs,) was born in Dutches county, N. Y., September 25, 1800. When the subject of this sketch was about five years old, his father purchased the mansion and farm now known as the *Childs Place*, four miles north of the Litchfield Court House, and at once removed his family there. Dr. Childs graduated at the Medical College in Pittsfield, Mass., and subsequently pursued his studies at the Institution connected with Yale College. In May, 1825, he commenced the practice of his profession in this village, and remained here until January, 1832, when he removed to the city of New York, where he soon had an extensive and lucrative business. He was appointed Physician to the City Dispensary, one of the Surgeons of the Eye and Ear Infirmary, Physician to the Bellvue Hospital, Health Officer of the city, &c. Though enthusiastically attached to his chosen profession, and one of its most learned and skillful practioners, his energies have not been devoted exclusively to it. In 1838, he was appointed one of the Commissioners of the Croton Water Board. The magnitude of the work committed to their care will be appreciated, when it is known that it required the expenditure of some $10,000,000, all of which passed through their hands. He was long a member of the Board of Education; and two or three times he was nominated for Congress in the Third District, but declined. In 1840, and again in 1853, Dr. Childs visited Europe, pursuing his professional investigations in the various hospitals of that country. With an ample fortune, he has retired to a beautiful residence near Saratoga Springs. Colonel HEMAN W. CHILDS, his brother, after being for several years a merchant and manufacturer in Litchfield, removed to New York in 1834, where he was chosen a Representative, Collector of the City Revenue, and Commissioner of Streets and Lamps; he died in 1851.

GALPIN, Robert E., (son of Mr. Amos Galpin,) was born in Litchfield; settled in Stockbridge, Mass., where he still resides. Besides holding various town offices, he was chosen a Representative in 1844 and again in 1845; and for the last twelve years, he has been a Justice of the Peace. In 1852, he was elected President of the Housatonic Agricultural Society.

STOWE, Mrs. Harriet Beecher, (daughter of the Rev. Lyman Beecher, *D. D.*,) was born in Litchfield, and married the Rev. Dr. Stowe, now Professor in the Theological Seminary at Andover. She is the author of *The May Flower*, *Uncle Tom's Cabin*, *Dred—a Tale of the Dismal Swamp*, *Sunny Memories of Foreign Lands*, &c. Each of these works, except the first, is published in two volumes. Uncle Tom's Cabin has had a much more rapid sale than any other American work. Her tour through England and Scotland, a few years since, was like a continued ovation. Wherever she went, she was welcomed with public addresses, private invitations, assemblies and festivals; indeed, the aristocracy and peasantry seemed to vie with each other in their efforts to do honor to their distinguished guest. No other lady from this side of the ocean was ever received by them with such enthusiasm.

WADSWORTH, General Elijah, was born in Hartford, Nov. 14, 1747: settled in Litchfield previous to the Revolution; was Captain in Sheldon's Regiment of Light Dragoons during nearly the entire war. In 1795, he associated himself with Messrs. Ephraim Kirby, Elijah Boardman, Uriel Holmes, sen'r and jun'r, and Samuel A. Law, in organizing the Connecticut Land Company and purchasing the Western Reserve; and the town of Wadsworth, in Medina county, was named from him. On the 15th of September, 1802, he started from Litchfield with his family for Ohio, arriving at Canfield on the 17th of October—thus making the journey in 33 days. In January, 1803, he was elected Sheriff of Trumbull county; and about a year later, he was appointed by the Legislature Major General of the 4th Division. By the surrender of Hull in August, 1812, the defense of the entire North Western Frontier of Ohio devolved upon General Wadsworth. He soon organized a force 1,500 men from his Division, placed them under the command of Brig. Gen. Perkins, who reported them to General Harrison. In November, General Wadsworth returned from the frontiers in feeble health—having reached the age of 65. In the summer of 1815, he had a paralytic shock which disabled him thereafter. He died in Canfield, Ohio, Dec. 30, 1817, in his 71st year. He married Rhoda Hopkins, of Litchfield, Feb. 16th, 1789, and had five children, all born in this town. One of these, FREDERICK, of Akron, Ohio, was Major and Inspector in the war of 1812; has since been Sheriff of Portage County, Senator, &c.

WRIGHT, George F., the celebrated artist, was born of Litchfield parents in the adjoining town of Washington, and was brought up from childhood in this town. In 1856, he received a commission from the Legislature of his native State, to paint the portraits of all the chief magistrates who have filled the executive chair of Connecticut. This important and interesting work he accomplished in such a manner as to give universal satisfaction. These portraits now adorn the Senate Chamber at Hartford. Mr. Wright has since spent two years at Rome and Munich, during a large part of which time he was a pupil of the celebrated Kaulbach. He is the inventor of an entirely new system of coloring, which is said by competent judges to be superior to anything hitherto in use. A well known amateur, writing recently from Europe to the New York *Home Journal*, says —"I saw in a studio, a few days since, two small works by a Connecticut artist named Wright, which impressed me by their wonderful beauty of color. I hesitate not to say, that one of them equalled any piece of flesh painting I ever saw, and I know of no approach to them in modern art. If these two productions are fair specimens of his system and powers, there has been no greater colorist since Titian." Mr. Wright is now pursuing his profession in Hartford.

WESSELLS, Henry W., Major U. S. Army, (son of Dr. Ashbel Wessells,) was born in Litchfield, February 20, 1809, graduated at West Point in 1833, and entered the army as brevet second lieutenant. He was actively engaged in the Creek war, in the Florida war, and in the war with Mexico. For his gallant services in the latter war, he was promoted to his present rank, and the Legislature of Connecticut, in the name of the State, presented him with a splendid sword.

BUTLER, Rev. David, *D. D.*, a native of Harwinton, was ordained Deacon by Bishop Seabury, June 10, 1792, and Presbyter June 9, 1793. From November 28, 1794, to February 21, 1799, he was Rector of St. Michael's Church in this town—during which time he lived in the large red house which then stood on the West Plain opposite the present residence of Col. Edwin Wadhams, but which has recently been moved farther south and converted into a barn. On leaving Litchfield, Dr. Butler was for a few years settled in Fairfield county, and thence removed to Troy, N. Y., where he became Rector of Trinity Church. He received the degree of D. D. at Washington (now Trinity) College in 1832; and died in Troy, July 11, 1843, aged 80 years. He married a Litchfield lady, and had ten children—one of whom, the Rev. Clement M. Butler, *D. D.*, was recently chaplain of the United States Senate.

DICKINSON, Anson, a celebrated miniature artist, was born in Litchfield, April 9, 1779; and, after residing abroad for about forty years, he returned to his native town, and died here, March 9, 1853. His brother, Andrew Dickinson, born in this town January 13, 1802, resides in Brooklyn, N. Y. He is the author of *The City of the Dead, and Other Poems;* and of an interesting volume entitled, *My First Visit to Europe*, which has reached a third edition.

GUERNSEY, Egbert, *M. D.*, (son of Mr. Noah Guernsey, or Garnsey,) was born in Litchfield, July 8, 1823, and received his medical degree at the New York University in 1846. He is the author of a *History of the United States*, for the use of Schools, (500 pages,) of which about 75,000 copies have been sold; also, of a work entitled, *Practice of Medicine*, (600 pages,) which has reached a third edition in this country, and has been re-published in England. His *Gentleman's Hand-Book of Homeopothy*, first published in 1855, has reached a second edition. Dr. Guernsey is Professor of the Principles and Practice of Medicine in the American College of Medical Science, and a medical practitioner in the city of New York.

PARMELEE, David, from Durham, married Lucy, daughter of of Ozias Lewis, Esq., of this town, Jan. 22, 1795, and immediately settled here as a lawyer. In 1806, he was appointed by President Jefferson to the office of Judge of the Court for the settlement of Land Claims in the then newly-acquired Territory of Louisiana. The Monitor (a federal paper) of March 19, of that year, in announcing the appointment, expresses its belief that "a more correct, judicious and unexceptionable appointment to office, has never been made by Mr. Jefferson." Judge Parmelee died in this town in May, 1811, aged 45—leaving six children, viz., David L., (now pastor of the church in South Farms,) Julia, (m. Hosea Webster, Esq., of Brooklyn, N. Y.,) Thomas J., Caroline, Albert O., and Celeste.

SMITH, Truman, a native of Roxbury, and a graduate of Yale college, resided in Litchfield nearly forty years, but removed to Stamford in 1854. While one of our citizens, he served as a Representative three years, a member of Congress eight years, and U. S. Senator five years—having resigned the latter office in 1854. In

1850, President Taylor tendered him a place in his cabinet as Secretary of the Interior, but, as he preferred remaining in the Senate, the offer was declined. Mr. S. is one of the ablest lawyers in the Union.

WELCH, Wm. H., (son of John Welch, Esq.,) was born in Litchfield, June 1, 1805; graduated at Yale College in 1827; was for some years a lawyer in Kalamazoo, Michigan, and while there, was chosen a member of the Constitutional Convention of that State. Removing thence to Minnesota, he was appointed Chief Justice of that Territory by President Pierce, and continued in office until her admission into the Union as a State.

Clerks and Treasurers of the 1st Episcopal Society in Litchfield, 1785 to 1859.—CLERKS.—Seth Landon, Ozias Seymour, Emanuel Russell, Ozias Lewis, David C. Sanford, Origen S. Seymour, Francis Bacon, A. S. Lewis. TREASURERS.—Heber Stone, Samuel McNiel, Lewis Kilbourn, Moses Seymour, Jr., Moses Seymour, Ozias Lewis, D. C. Sanford, Elihu Harrison, Wm. Porter, J. G. Beckwith.

☞ The following resident-Physicians of Litchfield have been Presidents of the County Medical Society, viz., William Buel, 1818, seven years; Reuben S. Woodward, 1831, one year; Samuel Buel, 1837, one year; Manly Peters, 1842, one year; Charles Vaill, 1843, one year; Reuben M. Woodruff, 1844, one year; George Seymour, 1857, one year. *Clerks.*—Samuel Buel, Samuel R. Childs, Moses A. Lee, J. G. Beckwith, George Seymour, Henry W. Buel, David E. Bostwick.

A MEETING of the GIBBS FAMILY was held at the Mansion House in Litchfield Feb. 4, 1847—at which *The Gibbs Association of Connecticut* was formed. An address was made by John Cornelius Gibbs, Esq., of Liverpool, England, relative to certain property in that country said to belong to the Gibbes of America. Frederick Whittlesey, Esq., of South Farms, was chosen President of the Association; and Frederick Gibbs, of Litchfield, Treasurer.

The Gibbs Family was formerly very numerous in Litchfield, though but few now remain among us. I am informed that Frederick Gibbs, Esq., resides on a farm which has descended from father to son, in his line, for 138 years. The "Birch Staddle," which formed one of the corner bounds of the farm in the early surveys, continued to stand as a bound-mark until the autumn of 1858, when, having become a venerable, decayed and moss-grown tree, it fell!

PERPETUAL MOTION.—At the October session of the Legislature, 1783, the exclusive right to manufacture Air Clocks was granted to Mr. Benjamin Hanks, of Litchfield. The Memorial of Mr. Hanks states that "he has invented and executed a Clock which winds itself up by the effects of air, and will continue so do without any other assistance, until the parts thereof are destroyed by friction."

SOUTH FARMS.—Just as the last form of this book was ready for the Press, this parish was, by an Act of the Legislature, incorporated as a Town, and named MORRIS, in honor of the late JAMES MORRIS, Esq. With a feeling of unaffected regret, we part with her broad and beautiful domains, and bid farewell to her many noble citizens. Thus far her history belongs to Litchfield—the Future is all her own. May her career be as glorious in the ages to come, as her Past has been honorable!

www.ingramcontent.com/pod-product-compliance
Lightning Source LLC
LaVergne TN
LVHW020540100826
845148LV00010B/1554

9781596411029